Best Hikes Colorado Springs

Help Us Keep This Guide Up to Date

Every effort has been made by the author and editors to make this guide as accurate and useful as possible. However, many things can change after a guide is published—trails are rerouted, regulations change, techniques evolve, facilities come under new management, etc.

We appreciate hearing from you concerning your experiences with this guide and how you feel it could be improved and kept up to date. While we may not be able to respond to all comments and suggestions, we'll take them to heart and we'll also make certain to share them with the author. Please send your comments and suggestions to the following address:

FalconGuides
Reader Response/Editorial Department
246 Goose Lane, Suite 200
Guilford, CT 06437

Thanks for your input, and happy trails!

Best Hikes Colorado Springs

The Greatest Views, Wildlife, and Forest Strolls

Second Edition

Stewart M. Green

GUILFORD, CONNECTICUT

FALCONGUIDES®

An imprint of The Rowman & Littlefield Publishing Group, Inc.
4501 Forbes Blvd., Ste. 200
Lanham, MD 20706
www.rowman.com

Distributed by NATIONAL BOOK NETWORK

All photographs are by Stewart M. Green.
Maps: Trailhead Graphics © Rowman & Littlefield

British Library Cataloguing in Publication Information available

Library of Congress Cataloging-in-Publication Data available

Library of Congress Cataloging-in-Publication Data Names: Green, Stewart M., author.
Title: Best hikes Colorado Springs : the greatest views, wildlife, and
forest strolls / Stewart M. Green.
Description: Second edition. | Guilford, Connecticut : FalconGuides, [2020]
| Revised edition of: Best hikes near Colorado Springs / Stewart M.
Green. c2014. | Includes bibliographical references. | Summary:
"Discover the most epic hikes close to town. With Best Hikes Colorado
Springs, readers have everything they need for the adventure they seek,
from an easy nature walk to a multi-day backpack. Complete with maps and
full-color photos, hike descriptions provide everything you need to know
before hitting the trail: location, length, hiking time, level of
difficulty, canine compatibility"– Provided by publisher.
Identifiers: LCCN 2020011121 (print) | LCCN 2020011122 (ebook) | ISBN
9781493047406 (paperback) | ISBN 9781493047413 (epub)

∞™ The paper used in this publication meets the minimum requirements of American National Standard for Information Sciences—Permanence of Paper for Printed Library Materials, ANSI/NISO Z39.48-1992.

The author and The Rowman & Littlefield Publishing Group, Inc. assume no liability for accidents happening to, or injuries sustained by, readers who engage in the activities described in this book.

Contents

The Hikes

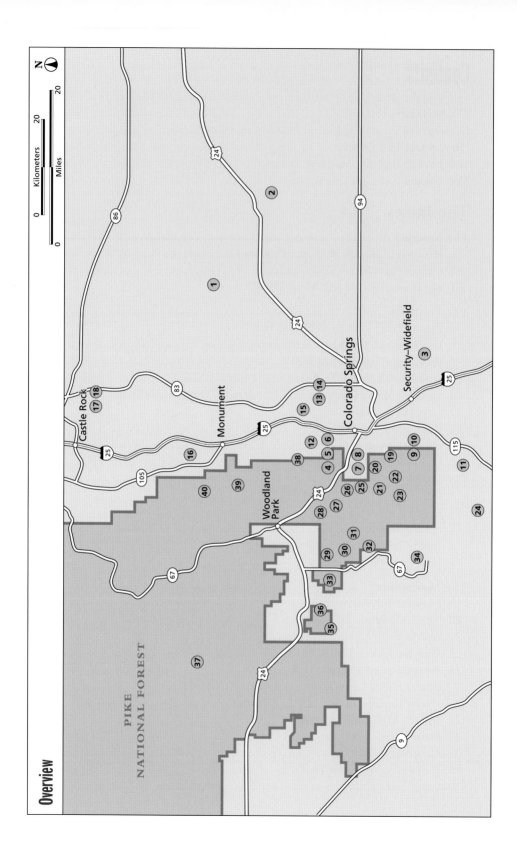

Overview

Acknowledgments

Best Hikes Colorado Springs is an exploration of the wild lands surrounding my hometown. Almost every day in summer when I grew up near North Cheyenne Cañon, I would pack a lunch, fill my steel army canteen with water, and shoulder an Austrian rucksack for the day's adventure.

I would walk in the cool morning to the pine forests at the canyon entrance. Some days I puttered along the creek, taking off shoes and wading in glassy water. Other days I watched 10th Mountain Division soldiers give climbing exhibitions at an amphitheater below the Pinnacle. But usually I logged miles on my boots, hiking Columbine Trail, then branching to St. Mary's Falls and the summit of Mount Rosa or hoofing it up to Captain Jack's, Tenney Crags, and Mount Arthur. I would arrive back home in the evening—footsore, tired, but always happy.

This book details those hikes I did as a boy and more. There is no shortage of great hikes near Colorado Springs. The city park system is simply one of the best in the United States. There aren't many cities that offer so much hiking on public lands. The Springs was fortunate to have General William Jackson Palmer, its forward-thinking founder, donate natural areas as parks but also to have a wealth of undeveloped land for recreation, including El Paso County parklands, Colorado state parks, and Pike National Forest. My thanks to the general, as well as other residents who love Pikes Peak Country and work to preserve and protect its natural values and diverse trails.

Thanks to all of my trail companions over the years as well as other hiking experts, FalconGuides editors, and park staff at state and city parks who reviewed the manuscript, offered advice, proofread sections, and added their ten cents, including Deb Acord, Kevin Baker, Howard Brooks, John Burbidge, Bob D'Antonio, Jimmie Dunn, Dave Golec, Aubrey Green, Ian Green, Isaac Hamilton, Doug Hatfield, Mike and Sherry Heinrichs, Bob Hostetler, Dennis Jackson, Jewels Johnson, Mitch Martin, Cindy McCaffrey, Martha Morris, Max Phelps, Brian Shelton, Bill Springer, Spencer Swanger, Autumn Thorpe, and Jeff Wolin.

Introduction

Walking is one of the most basic human activities. Walking is physical exercise that any able-bodied person can do, yet all too often we get in the car and drive somewhere when we could walk instead. There is great joy in walking or hiking for pleasure—in putting on lightweight boots, shouldering a pack, and setting off on foot into the world and into the wild.

The way of the trail is a great American tradition. The Native Americans followed ancient worn paths across Colorado's mountains, plateaus, and plains. Later trappers, traders, miners, and settlers trod the Santa Fe Trail, Smoky Hill Trail, and Cherokee Trail into this vast untrammeled land, taking to heart the words of the great nineteenth-century poet Walt Whitman: "Afoot and light-hearted I take to the open road. Healthy, free, the world before me. The long brown path before me leading wherever I choose."

One of the best ways to enjoy, understand, and appreciate the beauty and diversity of the Pikes Peak region is by hiking across its varied landscapes. Footpaths take you away from highways, roads, and suburbs and into ancient places preserved in the rarefied air, past lakes ringed by windswept grass and in the shadow of shining mountains. Anyone interested in Colorado's different ecosystems, from plains to peaks, can learn much by hiking the area's many trails.

A hiker crosses a broad meadow on the Aiken Canyon Trail (hike 11).

The Pikes Peak region, including the city of Colorado Springs, is simply one of America's best areas for hiking and trails. Over a thousand trail miles thread across prairie, peak, and canyon, climbing to cloud-scraping summits, ending at tumbling waterfalls, crossing wildflower-strewn meadows, and finding silence and solitude on wild lands within sight of a major city.

It is hard to decide what are the best hikes in Pikes Peak country and the best within an hour's drive of Colorado Springs, since there is no shortage of great hikes. There are no objective criteria that can be used to determine the best hikes, but the forty hiking adventures in *Best Hikes Colorado Springs* offer outdoor rewards for hikers of every ability, from beginners seeking an easy 2-hour day trip to intrepid trekkers who want to hike to the back of beyond.

You will find amazing hikes that wind among the soaring sandstone formations at the Garden of the Gods, follow tumbling creeks in Lost Creek Wilderness Area and North Cheyenne Cañon, and reach lofty summits like Mount Herman and Pikes Peak.

The hikes are divided among the region's three geographic provinces: prairie, foothills, and mountains. The mostly easy prairie hikes traverse open plains and climb bluffs with views of distant mountains. The foothills hikes, including the city of Colorado Springs, lie in a long strip of land sandwiched between the plains and the mountains. These hikes are easily accessible for year-round expeditions. The mountain hikes, the largest number in the book, explore the rugged Front Range peaks and valleys. These diverse hikes, taking you to scenic vistas and through gorgeous terrain, are of varied distances, difficulty, and steepness.

AMERICA THE BEAUTIFUL

When you stand atop Pikes Peak after hiking up, a vault of sky and clouds fills the heavens above. Far below to the east, cloud shadows trail across shimmering Colorado Springs and the distant prairie horizon edges the earth. Beneath the open sky, you feel on top of the world and sense the ancient eternal earth, the original Colorado.

In the summer of 1893, that same primeval Colorado prompted Katharine Lee Bates, a young English professor at Wellesley College, to write "America the Beautiful," the country's unofficial anthem, after riding to the top in a wagon and then a mule. On the summit she penned, "O beautiful for spacious skies, for amber waves of grain, for purple mountain majesties above the fruited plain."

"The opening lines of the hymn floated into my mind," Bates later recalled, "as I was looking out over the sea-like expanse of fertile country spreading away so far under those ample skies."

Colorado Springs, the forty-first-most populous city in the United States with a 2018 population of 464,474, spreads across plains and valleys beneath a looming escarpment of mountains. The city's park system, run by the City of Colorado Springs Parks, Recreation, and Cultural Services Department, is simply one of the best and largest in the United States.

There just aren't many major American cities that offer so much hiking on public lands and trails. The Springs was fortunate to have many benefactors who donated scenic gems to the city as public parkland. General William Jackson Palmer, the city's forward-thinking founder, in 1871 donated some of its best natural parks, including Palmer Park and North Cheyenne Cañon Park.

Charles Eliot Perkins, a friend of General Palmer and fellow railroad man, bought 480 acres at the Garden of the Gods and wished to give it to the city but died before it was included in his will. His six children honored his wishes and conveyed those acres in 1909 to Colorado Springs as the seed of today's Garden of the Gods Park with the stipulation that it would always remain free to the public.

There is a wealth of undeveloped public land in Pikes Peak country that is available for recreation and hiking, including El Paso County parks, Colorado state parks, Pike National Forest, and Bureau of Land Management (BLM) lands. There are also many urban trails and trail corridors that follow old rail beds and abandoned rights-of-way, including the Santa Fe Trail or Pikes Peak Greenway. This multiuse 30-mile trail, not included in this book, runs from Fountain Creek Nature Center south of Colorado Springs to Palmer Lake along the old Santa Fe Railroad bed and provides branches and linkups to other urban trails in Colorado Springs.

The city parks are also dog friendly with lots of off-leash areas for Fido to romp unfettered; the best dog areas are at Red Rock Canyon Open Space, Garden of the Gods Park, Palmer Park Dog Park, and the very popular Bear Creek Dog Park. Remember, however, to keep your dog under voice control to avoid unpleasant contact with other dogs and hikers and to always pick up and dispose of your dog's waste. It's the polite thing to do.

Pikes Peak Defines Geography

The Pikes Peak region is roughly bounded by the short-grass prairie east of Colorado Springs, the Arkansas River and Cañon City to the south, the Puma Hills and South Park to the west, and the South Platte River and Palmer Divide to the north. Geography dictates the landscape, a place of textbook geological formations including billion-year-old bedrock granite, thick layers of Mesozoic sandstone uplifted into soaring hogbacks, and coarse gravels deposited by runoff during recent ice ages.

Geography, geology, and the huge range of elevations from below 6,000 feet to 14,115 feet conspire to make Pikes Peak country an ecological melting pot. The diversity of animal habitats and plant communities are molded by variable temperatures,

Looking across East and West Beaver Creek Canyons from high on the Powerline Trail (hike 24)

precipitation patterns, and elevation. Indeed, traveling from the arid desert south of Colorado Springs to the frigid ice-bound summit of Pikes Peak is like taking a telescoped journey from Mexico to beyond the Arctic Circle in less than 30 miles and in over 8,000 feet of elevation difference.

The region is, of course, dominated by Pikes Peak, Colorado's thirty-first-highest mountain. From everywhere within 50 miles, the great Peak dominates the central Colorado landscape and the skyline of Colorado Springs, etching its snowcapped crown against a blue sky horizon. Pikes Peak stands alone as a silent granite sentinel, proudly rising above the tawny eastern plains and the lower forested mountains and valleys that surround it.

The storied mountain shapes more than the land and its natural history—it also exerts a powerful influence on the region's history, culture, and economics. The Peak is always there—serene, eternal, and a constant reminder of the wild out there beyond the city limits.

Pikes Peak is sacred to the native Ute Indians, who called it *Tava* (sun) as well as *Tavakiev* (sun mountain). The Utes, calling themselves *Tabeguache* (people of the sun), revered the mountain and lingered at the "boiling springs" at its base and camped among the sculptured sandstone formations at the Garden of the Gods. Even today the Utes come and leave ritual offerings at sacred sites and twisted prayer trees, some hundreds of years old.

Later, during the 1859 gold rush to the diggings at Central City, west of Denver, the famous mountain was a slogan—"Pikes Peak or Bust!"—for fortune seekers who marched across the Great Plains, including over 100,000 in a three-month period.

THE TEN ESSENTIALS

The Ten Essentials are easy to carry and will help you survive. The purpose of carrying the Ten Essentials is twofold: to allow you to respond positively to an accident or emergency situation and to allow you to survive one or more nights outside. It's best to carry most of the Ten Essentials in your hiking pack on a major trek like the Devil's Playground Trail up Pikes Peak, even though the highway parallels half of the trail.

These are the essential items to carry:

1. **Navigation.** Bring a map, compass, GPS unit, and extra batteries.

2. **Sun protection.** Sunscreen is essential to protect from the burning rays of the high-altitude sun as well as lip balm and either baby powder or Gold Bond powder for chafing.

3. **Insulation.** Bring plenty of clothing and dress in layers. Waterproof outer gear is essential.

4. **Illumination.** Bring a headlamp and extra batteries if you have to hike down in the dark.

5. **First-aid supplies.** A small first-aid kit with bandages, Band-Aids, and basic medical supplies is important.

6. **Fire.** Bring a lighter and box of matches to start a fire for warmth if you are benighted.

7. **Repair kit and tools.** A multiuse tool or pocketknife along with some duct tape can repair torn gear.

8. **Nutrition.** Pack plenty of food. Bring extra energy bars to stash in your pack. You may need them if you get lost.

9. **Hydration.** Bring plenty of water. In summer bring a minimum of three quarts of water. You can substitute a sports drink for one of them or bring powder to mix in water. You can refill your water bottles or CamelBak at the Pikes Peak Summit House or at the trailhead at many area parks.

10. **Emergency shelter.** It's easy to pack a lightweight space blanket or ultralight tarp for shelter from a storm.

The *St. Louis News* documented the peak obsession in a March 13, 1859, article: "Now they hear of nothing, dream of nothing, but Pike's Peak. It is the magnet to the mountains, toward which everybody and everything is tending. It seems that every man, woman and child, who is going anywhere at all, is moving Pike's Peakward."

Pikes Peak Country Trails and Hikes

Best Hikes Colorado Springs describes forty of the area's best hikes with informative text, GPS coordinates, and detailed maps within 50 miles of the city and Pikes Peak. It is difficult to narrow down all the wonderful trails in the region to only the select few, which were handpicked by the author, a native Colorado Springs resident, climber, and hiker.

There are some significant omissions, including Barr Trail, an arduous 12.6-mile trail up Pikes Peak's east side, and the fabulous Captain Jack's hike above North Cheyenne Cañon. Barr Trail was not included due to its length and difficulty and simply because the Devils Playground Trail is a better way to hike the Peak. The Captain Jack's hike was omitted because the Bear Creek area has been periodically closed by the USDA Forest Service to protect the endangered greenback cutthroat trout, the Colorado state fish. A 4-mile stretch of the creek southwest of Colorado Springs is the only remaining place with a genetically pure greenback population, and hikers using the creek area put those surviving fish at risk for extinction.

Also, the once-popular Waldo Canyon Trail was excluded because that trail has been closed until further notice, perhaps even permanently, as a result of the Waldo Canyon Fire, which burned over 18,000 acres in 2012. The 7-mile trail will eventually be reimagined and rebuilt with a different trailhead.

The hikes in this book are of varying lengths and difficulties so it is easy to pick out fun strolls for families, nature walks for kids, and barrier-free trails that are wheelchair accessible, as well as long, difficult hikes on rough terrain and in wilderness areas teeming with wildlife.

All of the trailheads are easily reached by driving, have parking lots, and often have facilities including water and restrooms. GPS coordinates are given for all of the parking areas and trailheads as well as in the Miles and Directions section for each hike's important trail junctions, points of interest, overlooks, and turnaround locations. The hikes are also rated by difficulty from easy to challenging so you can find trails for your ability and interest.

Best Hikes Colorado Springs is all about getting outside, walking for pleasure, and having a great adventure. So, pick a trail, put on your boots, and go hiking. If you put one foot in front of the other, you can go just about everywhere.

Practice Zero-Impact Philosophy

Colorado Springs is an outdoors-oriented city. The US Olympic Committee is headquartered in downtown Colorado Springs. World-class runners, Olympic speed skaters, triathletes, and mountain bikers train on Colorado Springs' trails. One of the region's biggest sporting events is the famed Pikes Peak Marathon—26 miles and 8,000 vertical feet up and down America's most famous mountain. In 2019 U.S. News & World Report rated Colorado Springs the third best "Best Place to Live" in the United States, while *Outside* magazine called it one of the "Top 10 Best Towns for High-Altitude Running in America." Colorado Springs and the Pikes Peak region provide simply a wonderful place to go outside and enjoy wild nature.

With all the hikers and outdoors enthusiasts in the Pikes Peak region, it's important to practice a zero-impact philosophy so that the area's natural resources and its

Helen Hunt Falls, named for the famed nineteenth-century writer, is at the western end of the Columbine Trail (hike 20).

trails are protected from overuse and to maintain a positive outdoor experience for all backcountry visitors. Use the following zero-impact suggestions to make both your own as well as everyone else's visit enjoyable and to protect our spectacular natural world.

Zero-impact is about responsible outdoor ethics, including staying on the trail, not cutting switchbacks, packing out litter, keeping your dog leashed and picking up its poop, disposing properly of human waste, and leaving the environment as pristine as possible. Mountain and prairie ecosystems and environments are fragile and sensitive to human use. The marks of man, including social trails and damage from ATVs and motorcycles, linger for years on this dry landscape.

Every hiker should adopt the zero-impact ethic to minimize his or her impact on this beautiful land. It's our responsibility to pay attention to our effect on the environment so that we can ensure that all these fabulous trails will remain as wild refuges from the urban environment.

FalconGuide Principles of Zero Impact

Always stay on the trail. Cutting switchbacks or traveling cross-country causes erosion and destroys plants. Often an area, like Garden of the Gods, is braided with social trails from careless hikers. Try to always follow the main route whenever possible. The mountains, especially steep slopes, are susceptible to erosion caused by unthinking off-trail hiking.

Pack it in—pack it out. Everything you carry and use, including food wrappers, orange peels, cigarette butts, plastic bottoms, and energy-bar wrappers, needs to come out with you and be deposited in a trash can. Carry a plastic bag for picking up other trash along the trail. Also remember to pick up your dog's waste and pack it out in a plastic bag. Too many thoughtless dog owners leave their pet's feces in the middle of the trail. That's just gross.

Respect public and private property, livestock fences, and mining claims. Federal laws protect all archaeological and historic antiquities, including Indian artifacts, projectile points, old ruins, petroglyphs, fossilized bone and petrified wood, and historic sites. Don't carve your name in a rock surface or on a tree. Leave all natural features, like flowers and rocks, where you found them. Enjoy their beauty but leave them for the next hiker.

Properly dispose of human waste. Dig a hole 4 to 6 inches deep and at least 300 feet from water sources and dry washes. Do not burn or bury toilet paper. Instead, pack it out in a plastic baggie. The best thing to do, of course, is to use the public restrooms that are found at many of the trailheads.

Take only photographs and memories. We can easily avoid leaving any evidence of our passage across this lovely and delicate mountain environment. With care and sensitivity, we can all do our part to keep the Pikes Peak region beautiful, clean, and pristine. Don't pick flowers, pick up rocks, or take anything with you when you leave.

Evening light on the Garden of the Gods from the Bretag Trail in Colorado Springs, Colorado (hike 4)

If everyone took just one item, it wouldn't be long before nothing special was left. Leave your souvenirs for other hikers to enjoy.

Be Prepared

Hiking, while immensely rewarding, also comes with hazards and inherent risks, especially for those who come unprepared. Respect the mountain environment and be prepared and you'll be safe. Remember that many dangers are found in the greater Colorado Springs area.

You must assume responsibility for your own actions and for your safety. Be aware of your surroundings and of dangers, including drop-offs, cliffs, and loose rock; the weather; and the physical condition of both your party and you. Never be afraid to turn around if conditions aren't right. Pay attention to those bad feelings—they keep you alive.

Here are a few suggestions to be prepared for emergency situations on your hike:

- Bring extra clothes and a raincoat, especially in the mountains. The weather can change in an instant. Heavy thunderstorms regularly occur on summer afternoons and cold wet clothing can lead to hypothermia.
- Colorado's Front Range has more lightning strikes than almost anywhere else in the United States. Pay attention to the weather and get off high places before a storm arrives. If you can hear thunder, you're probably not safe.
- The air is thin, and the sun is bright. Summer temperatures can be hot. Use sunscreen to avoid damaging sunburns and wear a hat.
- Carry plenty of water and sports drinks for electrolyte replacement due to sweating. Don't drink any water from streams unless you treat and purify it.

The upper section of the Mount Manitou Incline Trail reaches grades steeper than 60 degrees (hike 26).

- If you're coming from a lower elevation, watch for symptoms of altitude sickness, including headache, nausea, and loss of appetite. The best cure is to lose elevation.

- Allow enough time for your hike. If you start in late afternoon, bring a headlamp or flashlight so you can see the trail in the dark.

- Bring plenty of high-energy snacks for the trail and treats for the youngsters.

- Wear comfortable hiking shoes and good socks. Your feet will thank you for that. To avoid blisters, break in your shoes before wearing them in the backcountry.

- Enjoy wildlife you see along the trail but keep your distance and treat the animals with respect. Cute little animals can bite and spread diseases like rabies. Watchful mother animals, including deer and black bears, are protective of their babies. Rattlesnakes are found on low-elevation trails. Watch where you place your hands and feet. Don't feed wildlife as that can disrupt their natural eating habits.

- Carry a day pack to tote all your trail needs, including a raincoat, food, water bottle, first-aid kit, flashlight, matches, and extra clothes. A whistle, GPS unit, topo map, binoculars, camera, pocketknife, and FalconGuide identification book for plants and animals are all handy additions. And don't forget your *Best Hikes Colorado Springs* book!

How to Use This Guide

Take a close enough look, and you'll find that this guide contains just about everything you need to choose and enjoy a hike near Colorado Springs. Here's an outline of the book's major components.

Each hike starts with a short summary of the hike's highlights. These quick overviews give you a taste of the hiking adventures to follow. You'll learn about the trail terrain and what surprises each route has to offer.

Following the Overview you'll find the hike specs: quick, nitty-gritty details of the hike. Most are self-explanatory, but here are some details on others:

Distance: The total distance of the recommended route—one-way for loop hikes, the round-trip on an out-and-back or lollipop hike, point-to-point for a shuttle. Options are additional.

Hiking time: The average time it will take to cover the route. It is based on the total distance, elevation gain, and condition and difficulty of the trail. Your fitness level will also affect your time.

Difficulty: Each hike has been assigned a level of difficulty. The rating system was developed from several sources and personal experience. These levels are meant to be a guideline only and may prove easier or harder for different people depending on ability and physical fitness.

Easy—5 miles or less total trip distance in one day, with minimal elevation gain, and paved or smooth-surfaced dirt trail.

Moderate—Up to 10 miles total trip distance in one day, with moderate elevation gain and potentially rough terrain.

Strenuous—More than 10 miles total trip distance in one day, strenuous elevation gains, and/or rough or rocky terrain.

Trail surface: General information about what to expect underfoot.

Seasons: General information on the best time of year to hike.

Schedule: Days and hours the trail and visitor center, offices, and so forth are open to the public. Unless restrictions are stated, the trail is open 24 hours; and if the park is open, the trails are open.

Other trail users: Such as horseback riders, mountain bikers, inline skaters, and so on.

Canine compatibility: Know the trail regulations before you take your dog hiking with you. Dogs are not allowed on several trails in this book.

Land status: National forest, county open space, national park wilderness, and so on.

Fees and permits: Whether you need to carry any money with you for park entrance fees and permits.

Maps: This is a list of other maps to supplement the maps in this book. USGS maps are the best source for accurate topographical information, but the local park map may show more recent trails. Use both.

Trail contacts: This is the location, phone number, and website URL for the local land manager(s) in charge of all the trails within the selected hike. Before you head out, get trail access information, or contact the land manager after your visit if you see problems with trail erosion, damage, or misuse.

Other: Other information that will enhance your hike.

Special considerations: This section calls your attention to specific trail hazards, like hunting seasons or a lack of water, and other safety information.

The **Finding the trailhead** section gives you dependable driving directions to where you'll want to park, as well as GPS coordinates for the start of the hike.

The Hike is the meat of the chapter. Detailed and honest, it's a carefully researched impression of the trail. It also often includes lots of area history, both natural and human.

Under **Miles and Directions,** mileage cues identify all turns and trail name changes, as well as points of interest.

Options are also given for many hikes to make your journey shorter or longer depending on the amount of time you have.

Don't feel restricted to the routes and trails that are mapped here. Be adventurous and use this guide as a platform to discover new routes for yourself.

How to Use the Maps

Overview map: This map shows the location of each hike in the Colorado Springs area by hike number.

Route map: This is your primary guide to each hike. It shows all of the accessible roads and trails, points of interest, water, landmarks, and geographical features. It also distinguishes trails from roads, and paved roads from unpaved roads. The selected route is highlighted, and directional arrows point the way.

Trail Finder

Best Hikes for Views
6. Perkins Central Garden Trail
7. Red Rock Canyon Trail
22. Gray Back Peak Trail
31. Devils Playground Trail (Pikes Peak)
32. Pancake Rocks and Horsethief Falls Trails
37. Goose Creek Trail

Best Hikes for Waterfalls
20. Columbine Trail
21. St. Mary's Falls Trail
32. Pancake Rocks and Horsethief Falls Trails

Best Hikes for Kids
6. Perkins Central Garden Trail
9. Coyote Run Trail
18. Canyon View Nature Trail
35. Florissant Fossil Beds National Monument Trails

Best Hikes for Wildlife
11. Aiken Canyon Trail
24. Beaver Creek Loop Trail
33. Mueller State Park Loop
35. Florissant Fossil Beds National Monument Trails

Best Hikes for Photography
2. Calhan Paint Mines Trail
6. Perkins Central Garden Trail
30. Crags Trail
31. Devils Playground Trail
32. Pancake Rocks and Horsethief Falls Trails
37. Goose Creek Trail

Best Summit Hikes
22. Gray Back Peak Trail
29. Raspberry Mountain Trail
31. Devils Playground Trail
39. Mount Herman Trail
40. Palmer Reservoirs Loop with Cap Rock Option

Best Hikes for Solitude

Map Legend

Transportation

≡⟨25⟩≡   Interstate Highway

≡⟨24⟩≡   US Highway

≡⟨67⟩≡   State Highway

≡⟨621⟩≡   Forest/Paved/Improved Road

= = = =   Unpaved Road

+——+——+   Railroad

Trails

- - - - - -   Selected Route

- - - - - -   Trail/Fire Road

→   Direction of Route

Water Features

Body of Water

River or Creek

Intermittent Creek

Spring

Waterfall

Symbols

①   Trailhead

■   Building/Point of Interest

🅿   Parking

🚻   Restroom

   Scenic View/Overlook

❓   Visitor Center

⛽   Picnic Area

▲   Campground

•—•   Gate

   Bench

○   Towns and Cities

×   Spot Elevation

▲   Mountain/Peak

⌒   Cave

—   Dam

Land Management

National Park/Forest

State/Local Park

Wilderness Area

The Prairie

The wide, expansive prairie, stretching east from Colorado Springs to the Kansas border, is a Great Plains landscape of undulating hills broken by rocky bluffs and cottonwood-lined water courses. Much of the short-grass prairie near the Springs, once populated by vast herds of bison and migrating Native Americans, is now privately owned and divided into 5-acre ranchettes. Some exquisite pockets of prairie, however, offer scenic and unusual trails in both county and city parklands.

Colorful sandstone hoodoos stand above a dry wash at the Calhan Paint Mines (hike 2).

1 Homestead Ranch Regional Park Trail

The Homestead Ranch Trail is composed of two loops that form a 3.3-mile hike through pine woods and grasslands on a bluff northeast of Colorado Springs.

Start: Trailhead next to a building with restrooms at the northwest corner of the loop drive and parking lots
Distance: 3.3-mile double loop
Hiking time: About 2 hours
Difficulty: Easy
Elevation gain: 180 feet
Trail surface: Doubletrack dirt trail
Seasons: Year-round. Trail can be snowy and icy in winter.
Schedule: Open daily 5:00 a.m. to 9:00 p.m.

Other trail users: Horseback riders, mountain bikers
Canine compatibility: Leashed dogs only
Land status: El Paso County Park
Fees and permits: None
Maps: USGS Eastonville; El Paso County Park Map
Trail contact: El Paso County Parks, 2002 Creek Crossing, Colorado Springs 80906; (719) 520-7529; https://communityser vices.elpasoco.com/parks-and-recreation/homestead-ranch-regional-park/

Finding the trailhead: Drive east from Colorado Springs on US 24. Before reaching Peyton, turn left (north) on Elbert Road and drive 5 miles. Make a sharp right (east) turn on Sweet Road and drive 2.5 miles to Gollihar Road. Turn left on gravel Gollihar and drive 0.5 mile to the park. Turn left into the park on Person Drive and drive to a loop with several parking areas. Park at the northwest end of the loop in front of a building with restrooms. The trailhead is to the right of the building. The park's address is 16444 Gollihar Road (GPS: 39.074592, -104.523507).

The Hike

Homestead Ranch Regional Park, a 450-acre El Paso County regional parkland, protects a gorgeous slice of a high plains ecosystem northeast of Colorado Springs. The area includes pine-covered bluffs lined with sandstone cliff bands and broad meadows blanketed with tall grass and wildflowers. The park also offers expansive views toward Pikes Peak and the Front Range and distant views south to the ragged Sangre de Cristo Range and the Spanish Peaks.

The Homestead Ranch Trail, combined with the Rattlesnake Trail, makes two loops, an east loop and a west loop, connected by a short trail segment. Either loop can be hiked separately for a shorter outing or together for full value. The recommended and described hike is to do the east loop first and then the west.

The hike begins at the trailhead on the north side of the park building at the west side of the parking area. Walk up the doubletrack road past a playground on the left and continue through a broad meadow fringed with woods, passing a left turn and a short trail that descends to a spring-fed pond. The small pond, stocked with

Low broken cliffs rim bluffs along the trail at Homestead Ranch Regional Park.

bluegills and small bass, is a great fishing hole, especially for youngsters learning the art of fishing.

After almost 0.2 mile you reach a major trail junction. Keep right and continue hiking uphill toward the forested bluff ahead. The trail coming in from the left is on the west loop trail. After hiking the two loops, you will return to this point on the west loop.

The trail heads northwest and enters the ponderosa pine forest. Tall trees cast dappled shadows across the wide trail and thick grass on the forest floor. The final section of uphill trail climbs steeply and, after climbing 195 vertical feet from the parking lot, reaches the top of the bluff. Continue hiking and after 0.5 mile reach a trail junction. Go right to start the east loop trail on the Homestead Ranch Trail. The west loop goes left at this junction.

The sandy trail hooks right and heads northeast through a meadow above a wooded draw. At 0.55 mile the trail passes a spinning windmill with a water tank for horses, a hitching rack, picnic table, and a stone marker with a brass plaque placed by the El Paso County Horseman's Council. One of the quotes on the plaque reads "There's nothing better for the inside of a person than the outside of a horse." Continue hiking east to a Y-shaped trail junction and the start of the east loop trail at 0.6 mile.

Go left at the junction so that you will get the best mountain views as you hike along the bluff edge on your return to this spot. The trail swings below a low-browed hill rimmed with broken rock and scattered pines. It slowly climbs east to the top of a flat hill and continues across an open meadow to a trail junction at the northeast

A small horned lizard perches on a hand along the trail.

corner of the park. Go right on the Rattlesnake Trail, which forms an open loop. The trail that goes straight east travels 0.1 mile to the park boundary and a small parking area at the end of Lovaca Drive.

This next trail segment is the best part of the entire hike, edging along the cliffed rim of the bluff escarpment and offering wide views of the prairie to the south, distant mountain ranges, and broad-shouldered Pikes Peak. The trail heads south and quickly reaches the bluff's rim. Scattered ponderosa pine rise above the grassy meadows, while a dense piney forest spills down the side of the bluff. Just after the trail reaches the rim, take a break and look southeast through a break in the trees toward Rattlesnake Butte, an unranked 7,410-foot flat-topped peak that lies within the park.

Continue southwest along the bluff edge to a great viewpoint atop a rocky cliff. Stop for a breather to enjoy the wide vista, with Pikes Peak anchoring the western horizon. Beyond on the distant edge of the limitless prairie are the landmark Spanish Peaks, the dark Wet Mountains, and the sawtooth Sangre de Cristo Range. The exposed rock here is Dawson arkose, a coarse sandstone that is also seen in Colorado Springs at Pulpit Rock and Palmer Park. It is a Tertiary-age formation that is some 50 million years old.

The trail continues twisting along the bluff edge, heading northwest in both grassland and pine forest. After 1.5 miles you return to the Y junction. Keep left and hike back on the connector trail past the windmill to a major trail junction at 2.1 miles. Keep right to start the west loop on the Homestead Ranch Trail. **Option:** If you don't want to do the west loop, go left and follow the trail back to the parking lot.

The west loop trail follows the edge between bluff and prairie. Right of the trail stretches a high grassland swept by wind, while to the left is the ponderosa pine woodland, which covers the bluff edge and the steep hillsides below. The trail follows the rim for about a half mile before making a sharp left bend to the south and descending the steep hillside.

Just before the trail begins its descent, look on the left side of the trail at a twisted ponderosa pine. This tall pine is a Ute prayer tree, deformed by Ute Indians who lived here centuries before Anglo-Americans settled. On pilgrimages to Pikes Peak, a sacred mountain to the Utes, a tree sapling was tied to the ground, with the bend pointing toward the sacred peak. This tree was tied where it bends sharply upward. After the tree was bound, the group of Utes circled the tree and prayed. They believed the tree would hold their prayers for 800 years and each gust of wind would give their prayers new breath and life.

Homestead Ranch Regional Park Trail

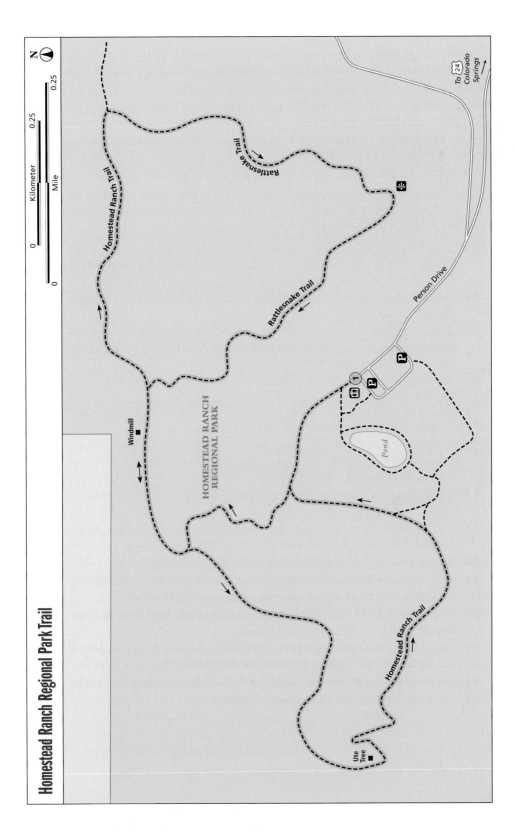

The trail descends steeply across a rocky slope, making a couple of switchbacks, before descending a shallow draw and emerging on gentler slopes below. Continue hiking southeast through meadows along the forest edge before the trail tops a low rise and bends northeast. The last trail section runs across a slope above the fishing pond until it reaches a junction with the trail you initially used to climb the bluff face. Turn right at the junction and descend 0.2 mile back to the trailhead, restrooms, and the parking area. If your kids still have pent-up energy after the 3.3-mile hike, let them loose on the playground equipment and they're guaranteed to sleep on the drive home.

Miles and Directions

0.0 The trailhead is at the northwest corner of the road and parking areas (GPS: 39.074583, -104.523505). Hike up a doubletrack trail, staying on the main trail at a junction. *Option:* A left turn takes you to the pond.

0.2 Reach a major trail junction. Continue straight up the hill. The trail to the left is the return trail at the end of the hike.

0.4 The trail, after gaining 195 feet, reaches the top of the bluff escarpment. After a few hundred feet, you will reach a three-way trail junction (GPS: 39.077482, -104.527214). Go right and hike north and then east.

0.55 The trail passes a windmill with a water tank for horses and a picnic table (GPS: 39.078474, -104.524595).

0.6 Reach a three-way trail junction (GPS: 39.078248, -104.523625). Keep left and begin hiking the lollipop loop, which will bring you back to this junction.

1.0 At a trail junction at the northeast corner of the park, go right (south) on Rattlesnake Trail at a three-way junction (GPS: 39.078964, -104.517446). The left fork goes 100 yards to a trailhead near houses.

1.3 The trail follows the eastern edge of the bluff, offering views across a valley to Rattlesnake Butte.

1.4 Stop at a rim overlook for great views south toward the Spanish Peaks, Wet Mountains, Sangre de Cristo Range, and Pikes Peak (GPS: 39.073839, -104.519545).

1.8 Reach a three-way junction where the loop started. Go left toward the windmill.

2.1 Reach the three-way junction where the uphill trail from the parking lot reaches the bluff top. Keep right on the Homestead Ranch Trail for the second leg of the hike.

2.5 Begin descending a steep slope from the top of the escarpment. Pass a bent Ute prayer tree.

2.9 Reach a trail junction (GPS: 39.073255, -104.526903). Go straight on the doubletrack trail. *Option:* The right singletrack trail drops east to the pond below.

3.1 End the second loop at a junction. Go right toward the trailhead, restrooms, and parking.

3.3 End at the trailhead by the parking lots and restrooms.

2 Calhan Paint Mines Trail

The Paint Mines Trail is a spectacular loop hike that crosses open prairie grasslands to eroded badlands of colored sandstone used by ancient Native Americans for paint and pottery. The trail offers panoramic views of the surrounding prairie as well as distant Pikes Peak on the western horizon.

Start: Paint Mines Interpretive Park Trailhead on the west side of the park
Distance: 3.7-mile loop
Hiking time: 1.5 to 3 hours
Difficulty: Easy
Elevation gain: 205 feet
Trail surface: Single- and doubletrack dirt path
Seasons: Year-round. Summers are hot. Winter days can be snowy and windy.
Schedule: Open daily, dawn to dark
Other trail users: Hikers only
Canine compatibility: Dogs not permitted
Land status: Paint Mines Interpretive Park, El Paso County Park
Fees and permits: None

Maps: USGS Calhan; park map on El Paso County Parks website
Trail contact: El Paso County Parks, 2002 Creek Crossing, Colorado Springs 80906; (719) 520-7529; https://communityser vices.elpasoco.com/parks-and-recreation/ paint-mines-interpretive-park/
Special considerations: Use extreme caution in the badlands area. Stay on the trails to avoid damaging the fragile rock formations. Watch children around drop-offs. Watch for rattlesnakes in summer. Summer can be hot; no shade along the trail. Wear a hat and bring plenty of water as none is found along the trail.

Finding the trailhead: Drive east from Colorado Springs on US 24 for 25 miles to Calhan. On the east side of Calhan, turn right (south) on Yoder Street, which becomes Calhan Highway. Drive south on the road for 0.5 mile to Paint Mine Road. Turn left (east) on Paint Mine Road and drive to a large parking area and the trailhead on the left (GPS: 39.020443, -104.274103). Park address is 29950 Paint Mine Road, Calhan. A restroom is at the parking area. Another parking lot is 0.6 mile farther along the road on the south side of the park.

The Hike

The 3.7-mile-long Paint Mines Trail offers a wonderful hike that explores the high prairie and unusual badlands south of Calhan in eastern El Paso County. The single- and doubletrack trail has easy grades, several interpretative sites, and lots of Colorado history.

The Paint Mines, a small eroded badlands south of Calhan and US 24, is one of those unknown off-the-beaten-track places that amazes when you first visit it. Eroded into the flank of a bluff, the mines are a wonderland of narrow sharp canyons, rounded alabaster-white boulders, and rainbow-dyed hoodoos. The colorful mines, however, are only one part of the 753-acre Paint Mines Interpretive Park, an El Paso

Hoodoos and shale cliffs line a shallow canyon in the heart of the Paint Mines.

County park, which spreads across a broad grassy valley and protects a swath of short-grass prairie.

The Paint Mines form a miniature painted desert that was frequented by Native Americans, including Paleo-Indians for as long as 10,000 years and, in the past 700 or 800 years, the Cheyenne and Arapahoe tribes. They mined the colored clay for ceramics and to paint pottery and used petrified wood to make projectile points and scrapers. Later, settlers in the 1800s used the clay for bricks. The Calhan Paint Mines Archeological District is listed on the National Register of Historic Places for their prehistoric significance.

Begin the hike at the trailhead on the east side of the parking lot off Paint Mine Road south of Calhan. A restroom is at the parking area, but there's no water. The hike goes clockwise, following two loop trails across the rolling prairie before finishing at the Paint Mines area. Hike east 0.1 mile to a three-way T intersection. Go straight (east). **Option:** A right turn, however, travels 0.7 mile south to the Paint Mines if you want to go there first.

The first trail segment makes a 1.1-mile loop across prairie and up a dry drainage. Hike northeast on the wide trail and after 0.4 mile reach an interpretive sign that explains Colorado prairie ecology. Drop into a broad dry wash and turn southwest. The sandy singletrack trail twists up a willow-filled arroyo between clay banks until it reaches a four-way trail intersection. Go left (southeast).

The next 1.3-mile trail section makes a wide-open loop across the southeastern part of the park to a junction just north of the southern parking lot. The trail quickly leaves the wash and climbs to a bench that overlooks eroded white badlands, with dry eroded hummocks of soft sandstone. Bend left here and follow the trail as it contours northeast across a basin to an eroded badlands and an old quarry where clay was excavated for bricks. The trail continues uphill left of the badlands to a bench, an interpretive sign detailing human habitation here, and a great view west across the park to distant Pikes Peak.

The trail turns southwest and gently climbs to a Y-fork trail junction at 2.4 miles. Go right (west) on the next 0.6-mile trail segment, which ends at the Paint Mines. The south parking lot is 0.1 mile to the southwest on Paint Mine Road from this junction. Back on the main trail, hike west and reach another Y junction after a few hundred feet. Keep left on the main trail, which descends onto north-facing slopes and contours west across a shallow ravine. At 2.8 miles is a marvelous overlook above the Paint Mines. Drop down to the eastern edge of the Paint Mines to a metal bench and enjoy a view of the white, gray, yellow, orange, and ocher badlands below. Continue down the trail to the bottom of a deep wash and a trail junction.

Go left (south) and hike 0.2 mile up the bottom of the deep arroyo into the heart of the Paint Mines. All around you are twisted gullies, standing blocks of sandstone, hoodoos carved into fanciful shapes by erosion, and tumbled boulders all tinted by every color of the rainbow. The exposed rock here is Dawson arkose, a coarse sandstone interspersed with clay layers that was deposited 55 million years ago when this region was covered with a tropical hardwood forest. Don't climb on the fragile formations—they're easily damaged by human activity. Also control your children since there are lots of drop-offs.

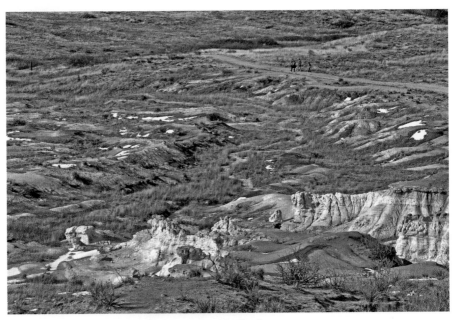

The trail bends north around the Paint Mines' badlands.

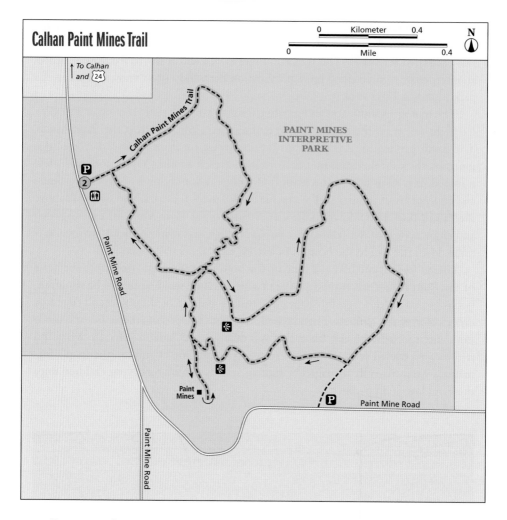

Calhan Paint Mines Trail

0   Kilometer   0.4

N

0   Mile   0.4

To Calhan
and 24

Calhan Paint Mines Trail

PAINT MINES
INTERPRETIVE
PARK

Paint Mine Road

Paint
Mines

P   Paint Mine Road

Paint Mine Road

Return to the intersection with the main trail and head north. The last 0.7-mile trail section climbs away from the Paint Mines and returns to the trailhead. Walk north along the sandy floor of the dry arroyo for 0.2 mile to a four-way junction. Go left (west).

The last 0.5-mile trail section begins with a gradual climb up a hill to a high metal bench and a good view south to the mines. Continue north on the trail as it gently descends an open grassland to a T junction. Go left (west) and walk another 0.1 mile to the hike's terminus at the trailhead and parking lot.

Miles and Directions

0.0   Trailhead at the parking lot on the east side of Paint Mine Road (GPS: 39.020451, -104.274082).

0.1 Trail junction (GPS: 39.020863, -104.273012). Go straight for the loop hike. (*Option:* For a short hike, go right to the Paint Mines.)

0.4 Interpretive sign about ecology.

1.1 Four-way trail intersection (GPS: 39.017359, -104.268546). Go left on the loop hike.

1.2 Reach a ridge overlooking the Paint Mines.

2.4 Reach a T-shaped trail junction on a high grassland (GPS: 39.014091, -104.261903). Go right. South parking area is 0.1 mile to the left.

2.8 Reach the crest of the trail and a great view of the Paint Mines (GPS: 39.014107, -104.267976).

3.0 Reach a trail junction in the bottom of a dry wash (GPS: 39.014879, -104.269186). Go left to the Paint Mines (or right to the trailhead). After exploring the mines return to this junction and go north down the wash.

3.2 Leave the wash and go left up a slight grade to a trail junction (GPS: 39.017213, -104.269554). Go left (west) on the uphill trail.

3.7 Arrive back at the trailhead and parking lot.

3 Big Bluestem Trail and Meadowlark Loop

This easy trail, crossing open grass prairie and through a prairie-dog town, makes a lollipop loop hike on the east side of Big Johnson Reservoir southeast of Colorado Springs.

Start: Trailhead at the Bluestem Prairie Open Space parking lot on the east side of Goldfield Drive

Distance: 8.3 miles lollipop

Hiking time: 3 to 4 hours

Difficulty: Moderate

Elevation gain: 350 feet of cumulative elevation gain

Trail surface: Double- and singletrack dirt trail

Seasons: Year-round

Schedule: Open daily, sunrise to sunset

Other trail users: Mountain bikers

Canine compatibility: Dogs not allowed because of wildlife and plague in prairie dogs

Land status: Public land; City of Colorado Springs Open Space

Fees and permits: None

Maps: USGS Ellsmere and Fountain quads

Trail contact: Colorado Springs Parks, Recreation and Cultural Services, 1401 Recreation Way, Colorado Springs 80905-1975; (719) 385-5940; https://coloradosprings.gov/parks/page/bluestem-prairie-open-space

Finding the trailhead: The Big Bluestem Trailhead is easily accessed from I-25 by taking South Academy Boulevard, exit 135, on the south side of Colorado Springs. Go east on South Academy about a mile, exit south on US 85/87, and drive south to Fontaine Boulevard. Turn left (east) and drive to Goldfield Drive. Turn left (north) on Goldfield and drive a short distance to the open space parking area and trailhead on the right (GPS: 38.743680, -104.694377).

The Hike

This 8.3-mile-long hike follows 2.1-mile Big Bluestem Trail around the east side of Big Johnson Reservoir to 4.1-mile Meadowlark Loop in the north part of 647-acre Bluestem Prairie Open Space. The trails and open space are located 10 miles southeast of downtown Colorado Springs and directly south of the Colorado Springs Municipal Airport. The easy trail, also used by mountain bikers, offers wildlife study, birdwatching, and expansive views of the mountain front. The Big Bluestem Trail is mostly level, while the Meadowlark Loop dips and rolls across grassy hills on the north side of the open space land.

The hike, like the Paint Mines Trail, crosses the open prairie, with the first trail section following a perimeter fence that blocks access to the reservoir, which is private property and not part of the City of Colorado Springs open-space parkland. The reservoir is owned and operated by Fountain Mutual Irrigation Company (FMIC), which stores and provides irrigation water for downstream farmers. The company drained the lake in 2016 to repair the outlet gates and to remove silt and sediment that was deposited in the lake over the last 100 years. When work is completed, FMIC will fill the reservoir to its maximum capacity by 2022, allowing the area's prolific waterfowl and birds to return.

The high plains, stretching east from Colorado Springs to Kansas, is an unsung landscape that most people speed through on highways to other places. The rolling plains, blanketed by mixed-grass prairie and scattered cottonwoods along dry creek beds as well as muddy creeks, is a land of little rain (which usually falls in torrential thunderstorms), wide temperature ranges, and a soaring vault of blue sky. Dry plains like those at Bluestem Prairie Open Space are, however, rich in plants, animals, and unique ecosystems.

Hiking the first segment on the Big Bluestem Trail at first glance might appear to be a boring trudge along a barbed wire fence a few hundred feet from the shore of Big Johnson Reservoir. But the place is magical if you come at the right time of day, like early morning or late evening when slanting sunlight reddens the grass and clumps of yucca. The open space is considered a significant regional grassland that protects a tallgrass prairie remnant composed mostly of big bluestem grass.

This prairie fragment, bordered by Powers Boulevard to the east and north, Fountain Valley School to the west, and Fontaine Boulevard to the south, provides important habitat for wintering bald eagles, migratory birds and waterfowl, and herds of fleet pronghorn antelope and mule deer as well as one of the largest black-tailed prairie-dog colonies near Colorado Springs. Also, watch for rattlesnakes sunning alongside the trail on warm days. Remember to bring a good pair of binoculars on your hike to watch the wildlife.

Bluestem Prairie Open Space, providing a buffer from encroaching suburbs in Widefield and Security on the southeastern edge of Colorado Springs, lies in a wide bowl-shaped valley that slopes gently westward toward Fountain Creek valley. The bottom of the valley, blocked by a long earthen dam, is filled with Big Johnson Reservoir, a private lake used for downstream irrigation on farms. No fishing is allowed. The trail and open space offer marvelous views of the mountain escarpment to the west, including 14,115-foot Pikes Peak, while the ragged snowcapped Sangre de Cristo Mountains scrape against the southwestern horizon.

The hike begins at the Bluestem Prairie Open Space Trailhead on the south side of the parking lot on the east side of Goldfield Drive south of the reservoir. The first 2.1-mile leg of the hike follows the Big Bluestem Trail to a junction with the Meadowlark Loop north of the reservoir. Walk through an open gateway in a split-rail fence and pass a sign with a map of the open-space land and a list of parkland regulations. From the sign, head east on the wide trail through a field of tall grass studded with narrowleaf yuccas to a sign that interprets the songbirds and shorebirds found in the open space and along the lake.

The trail heads southeast and enters a large tract of dusty land filled with cratered holes. This is a colony of about 200 black-tailed prairie dogs that inhabits the southeast corner of the open space and borders the trail on the south and east sides of the lake.

The Bluestem Prairie Trail traverses the southern bank of Big Johnson Reservoir.

The prairie dog is an important part of grassland ecosystems, with other species like burrowing owls and prairie rattlesnakes moving into abandoned burrows as well as being prey for predators like coyotes, hawks, and eagles. The prairie dogs are not amused as you pass through their colony, with watch dogs standing above their holes and whistling displeasure at your passage while, at the same time, keeping a wary eye on the sky to warn others of soaring raptors. An interpretive sign explains the importance of the prairie dog in plains ecosystems. The historic range of the black-tailed prairie dog covers the Great Plains, including eastern Colorado, from Canada to Mexico. These social animals were once considered the most abundant prairie dog in the central United States until systematic extermination by ranchers and farmers greatly reduced their numbers.

Continue hiking east on the trail, paralleling a fence that marks the boundary between the open space and the private reservoir land. After about 0.5 mile of hiking, the trail bends left and heads north on the sloping hillside between the lake and noisy Powers Boulevard on the top of the hill to the east. Stop at an interpretive sign for the Bluestem Prairie ecosystem, which explains the area's vegetation and wildlife.

The open space is considered a mixed-grass prairie, with a variety of native grasses including big bluestem, little bluestem, blue grama, buffalo grass, side-oats grama, sleepy grass, and needlegrass. Other plants include thistle, silver sage, rabbitbrush, yucca, and flowers like Easter daisy, sand lily, scarlet gilia, and prickly poppy. The big bluestem species is a rare and endangered grass species, making this protected parkland a valuable haven for its continued survival.

The trail continues north and after 1.2 miles passes another sign, which details the area's colorful history. In the early nineteenth century, trappers, traders, and Indians traveled along the old Cherokee Trail. This overland route, also called the Trapper's Trail, began in Oklahoma and traversed part of Kansas into the Colorado Territory along the Santa Fe Trail before striking north from today's Pueblo along the Front Range to Wyoming. A historic site along the old pioneer trail is just north of the open space at Jimmy Camp Creek. A trading post operated by trader James (Jimmy) Daugherty, who was murdered by Indians, was located here. Later the area was part of the 30,000-acre Banning-Lewis Ranch, a huge cattle ranch founded in 1897.

Past the history sign the trail bends across a dry wash on the northeast corner of the lake and crosses a wide sloping plain dotted with prairie dog holes. The trail twists northwest across low hills blanketed with tall grass and low sagebrush and after 2.1 miles reaches a Y-junction with the Meadowlark Loop. The singletrack trail, built in late 2019, makes a 4.1-mile loop over hills and broad valleys on the northern side of the open space. This description follows the loop in a counterclockwise direction and returns to the left side of the junction.

Go right on Meadowlark Loop and hike 2.8 miles on the trail, contouring over grassy slopes and dipping across a couple ravines and, after 4.9 miles, reach a T-junction with 0.1-mile Kestral Connector Trail on the far west side of the open space. This short trail goes west to a proposed trailhead at the intersection of Goldfield Drive and Bradley Road. Go left on Meadowlark Loop and descend gentle slopes east to the bottom of a wide swale. This 1.3-mile trail section parallels the northern edge of the private reservoir property.

At the bottom of the valley the trail passes the cottonwood-shaded ruins of a weathered ranch, including a tilting wooden building and a broken windmill, that operated here in the early twentieth century. Past the ranch the path slowly climbs back to the start of the loop trail and its junction with Big Bluestem Trail at 6.2 miles. Go right on Big Bluestem and follow it 2.1 miles along the east and south sides of the lake to the trailhead and parking lot.

GREEN TIP:
Carry a reusable water container that you fill at the tap at home or the trailhead. Bottled water is expensive; lots of petroleum is used to make the plastic bottles; and they're a disposal nightmare.

Big Bluestem Trail and Meadowlark Loop

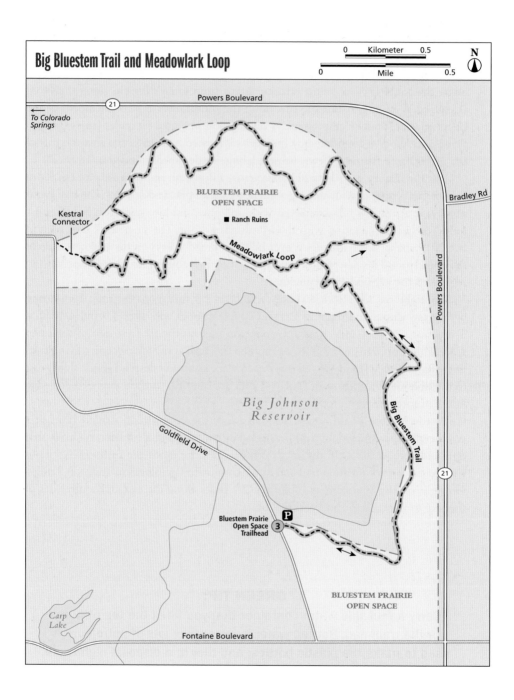

Miles and Directions

0.0 Start from the parking lot and trailhead on the east side of Goldfield Drive on Big Bluestem Trail (GPS: 38.74366, -104.694362).

0.5 Turn left, following the reservoir perimeter fence, and head north along the east side of the lake.

1.2 Reach a sign about the history of the area, including the Cherokee Trail, on the northeast side of the reservoir.

2.1 Reach the end of Big Bluestem Trail and a Y-junction with Meadowlark Loop (GPS: 38.757842, -104.691821). Go right to hike the trail counterclockwise.

4.9 Reach a T-junction with Kestral Connector Trail (GPS: 38.757900, -104.708411). Go left and hike east toward ranch ruins.

6.2 Return to the Y-junction with Big Bluestem Trail. Go right on Big Bluestem and hike along the reservoir perimeter fence.

8.3 Arrive back at the trailhead and parking lot on Goldfield Drive.

The Foothills

Colorado Springs spreads across the foothills below Pikes Peak. These low hills, rising sharply from the plains as rocky hogbacks and broad mesas, form distinctive landscapes. Some of the most spectacular natural features in the Pikes Peak region, including the famed sandstone formations at the Garden of the Gods as well as Red Rock Canyon Open Space and Palmer Park, lie within the foothills zone against the towering mountain escarpment. Numerous trails, mostly easy and moderate in difficulty, thread through these natural parks, offering quick and easy hiking getaways from the bustle of Colorado Springs, the thirty-ninth-largest city in the United States.

Afternoon reflections in a pond brimming with rainwater along the Red Rock Canyon Trail (hike 7)

4 Palmer Trail to Susan G. Bretag Trail Loop

This excellent loop hike follows four different trails around the spectacular rock formations in Garden of the Gods Park—the Palmer Trail, Scotsman Trail, Perkins Central Garden Trail, and Susan G. Bretag Trail. The loop offers fun, easy hiking on a good surface as well as spectacular views of the cliffs and Pikes Peak from rocky ridges and wooded valleys.

Start: Main parking lot at north end of Juniper Way Loop road
Distance: 2.6-mile loop
Hiking time: 1 to 2 hours
Difficulty: Moderate
Elevation gain: 200 feet
Trail surface: Singletrack dirt path and double-track paved trail
Seasons: Year-round
Schedule: Open daily; May 1 to Oct 31, 5 a.m. to 10 p.m.; Nov 1 to Apr 30, 5 a.m. to 9 p.m. Entrance gates are locked at night.

Other trail users: Equestrians on parts of the Scotsman Trail
Canine compatibility: Leashed dogs only. Pick up your dog's waste.
Land status: City of Colorado Springs park
Fees and permits: None; Colorado Springs city park rules apply
Maps: USGS Cascade; trail map available at the visitor center
Trail contact: Colorado Springs Parks, Recreation and Cultural Services, 1401 Recreation Way, Colorado Springs 80905-1975; (719) 385-5940; https://coloradosprings.gov/parks

Finding the trailhead: From I-25, take exit 146 and drive west on Garden of the Gods Road until it dead-ends at 30th Street against the mountains. Turn left (south) on 30th Street and drive 2 miles south to Gateway Road, opposite the Garden of the Gods Visitor and Nature Center. Turn right (west) on Gateway Road and follow it until it merges with Juniper Way Loop, a loop road that encircles the main Garden of the Gods zone. Turn right (north) on the one-way road and follow it to the large Main Parking Lot on the left (GPS: 38.881223, -104.880401). The trailhead is at the north side of the parking lot at a crosswalk (GPS: 38.881575, -104.880400).

Alternatively, approach from I-25 and downtown Colorado Springs by driving west on Cimarron Street / US 24 from I-25 to 10th Street. Exit right and follow North 31st Street north to a stop sign at West Fontanero Street. Turn right and drive to a stoplight at North 30th Street and turn left. Drive 1.2 miles north to Gateway Road. Turn left and drive to Juniper Way Loop, go right and drive to the Main Parking Lot on the north side of the park.

The Hike

This 2.6-mile hike loops around the perimeter of the Garden of the Gods, following parts of four different Garden trails—Palmer Trail, Scotsman Trail, Perkins Central Garden Trail, and Susan G. Bretag Trail. This is an interesting hike that offers scenic views of the park's iconic sandstone formations. The first hike section, following Palmer Trail, climbs onto wooded ridges west of North and South Gateway Rocks before dipping down to Scotsman Picnic Area. The next segment follows Scotsman Trail back to the central Garden zone, where it picks up the paved Perkins Central Garden Trail. The last part follows the Susan G. Bretag Trail north up a broad valley east of the rock formations and back to the parking lot and trailhead.

The trails are all singletrack except for a wide concrete sidewalk section through the central Garden zone. Expect spectacular scenery and a close-up, intimate experience with the different rock formations as well as the transitional ecosystems found at the Garden of the Gods. The trail is quiet with few other hikers, although the paved section through the main Garden is usually busy, especially on summer days when tourists jam the pavement. The trail also crosses the park roads four times. Use the designated crosswalks for safety.

Start the hike at the trailhead on the north side of the Main Parking Lot off Juniper Way Loop. Walk north across the road at a crosswalk to a trail junction.

Go left on the Palmer Trail. The trail coming in from the right, the Susan G. Bretag Trail, is the return trail. The first trail segment on the Palmer Trail, named for General William Jackson Palmer, an early settler and the founder of Colorado Springs, runs 1.2 miles from the junction to the Scotsman Picnic Area southwest of the central Garden zone.

The Palmer Trail, paralleling the road, heads northwest through copses of Gambel oak before bending south. It slowly gains elevation and after 0.3 mile reaches a scenic overlook and a superb photo opportunity. All the main rock formations—North Gateway Rock, South Gateway Rock, Gray Rock, Keyhole Rock, Montezuma Ruins, and the Three Graces—tower to the south, their ragged outlines etched against the sky.

Past the overlook the trail turns west and contours across a steep shallow canyon before climbing onto east-facing slopes opposite North Gateway Rock, the park's highest sandstone formation. The trail continues climbing through a piñon pine and juniper woodland until it reaches a high point and then descends to a shoulder. This is another fine viewpoint. Note the Kissing Camels, a small arch perched atop North Gateway Rock on the left, and the Weeping Indian, the white-rock profile of a Native American face on South Gateway Rock. Hike south down the rocky trail and, after 0.8 mile from the trailhead, reach a trail junction. From here a short trail heads left to the central Garden zone. Stay straight on the main Palmer Trail. Ignore another side trail that jogs over to the road 100 feet farther down.

The Palmer Trail passes beneath the west face of the Giant Footprints, a couple of tilted slabs composed of 220-million-year-old Fountain Formation sandstone, then descends southwest parallel to the park road through scrub-oak groves for 0.4 mile. When the trail reaches the edge of the road at 1.2 miles, you're opposite the Scotsman Picnic Area. Cross the road to a parking lot and walk over a bridge. A restroom, open in summer only, is to your left. Curve to the right on Scotsman Trail.

Follow the Scotsman Trail northeast for 0.35 mile. The sandy trail, often used by horse strings from a nearby stable, slowly climbs toward the Garden's rock formations.

The Tower of Babel towers above the Palmer Trail on the north side of the Garden of the Gods.

At an obvious trail junction, keep left and hike up to Juniper Way Loop road. Cross the road just north of a small parking area and follow a wide trail into the central Garden zone.

The next 0.5 mile of trail follows parts of the paved Perkins Central Garden Trail, the most popular and most scenic trail at the Garden of the Gods. Hike north and then east on the paved path, passing north of the Three Graces and Montezuma Tower, both slender spires that are popular with rock climbers. At an obvious Y junction, go left (north) and hike to the Gateway, the huge gap between North and South Gateway Rocks. At the trail junction here below the dedication plaque, which commemorates the gift of the Garden of the Gods from the children of Charles Eliot Perkins to the City of Colorado Springs in 1909, go right on a paved trail and walk 0.15 mile east to Juniper Way Loop.

The last trail segment follows the Susan G. Bretag Trail for 0.5 mile back to the trailhead and parking lot. Cross the road at a crosswalk and then turn north on the marked trail. Follow the wide trail north in a broad valley between white rock formations on the west and the Dakota Hogback to the east. The trail crosses an open meadow covered with grass and yucca.

After 0.3 mile it reaches a Y junction with the Dakota Trail. Keep left and follow the Bretag Trail, which bends northwest. End at the start of the Palmer Trail. Cross the road back to the trailhead and parking lot. If you're thirsty or need the facilities, a water fountain and restrooms are located on the southeast side of the parking lot.

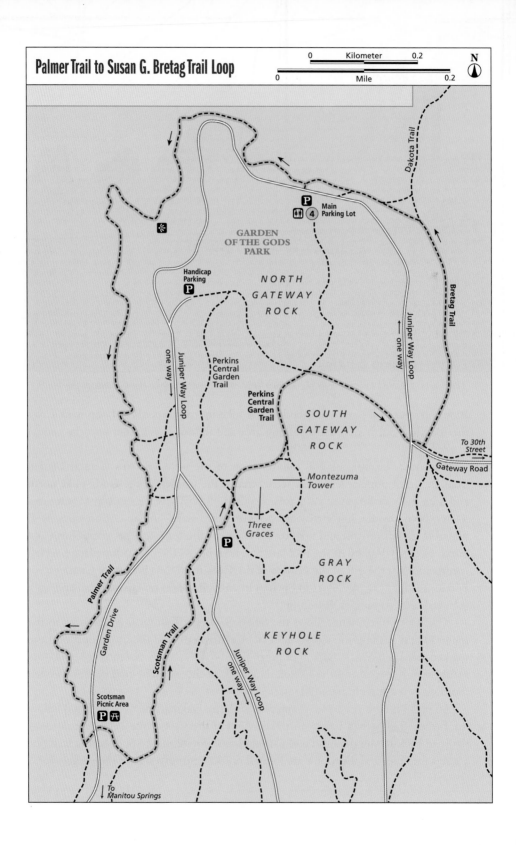

Palmer Trail to Susan G. Bretag Trail Loop

Kilometer
0   0.2

Mile
0   0.2

N

Dakota Trail

P
4 Main
Parking Lot

GARDEN
OF THE GODS
PARK

*NORTH
GATEWAY
ROCK*

Handicap
Parking
P

Juniper Way Loop
one way

Bretag Trail

Perkins
Central
Garden
Trail

**Perkins
Central
Garden
Trail**

*SOUTH
GATEWAY
ROCK*

Juniper Way Loop
one way

To 30th
Street

Gateway Road

Montezuma
Tower

P

*Three
Graces*

*GRAY
ROCK*

Palmer Trail

Garden Drive

Scotsman Trail

*KEYHOLE
ROCK*

Juniper Way Loop
one way

Scotsman
Picnic Area
P

↓ To
Manitou Springs

After doing this hike check out the other Garden of the Gods hikes detailed here—all are scenic and worth your footsteps.

Miles and Directions

0.0 Start at trailhead on the north side of the Main Garden Parking Lot (GPS: 38.88157, -104.880402). Cross the road to a T junction. Go left (west) on Palmer Trail.

0.3 Scenic overlook on the left (GPS: 38.881298, -104.883461). Walk down from the trail for the best photos.

0.8 Trail junction with short trail to Garden zone on left (GPS: 38.877218, -104.884248). Go straight.

1.2 Reach road opposite Scotsman Picnic Area (GPS: 38.872343, -104.885498). Cross road to the left at a crosswalk, then cross bridge to Scotsman Trail and restrooms (GPS: 38.872161, -104.884861). Go right.

1.6 End Scotsman Trail at Juniper Way Loop (GPS: 38.87569, -104.88253). Cross road at a crosswalk to the central Garden zone. Go left and follow a trail straight to the paved Perkins Central Garden Trail.

2.1 End the Central Perkins Garden Trail section at Juniper Way Loop on the east side of the park (GPS: 38.877193, -104.878011). Cross the road to the Susan G. Bretag Trail. Go left (north) up a wide valley on the Bretag Trail.

2.6 End the Susan G. Bretag Trail at its junction with Palmer Trail. Go left across the road to the trailhead and parking lot.

5 Ute Trail and Chambers Trail Loop

This short, fun hike explores the southeast side of the Garden of the Gods Park on a couple of excellent footpaths—the Ute Trail and Chambers Trail. The hike crosses broad meadows with tall grass and summer wildflowers, plunges through groves of Gambel oak, and passes beneath shady cottonwoods. Most of the hike follows the old Ute Trail, a route once followed by Ute Indians.

Start: South Garden Parking Lot at the southeast part of Juniper Way Loop road

Distance: 1.2-mile loop

Hiking time: About 1 hour

Difficulty: Easy

Elevation gain: 200 feet

Trail surface: Single- and doubletrack dirt trail

Seasons: Year-round

Schedule: Open daily; May 1 to Oct 31, 5 a.m. to 10 p.m.; Nov 1 to Apr 30, 5 a.m. to 9 p.m. Entrance gates are locked at night.

Other trail users: Multiuse trail with horses and mountain bikers

Canine compatibility: Leashed dogs only. Pick up your dog's waste.

Land status: City of Colorado Springs park

Fees and permits: None. Colorado Springs city park rules apply.

Map: USGS Cascade

Trail contact: Colorado Springs Parks, Recreation and Cultural Services, 1401 Recreation Way, Colorado Springs, CO 80905-1975; (719) 385-5940; https://coloradosprings.gov/parks gov.com

Finding the trailhead: From I-25 take exit 146 and drive west on Garden of the Gods Road until it dead-ends at North 30th Street against the mountains. Turn left (south) on North 30th Street and drive 1.5 miles south to Gateway Road opposite the Garden of the Gods Visitor and Nature Center. Turn right (west) on Gateway Road and follow it until it merges with Juniper Way Loop, a loop road that encircles the main Garden of the Gods zone. Turn right (north) on the one-way road and follow it past the Main Parking Lot on the left then down the west side of the park. Keep left at a junction and continue south past Keyhole Rock to a junction with Ridge Road. Keep left and bend around to the South Garden Parking Lot (#10) on the right (GPS: 38.869729, -104.878112). The trailhead is at the north side of the parking lot at an information kiosk (GPS: 38.870139, -104.878235).

Alternatively, approach from I-25 and downtown Colorado Springs by driving west on Cimarron Street / US 24 from I-25 to 31st Street. Exit right and follow North 31st Street north to a stop sign at West Fontanero Street. Drive 2 blocks east on Fontanero and turn left (north) on North 30th Street. Drive 1.2 miles to its junction with Gateway Road. Turn left (west) and follow the above directions to the South Garden Parking Lot.

The Hike

This short loop hike, following parts of the Ute Trail and Chambers Trail, is a marvelous and scenic excursion around the southeast corner of the Garden of the Gods Park. It offers spectacular views of soaring rock formations, tallgrass meadows, a pond (sometimes filled with rainwater) lined with cottonwood trees, and a historical link to the Ute Indians, the park's first residents.

Start the hike at the South Garden Parking Lot on the east side of Juniper Way Loop, a one-way scenic road that loops around the central Garden of the Gods zone. The trailhead is located at a ramada on the north side of the parking lot. Before hiking, be sure to read four interpretive signs at the ramada that provide information on the Utes, Zebulon Pike's expedition in 1806, the plants and animals that live at the Garden, and a 1930s photo of the park filled with cars at an Easter sunrise service.

Hike north from the trailhead on a dirt track. The trail parallels the park road and, after 250 feet, reaches a stone marker next to a small parking area. The granite stele, placed by the Daughters of the American Revolution in 1935, reads: "This Stone Marks the Indian Trail Used by the Plains Indians to Ute Pass." A famous photograph was taken in 1912 of a string of Utes riding horses single-file up the trail toward the stele.

From the marker, descend the wide trail through a broad meadow covered with tall grass and studded with spiky yuccas, clumps of skunkbrush, and scattered groves of Gambel oak. After crossing a bridge over a deep arroyo, which drains out of a rocky canyon, the trail passes beneath looming Gray Rock. This towering rock formation, also called Cathedral Rock and Kindergarten Rock, is composed of the upper layer of Lyons sandstone, a fine-grained sandstone with extensive cross-bedding, indicating that it was deposited in a sand dune environment during the Permian period between 225 million and 270 million years ago. Later during the Laramide orogeny, an intense mountain-building period about 70 million years ago, the horizontal sandstone was thrust upward as the Rocky Mountains slowly rose to the west. Erosion then attacked the rising layers, stripping off softer rock surrounding the Lyons and leaving today's bare-rock monuments.

The trail passes a couple of large boulders, tumbled down from Gray Rock, on the left. These room-size blocks, called the Snake Pit by climbers, is a popular spot for bouldering, the art of climbing difficult problems on small rocks. The east face of Gray Rock also offers lots of excellent climbing routes up its vertical faces. Check out *Rock Climbing Colorado* (FalconGuides, 2019) for route descriptions and information on climbing at the Garden of the Gods.

Hike north along the edge of the grassy meadow, and after 0.25 mile reach a trail junction with the right-hand loop of the Ute Trail. Continue straight on the Ute Trail. The sandy trail heads through broad meadows filled with wavering grass and gray with clumps of sage. At an obvious Y fork, take the right trail. The left one heads up to the loop road. After passing through a dense copse of Gambel or scrub oak, the trail bends right, crosses a small wooden bridge, and, at 0.45 mile from the trailhead, reaches a major three-way trail junction immediately south of the park entrance road. Take a sharp right turn here onto Chambers Trail. A post marks the junction with signs pointing out three trails.

THE HISTORIC UTE TRAIL

The Mountain Utes traveled along ancient trails down Ute Pass to the mineral springs and the Garden of the Gods. In his book *The Indians of the Pikes Peak* Region, early pioneer Irving Howbert wrote that the Native American trail through the Garden of the Gods was a branch of the old Ute Trail. This trail came down Ute Pass northeast of Pikes Peak to the springs in Manitou, then headed down Fountain Creek's canyon to today's Becker's Lane, where the trail climbed toward Ridge Road and the Garden of the Gods. It swung around a low hill, following today's park loop road, and passed by the South Parking Lot before descending a hill still followed by today's trail. The Ute Trail descended across the Rock Ledge Ranch east of the Garden's rock formations, climbed over the Mesa, and headed northeast along today's Fillmore Street before exiting the valley through Templeton Gap.

Howbert also remembered that more than 300 Utes camped near Balanced Rock in the cold winter of 1866-67. He wrote: "They did not bother us in Colorado City, and we felt no great alarm. They were more inclined to be friendly than otherwise. But one day a party of them came into town and made a demand upon us for 20 sacks of flour. They told us that they were nearly out of provisions and were in danger of starving. They said that they had come to ask that we give them the flour, but that so pressing was the need that if we were to refuse they would take it anyhow.

"The matter was talked over by the people of the town and not a person was found who did not think it the right thing to give them that for which they asked. It was the general belief that they were facing starvation and much sympathy was felt for them. So the 20 sacks of flour were presented and the Indians went away with it, grateful for the food."

Nothing exists of the historic Ute Trail today except a short section at the Garden of the Gods, which can only be documented by historic photographs that show Ute Indians riding up the trail.

Go southeast on Chambers Trail across the meadow, with great views of the red rock formations, including Gray Rock, South Gateway Rock, and North Gateway Rock, on the western skyline. The open trail eventually threads across a shale slope below the Dakota Hogback, a high elongated ridge to the left, before reaching the top of an old earthen dam above Rock Ledge Ranch on the east and a catchment basin on the right that fills with rainwater every ten years or so. On the north side of the dam is an obvious three-way trail junction. Continue straight across the dam on

Hikers pass beneath Gray Rock and Keyhole Rock on the Ute Trail.

ANCIENT ARTIFACTS

Evidence, including prehistoric hearths found in 1993, indicates that ancient people camped at the Garden of the Gods around 1330 BC, or 3,330 years ago, while radiocarbon dates from hearths and fire rings show that there were seasonal encampments at the Garden of the Gods beginning by 250 BC. Artifacts of early Native Americans here include broken pottery bits, stone tools, and projectile points or arrowheads.

short Valley Reservoir Trail. A sharp left turn is the Galloway–Homestead Trail, while the Chambers Trail continues down left to Rock Ledge Ranch Historic Site.

Option: The Rock Ledge Ranch is worth a short visit for the pioneer history of the Pikes Peak region if you have the time. Follow the Chambers Trail down to the ranch and meander around. It's best to visit on weekends when the place is buzzing with activity. The site was originally settled in 1867 by Scotsman Walt Galloway, who established a 160-acre homestead along Camp Creek. He built a rustic log cabin and planted a garden, irrigating it with water from the creek. Eventually he sold his property to the Chambers family, who built Rock Ledge Ranch. Elsie Chambers later called him ". . . a plain, plodding day laborer, but exemplified what persistence can do in securing a home in his own name, by staying in one place and cultivating the regulation patch of garden demanded by Uncle Sam."

Hike across the top of the dam and bend right, passing a junction with Niobrara Trail, which strikes up left onto the hogback. After 0.9 mile from the trailhead, you reach a junction with the Ute Trail loop, which comes in from the northwest. Go left at this Y junction on the Ute Trail and climb a slight hill for a couple hundred feet to the last junction. Go right (west) on Ute Trail Connection.

Follow this narrow track up and over a hogback, passing low tilted sandstone cliffs. At the top of a hogback is a short spur trail that trots north a few hundred feet to an overlook. Follow the main trail down a gentle slope on the west side of the hogback and end at a trailhead at the southern end of the South Garden Parking Lot.

Miles and Directions

0.0 Start at the trailhead at the north end of the South Garden Parking Lot (GPS: 38.870139, -104.878235).

0.2 Ute Trail stone marker beside park loop road and trail. Go north downhill.

0.25 Reach a trail junction with the loop formed by the Ute Trail (GPS: 38.872114, -104.877855). Go straight and pass another trail junction to the right. Continue straight (north).

0.45 After passing a social trail that goes left to the road, continue to a major three-trail junction just south of the park entrance road (GPS: 38.876764, -104.877576). Make a sharp right turn and head southeast on the Chambers Trail.

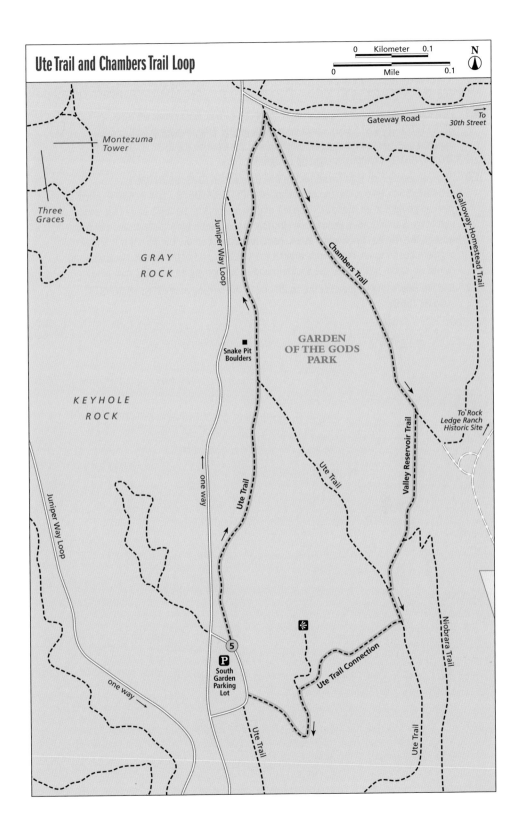

Ute Trail and Chambers Trail Loop

0   Kilometer   0.1

0   Mile   0.1

N

Gateway Road

To 30th Street

Montezuma Tower

Three Graces

GRAY ROCK

Juniper Way Loop

Chambers Trail

Galloway-Homestead Trail

Snake Pit Boulders

GARDEN OF THE GODS PARK

KEYHOLE ROCK

To Rock Ledge Ranch Historic Site

one way

Ute Trail

Ute Trail

Valley Reservoir Trail

Juniper Way Loop

5

P

South Garden Parking Lot

Ute Trail Connection

Niobrara Trail

one way

Ute Trail

Ute Trail

0.8 Reach a junction with the Galloway-Homestead Trail and the Valley Reservoir Trail (GPS: 38.873036, -104.875063). Go right on Valley Reservoir Trail and hike across the top of an old dam. The Chambers Trail continues southeast, descending down to the southern end of Rock Ledge Ranch.

0.9 Past the old dam, reach a junction with the Niobrara Trail, which goes left (GPS: 38.871356, -104.875326). Continue straight on the Valley Reservoir Trail. In a few hundred feet, you will reach a trail junction with the Ute Trail (GPS: 38.870713, -104.875519). Continue straight up a slight hill.

1.0 At a trail junction go right (west) on Ute Trail Connection (GPS: 38.870353, -104.875354). Hike to the top of a hogback (GPS: 38.869678, -104.876867), where you can go right to an overlook. Keep left and go downhill to the trail's end at the south end of the South Garden Parking Lot. (***Option:*** If you want a longer hike, instead of going west on the Ute Trail Connection cutoff, continue straight on the Ute Trail. This 0.5-mile trail segment heads south, then bends around the southern end of the rounded hogback and climbs up to the trailhead at the southern end of the parking lot for a 1.7-mile hike.)

1.2 End the hike at the trailhead at the south end of the parking area (GPS: 38.869377, -104.877859).

6 Perkins Central Garden Trail

This short loop hike follows a paved wheelchair-accessible trail that explores the scenic heart of the Garden of the Gods Park, a spectacular natural wonder of uplifted sandstone rock formations on the west side of Colorado Springs. The trail is one of the best easy hikes in the Colorado Springs area and one that every visitor and resident should do.

Start: Main Parking Lot at the north end of Juniper Way Loop
Distance: 1.2-mile lollipop
Hiking time: 30 minutes to 1 hour
Difficulty: Easy; wheelchair- and stroller-accessible
Elevation gain: Minimal
Trail surface: Concrete sidewalk
Seasons: Year-round
Schedule: Open daily. Nov 1 to Apr 30: 5 a.m. to 9 p.m.; May 1 to Oct 31: 5 a.m. to 10 p.m. Entrance gates are locked at night.

Other trail users: Hikers only
Canine compatibility: Leashed dogs only
Land status: City of Colorado Springs park
Fees and permits: None
Maps: USGS Manitou Springs; Garden of the Gods park trail map
Trail contact: Colorado Springs Parks, Recreation and Cultural Services, 1401 Recreation Way, Colorado Springs 80905-1975; (719) 385-5940; https://coloradosprings.gov/parks

Finding the trailhead: From I-25 take exit 146 and drive west on Garden of the Gods Road until it dead-ends at 30th Street against the mountain front. Turn left (south) on 30th Street and drive south to Gateway Road opposite the Garden of the Gods Visitor and Nature Center. Turn right (west) on Gateway Road and follow it until it merges with Juniper Way Loop, a loop road that encircles the main Garden of the Gods zone. Turn right (north) on the one-way road and follow it to the large Main Parking Lot on the left (south) side of the road. The trailhead is at the southeast corner of the lot (GPS: 38.880916, -104.880163).

Alternatively, approach from the south by driving west from I-25 on US 24 to 31st Street. Exit right and follow 31st Street north to a stop sign at West Fontanero Street. Turn right on Fontanero, drive 2 blocks, and make a left turn on 30th Street. Follow 30th Street north to Gateway Road. Turn left on Gateway Road opposite the park visitor center and follow the directions above to the trailhead.

The Hike

The Perkins Central Garden Trail, a 1.2-mile hike that follows a paved path that loops around the major rock formations in the Garden of the Gods, a Colorado Springs city park, gets you up close and personal with the Garden's soaring sandstone rock formations. The wide trail, accessible to both wheelchairs and strollers, has gentle gradients and plenty of spectacular scenic views, some of the best in Colorado. This short hike is simply one that every resident of and visitor to Colorado Springs should enjoy. The trail is accessible year-round, with every time of day and every season offering new perspectives, views, and experiences.

The Garden of the Gods, nestled against the southern end of the Rampart Range on the west side of Colorado Springs, is a huge outdoor sculpture garden dominated by towering rock monuments. Here rise twisted, faulted, and uplifted layers of sandstone that tell the geologic story of the constantly changing earth—the uplift and erosion of ancient mountain ranges, periodic inundations by seas, and the comings and goings of different lives.

The story of the earth from a couple billion years ago until the present is seen at the Garden of the Gods. Few other places in the United States boast the variety and age of exposed rock like the Garden. Every different rock stratum is a page from a great book, each showing its own story from its own world.

Begin the paved trail at the southeast corner of the large Main Parking Lot on the north side of the Garden of the Gods off Juniper Way Loop, a one-way road that encircles the main Garden zone. Restrooms, open year-round, and a water fountain are left of the trailhead. To the right is a ramada with an interpretive display.

The first 0.2-mile trail segment heads south down the paved path to a viewpoint surrounded by a circular stone wall. North Gateway Rock, also called Gate Rock, towers above the trail to the west. This huge salmon-colored formation is the highest in the Garden, looming over 300 feet above the footpath. The long, ragged ridge of White Rock rims the shallow canyon on its east side. Continue down the trail to The Gateway, a broad open gap between North Gateway on the right and South Gateway Rock on the left.

A couple of squat pinnacles, Red Twin Spire and White Twin Spire, sit on the west side of The Gateway. On the right side of the trail before The Gateway is Signature Rock, a boulder covered with inscriptions, some dating back to early park visitors in the nineteenth century. Over 600 historic names once covered the boulder's face but most have eroded away. The oldest signatures date from 1858 when the Lawrence party passed through on their way to the goldfields near Central City. Another interesting name on the rock is Edwin "Fatty" Rice who ran a saloon and shop on the eastern edge of the Garden of the Gods in the 1890s.

A large plaque on the narrow south face of North Gateway Rock details the gift of the Garden of the Gods to the City of Colorado Springs and honors its benefactor, railroad magnate Charles Elliott Perkins. Perkins purchased most of the Garden in 1879 but allowed public visitation. Two years after Perkins's death in 1907, his children donated the land to the city as a park that would "be kept forever open and free to the public." From Perkins's original 480 acres, the Garden of the Gods Park, now a designated National Natural Landmark, has grown to 1,334 acres.

The rock formations were long a sacred place to Native Americans, who first camped here as long as 3,300 years ago and undoubtedly scrambled to the lofty summits. The Garden was later sacred to other tribes, including the Apache, Arapaho, Cheyenne, Comanche, Kiowa, Pawnee, Shoshone, and Ute peoples. The Utes, a

Hikers enjoy a brisk winter morning below South Gateway Rock.

Colorado mountain tribe, particularly revered the Garden of the Gods and camped below the formations. Evidence of their passage includes a few petroglyphs pecked onto sandstone surfaces and historic photographs of Ute visitors taken in the nineteenth century.

Park visitors always wonder how the Garden received its name. Early visitors first called the area Red Rock Corral. In the summer of 1859, surveyors M. S. Beach and Rufus Cable visited the site while laying out what is now Old Colorado City. Inspired by the scenery, Beach told his friend, "Rufus, this is a capital place for a beer garden." Cable, however, fittingly replied, "A beer garden? No, this is a fit place for the gods to assemble. We should call it Garden of the Gods!"

At The Gateway the trail splits. Take the left fork and hike beneath the sharp northern edge of South Gateway Rock and past Red and White Twin Spires on the right. A low stone wall here makes a good bench to have a drink of water and watch rock climbers clamber up the spires. The trail bends left into the central Garden, a broad valley with open grasslands, groves of Gambel oak, scattered juniper trees, and grazing mule deer. Follow the trail past the vertical west face of South Gateway Rock on the left to a junction. Keep left and pass below the sheer east face of Montezuma Tower on the right. (**Option:** Stay to the right and cut off 0.1 mile from the hike by

SACRED GROUND

The Garden of the Gods, with its soaring sandstone formations and strange aura of serenity, silence, and a touch of eternity, was undoubtedly a sacred place to Native Americans. The mythology of many tribes, including the Kiowa, Pawnee, Cheyenne, Arapaho, Comanche, Apache, Shoshone, and Ute groups, describes this as a special place.

The Mountain Utes were particularly fond of the Garden of the Gods, often camping among the rocks, hunting for deer and elk, and soaking and drinking from the sacred bubbling waters in today's Manitou Springs. Several accounts by early settlers document that the Utes often camped at the Garden of the Gods, particularly in winter. Buckskin Charley, their famed chief after Ouray in the late nineteenth century, was auspiciously born at the Garden. He was awarded the Rutherford Hayes Peace Medal by President Benjamin Harrison in 1890 and rode beside the Apache chief Geronimo in President Teddy Roosevelt's inauguration parade in 1905.

passing northwest of Montezuma Tower and the Three Graces. Keep right at the next two intersections to return to the Perkins Trail and continue the hike.)

Option: If you want to add a short scenic 0.2-mile loop to the hike, take a left off the main trail at the next three-way intersection and hike up a dirt trail, which climbs south to a rocky overlook north of Keyhole Rock. Expect spacious views here of the Garden's rock formations and Pikes Peak to the west. Don't scramble onto the ledges on Keyhole Rock south of the overlook: It's an area reserved for technical climbing and is dangerous, especially for children, with drop-offs. From the overlook descend west through a grove of thousand-year-old junipers and rejoin the paved trail just west of Three Graces Plaza.

Three Graces Plaza is a small open area flanked by low stone walls at the southern end of the paved trail. Looming above the circular plaza is 135-foot-high Montezuma Tower, a tall, frail spire on the right, and the three narrow fins of the Three Graces directly above the plaza. This is a great spot to sit on a wall and marvel at the soaring sandstone formations. Helen Hunt Jackson, a nineteenth-century writer and author of *Ramona*, described the Garden of the Gods this way: "You wind among rocks of every conceivable and inconceivable shape and size . . . all bright red, all motionless and silent, with a strange look of having been just stopped and held back in the very climax of some supernatural catastrophe."

From the plaza, hike west on the paved trail down a gentle slope. A side trail goes left to the park road and two small roadside parking lots. At a three-way junction, go left and continue north on the main Perkins trail for 0.3 mile, paralleling the park loop road to the left. Benches along the way allow you to rest and marvel at the rock formations. From the earliest days the bizarre rocks have teased the imaginations of countless visitors who saw fanciful shapes, some reflected by names including

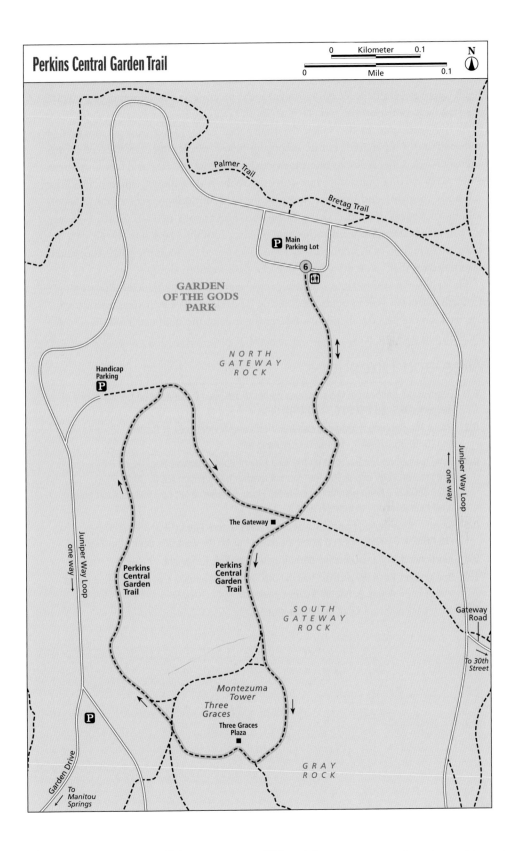

Perkins Central Garden Trail

0   Kilometer   0.1

0   Mile   0.1

N

Palmer Trail

Bretag Trail

P Main Parking Lot

6

GARDEN OF THE GODS PARK

NORTH GATEWAY ROCK

Handicap Parking **P**

Juniper Way Loop
one way

The Gateway ■

Juniper Way Loop
one way

Perkins Central Garden Trail

Perkins Central Garden Trail

SOUTH GATEWAY ROCK

Gateway Road

To 30th Street

Montezuma Tower
Three Graces

Three Graces Plaza ■

P

GRAY ROCK

Garden Drive

To Manitou Springs

Weeping Indian and Kissing Camels. Take a look across the grassy vale to see if you can spot these two shapes. Kissing Camels is a fragile skyline arch perched high atop North Gateway, while the Weeping Indian is the profile of a chief composed of white rock that faces north on the west face of South Gateway Rock.

At the north end of the valley, the trail bends east, passing through thickets of scrub oak and juniper trees before emerging below the abrupt west face of North Gateway Rock. Check out an interpretive exhibit below the face and take a moment to watch the darting flights of white-throated swifts and swallows, which nest on the rock walls. In spring and summer, you may hear the shrieking cry of a prairie falcon looking for a meal of mouse, snake, or pigeon. The falcons nest on North Gateway Rock in spring and summer. Another rare inhabitant of the Garden of the Gods is the honey ant, which lives in a handful of colonies scattered through the park. Also, watch for rattlesnakes that sometimes stray onto the paved trail in summer.

The trail turns southeast at the interpretive sign and passes beneath the west face of North Gateway Rock, before reentering The Gateway. From here, retrace your steps back on the paved trail, northward, for 0.2 mile to the trailhead, restrooms, water fountain, and parking area.

Miles and Directions

0.0 Begin at the trailhead at the southeast corner of the Main Parking Lot on the north side of the park (GPS: 38.880916, -104.880163).

0.2 Reach The Gateway, a wide gap between North and South Gateway Rocks, and a trail junction (GPS: 38.878426, -104.880322). Keep left.

0.3 Enter the central Garden zone on the west side of South Gateway Rock. Keep left at a junction. After about 500 feet you will reach a trail junction (GPS: 38.875929, -104.880857). Keep right to Three Graces Plaza. (**Option:** A left turn follows a dirt trail up a hill to an overlook at Keyhole Rock.)

0.5 Reach a three-way trail junction west of the Three Graces Plaza (GPS: 38.876376, -104.882078). Keep left and follow the paved trail on the west side of an open meadow.

0.8 Junction with trail to accessible parking area on the left. Keep right.

1.0 Trail junction. Keep left on main trail through Gateway. At a major trail junction on the east side of The Gateway, go left toward the parking lot.

1.2 Arrive back at the trailhead and parking lot.

7 Red Rock Canyon Trail

This out-and-back classic hike is flanked by towering sandstone walls and follows an old road in the heart of Red Rock Canyon, the centerpiece of Red Rock Canyon Open Space on the west side of Colorado Springs. A spur trail climbs to a historic stone quarry, then returns to the main trail.

Start: Eastern end of the park road off Ridge Road

Distance: 2.6 miles out and back on two trails

Hiking time: 1 to 2 hours

Difficulty: Easy

Elevation gain: 150 feet

Trail surface: Doubletrack dirt trail up a closed road

Seasons: Year-round. Trail can be muddy or snowy in winter.

Schedule: Open daily. Nov 1 to Apr 30: 5 a.m. to 9 p.m.; May 1 to Oct 31: 5 a.m. to 10 p.m.

Other trail users: Runners, mountain bikers, equestrians

Canine compatibility: Leashed dogs only

Land status: City of Colorado Springs

Fees and permits: None

Maps: USGS Manitou Springs; Colorado Springs RRCOS map at https://colorado springs.gov/

Trail contact: Colorado Springs Parks, Recreation and Cultural Services, 1401 Recreation Way, Colorado Springs 80905-1975; (719) 385-5940; https://coloradosprings.gov/parks

Special considerations: Don't leave valuables, including purses and cameras, visible in your vehicle at the parking areas. Break-ins do occur. Bring everything of value with you on your hike.

Finding the trailhead: Red Rock Canyon Open Space is south of the Garden of the Gods Park and US 24. To access the park from downtown Colorado Springs and I-25, take the Cimarron Street / US 24 exit (exit 141) and drive west 3.5 miles toward the mountains. Access the parking areas and trailheads by turning left (south) on South Ridge Road from US 24, which is the only left turn between 31st Street and the first Manitou Springs exit. Use extreme caution turning across the busy highway. Drive south on Ridge Road for 0.1 mile and turn left into the park. Drive through a roundabout and follow the park road to a large parking area on the right (GPS: 38.853605, -104.880551). Portable toilets and a trail map are available at a trailhead at the east end of the parking lot (GPS: 38.853327, -104.879257). You can also park in another lot at the end of the park road to the southeast.

The Hike

The 1.1-mile-long Red Rock Canyon Trail explores Red Rock Canyon, the scenic centerpiece of 1,474-acre Red Rock Canyon Open Space. The city of Colorado Springs purchased the park's initial 787 acres in 2003, saving the area from trophy homes, a golf course, and resort development. Red Rock Canyon, splitting the center of the parkland from south to north, is a mile-long canyon lined with tall sandstone cliffs and floored with groves of scrub oak, cottonwood trees, and meadows blanketed with tall grass and wildflowers. Besides its natural beauty and dramatic geology, Red Rock Canyon also harbors archaeological and historical sites including an old stone quarry that operated from 1886 until 1915.

Red Rock Canyon Trail is an easy hike up the canyon from the parking lot, following a closed dirt road. The trail has easy grades and great scenery and is popular, especially on weekends. While the described hike ends at the start of the Roundup Trail in the south part of the canyon, it can be combined with it or Red Rock Rim Trail to create a longer loop hike. Download a trail map from the Friends of Red Rock Canyon at their website www.redrockcanyonopenspace.org.

Begin the hike from the trailhead at the east side of the main parking lot, on the north side of the park opposite US 24. Portable toilets and a trail map are available at the trailhead. An alternative parking area is located to the east past the first large parking lot at the end of the park road below Red Rock Canyon itself. If you park there, knock 0.2 mile off your hike.

The first trail segment runs east and then south for 0.4 mile before joining an old closed road. East of the trailhead is a junction with the Mesa and Greenlee Trails, which head south up another closed road. Continue hiking straight and pass the left side of a freestyle-biking area. Here the wide gravel trail bends south. Follow the trail between the south parking area and a sandstone cliff that was quarried in the nineteenth century. The trail slowly climbs and then bends east to join the old Red Rock Canyon road. If you hike from the south parking area, it's 0.2 mile to this point.

Hike up the road for 0.1 mile, passing a locked gate, to the site of the old Bock house, now a shaded pavilion. The Red Rock Canyon property once belonged to John George Bock, who acquired it during the 1920s. Bock started with a tourist camp and stables by Fountain Creek and then bought the other land from quarrying companies, paying only back taxes. After Bock's death, his two sons, John and Richard, wanted to build a World Trade Center here with two golf courses, luxury homes and condos, a shopping center, office buildings, a sports arena, and thirteen lakes. They were unable to get the area rezoned, so in the 1970s they turned it into a landfill for Colorado Springs trash and gravel pit. In the 1990s another large developer attempted to resurrect the Bock plan but was denied annexation by both Manitou Springs and Colorado Springs, leaving the door open for its purchase as a Colorado Springs park. Colorado Springs initially acquired 789 acres and then later purchased adjoining Section 16 and White Acres properties.

The next trail segment follows the closed road up the east side of Red Rock Canyon for 0.4 mile to its junction with Quarry Pass Trail.

Option: For an alternative hike, go right at the pavilion and descend down to a small pond. Follow the singletrack 0.5-mile Red Rock Canyon Path, a hiker-only trail, along the west side of the canyon to the Quarry Pass Trail Junction.

Sandstone hogbacks reflect in a pond at Red Rock Canyon. ▶

RED ROCK CANYON'S HISTORIC QUARRIES

The ruddy Lyons sandstone, forming the west wall of Red Rock Canyon, became a popular building stone in the 1880s and was used for construction in Colorado Springs, Manitou Springs, and Denver, including the Redstone Castle in Manitou and the Molly Brown House in Denver. The rock, then called Manitou sandstone, was popular for its red color, easily carved, and sometimes used as an accent with other stone.

The canyon had two main quarries—the Kenmuir and Snider Quarries. The Kenmuir Quarry, the large quarry in the middle of the canyon, was operated by the Greenlee Company and employed hundreds of workers, who used steam equipment and drills to excavate blocks of stone. Many workers lived in the canyon. In 1886 the Colorado Midland Railroad built a spur line into the canyon; blocks were loaded by crane onto flatcars and transported around Colorado and to other states.

A decline in the use of stone around 1900 coupled with the growing use of concrete and steel as building materials forced the quarries to close, leaving their stair-stepped walls as a historic legacy of early Colorado Springs' industry.

Whether you took the option or stayed on the main featured trail, at the junction go right and follow Quarry Pass Trail for 0.1 mile up into Kenmuir Quarry, a nineteenth-century stone quarry and historic site. The Lyons sandstone blocks quarried here were loaded onto train cars on a railroad spur that ran into the canyon. The stone was then shipped to Colorado Springs as well as Denver, Kansas, and Texas for buildings and foundations. Many buildings in Denver were built with the striking red sandstone blocks from here. The stone, however, didn't weather well, and the canyon's quarries, operated by the Greenlee family in Denver, closed down by 1915. Most of the sandstone was quarried between 1888 and 1893. This side trail climbs up to the quarry. Make sure you climb the staircase chopped into bedrock to enter the quarry. After visiting it retrace your steps back to the main trail.

The last trail segment continues south for 0.20 mile on the old road, steadily climbing a long hill to a major trail junction and the Red Rock Canyon Trail turnaround point at 6,400 feet. Take a minute to enjoy the view. Directly west across the wooded canyon is the Wiggins Wall, named for the late Earl Wiggins, a famous local rock climber, and a deep defile called Black Bear Canyon. This and the other cliffs in Red Rock Canyon are popular with rock climbers, who enjoy over one hundred established climbing routes in the canyon. From this high point, retrace the trail north for 1.3 miles to the parking lot.

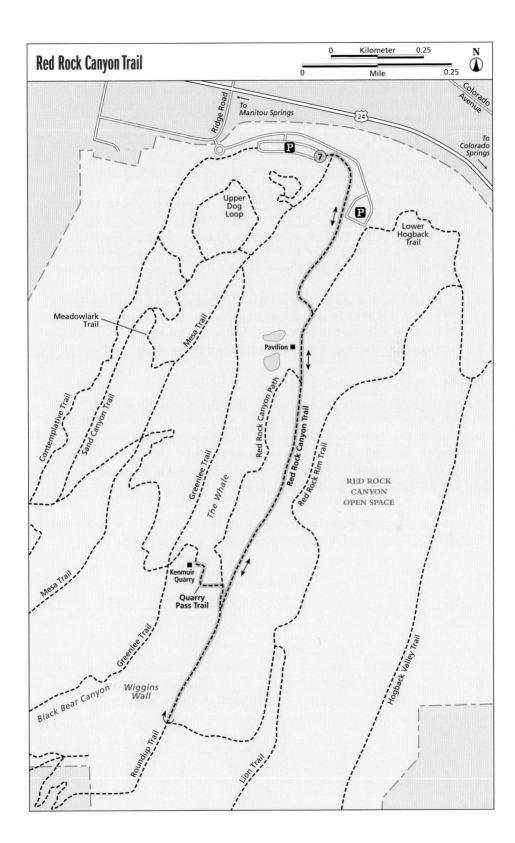

Miles and Directions

0.0 Begin at the trailhead at the east end of the park's main parking lot (GPS: 38.853327, -104.879257). Restrooms and a trail map are here. Hike southeast on a wide trail, passing a freestyle-biking area and another parking area.

0.4 Climb a gradual hill and reach a junction with a closed dirt road (GPS: 38.84971, -104.879644). Turn right (south).

0.5 Hike south past a gate to a stone pavilion (GPS: 38.848932, -104.880134) and a small pond on the right. Stay on the road and continue hiking south up the east side of the canyon. (**Option:** Red Rock Canyon Path, a singletrack trail, begins at the pavilion and follows the west side of the canyon to the Quarry Pass Trail junction.)

0.9 After hiking below tall cliffs above the trail, arrive at the junction with Quarry Pass Trail (GPS: 38.843297, -104.882469). Go right on Quarry Pass Trail and hike 0.1 mile up to the historic quarry site. After viewing, return 0.1 mile to the junction and continue straight south on the main trail.

1.3 End the first half of the hike at the top of a hill at a junction with Red Rock Rim Trail (GPS: 38.840008, -104.884362), which goes left (east). Turn around and hike back to the trailhead. (**Two options are available at this point; see Options below**.)

2.6 After hiking north down the main canyon trail, arrive back at the trailhead.

Options

For extra credit you can continue hiking on trails from the turnaround point. Several loop hikes fan out from the end of the Red Rock Canyon Trail. The best hike continues south up the canyon for 0.2 mile before turning west up a deep canyon. Follow the 1.3-mile Roundup Trail out of the canyon, then dip across the heads of a couple shallow canyons before descending north to the southern end of the Contemplative Trail, which is followed back to the main parking lot. This creates an excellent 3.5-mile loop hike.

Another good option from the junction at the end of the trail is to go left and follow the Red Rock Rim Trail for 1.4 miles back to the upper parking lot.

8 Contemplative, Roundup, and Red Rock Canyon Trails Loop

This excellent loop hike, combining parts of four trails, offers a grand walking tour that winds among soaring sandstone formations and threads through canyons in the western sector of Red Rock Canyon Open Space.

Start: West side of large parking lot on north side of the park. Hike ends at east side of parking lot.

Distance: 3.3-mile loop following 4 different trails

Hiking time: 1.5 to 2 hours

Difficulty: Easy with gradual grades

Elevation gain: 450 feet

Trail surface: Singletrack dirt trail and closed dirt road

Seasons: Year-round. Trail can be icy in winter; bring spikes and trekking poles.

Schedule: Open daily. Nov 1 to Apr 30: 5 a.m. to 9 p.m.; May 1 to Oct 31: 5 a.m. to 10 p.m.

Other trail users: Hikers only on the Contemplative Trail. Mountain bikes and horses allowed on other trail segments.

Canine compatibility: Leashed dogs only

Land status: Public land in a Colorado Springs open space

Fees and permits: None

Maps: USGS Manitou Springs; Colorado Springs RRCOS map

Trail contact: Colorado Springs Parks, Recreation and Cultural Services, 1401 Recreation Way, Colorado Springs, CO 80905-1975; (719) 385-5940; https://coloradosprings.gov/parks

Special considerations: Don't leave valuables, including purses and cameras, visible in your vehicle at the parking areas. Break-ins do occur. Bring everything of value with you on your hike.

Finding the trailhead: Red Rock Canyon Open Space is south of Garden of the Gods and US 24. To access the area from downtown Colorado Springs and I-25, take the Cimarron Street / US 24 exit (exit 141) and drive west 3.5 miles toward the mountains. Access the parking lot and trailhead by turning left (south) on Ridge Road from US 24, which is the only left turn between 31st Street and the first Manitou Springs exit. Use extreme caution turning since the highway is busy. Drive south on Ridge Road for 0.1 mile and turn left into the park. Drive through a roundabout and go left. Park at the first lot near its western end. The trailhead is at the west end of the lot (GPS: 38.853555, -104.881386). The end of the hike is at the trailhead on the east side of the lot, which is 0.25 mile east of the hike start.

The Hike

This fantastic 3.3-mile hike, combining 0.2 mile of the Sand Canyon Trail, the 0.6-mile Contemplative Trail, the 1.1-mile Roundup Trail, and the 1.3-mile Red Rock Canyon Trail, forms a loop hike on the west side of Red Rock Canyon Open Space. The easy hike wanders through soaring fins of sandstone, dense thickets of scrub oak, open ponderosa pine woods, and, in summer, flower-strewn meadows.

PIKES PEAK REGION GEOLOGY

The Pikes Peak region, including the Garden of the Gods and Red Rock Canyon, is renowned among earth scientists for its unique geological value. Colorado Springs offers more exposed geological history within its city limits than any other American city, with every geologic period represented except the Silurian. The exposed rock formations form the pages of a book that tells the story of the earth's history with stone evidence of a constantly changing planet—the uplift and erosion of great mountain ranges; an inundation of seas; great fields of sand dunes; and the evolution of life from fish to dinosaur to mammal. The age of the rocks ranges from Pikes Peak granite formed in a batholith 1.08 billion years ago to recent Quaternary gravel deposits left by streams swollen with glacial snowmelt within the last 30,000 years.

Interpretive signs and a map are available at the trailhead, located on the western side of the large parking area on the north side of the park and east of the roundabout on the park entrance road. The trailhead where the hike ends is at the east side of the parking area, 0.25 mile from the western trailhead. Portable toilets and a park trail map are available at the east end of the lot.

Hike west from the trailhead, passing a roundabout on the road at the park entrance off Ridge Road, and bend south on the first part of the Sand Canyon Trail. Bock Fin, a towering rock hogback composed of coarse 300-million-year-old Fountain Formation sandstone, looms above the trail. After 0.2 mile you reach a trail junction. Continue straight on the Contemplative Trail. The Sand Canyon Trail jogs left at the junction and climbs east.

The 0.6-mile Contemplative Trail segment twists south beneath tall rock formations, dipping across shallow valleys and climbing short hills. One spectacular trail section squeezes through a rock-walled passageway. Tall ponderosa pines, groves of Gambel oaks, and pocket meadows of tall grass and wildflowers fill shady vales below the rocks. Occasional cliff overlooks offer great views across wide Sand Canyon and north to the Garden of the Gods and the Rampart Range. Watch for grazing mule deer or an occasional black bear rambling down the valley. At its southern terminus the trail climbs timber steps and ends at Sand Canyon Trail, here an old roadbed.

Go straight (south) from this trail junction on the Roundup Trail. This 1.35-mile segment heads steadily uphill through pines and oaks, slowly climbing and switchbacking for 0.5 mile onto a wide ridge and a junction with Mesa Trail. Continue south on the Roundup Trail for 0.2 mile, dipping across the head of a shallow valley and reaching a junction with Greenlee Trail.

A hidden arch tops a sandstone fin above the Contemplative Trail.

Continue straight on the Roundup Trail and traverse across the head of Black Bear Canyon, which drains east into Red Rock Canyon. After 0.25 mile the trail again reaches Mesa Trail, which goes left to end atop a rocky hogback. From the junction descend a steep slope on a couple of wide switchbacks and follow the trail to the bottom of a narrow canyon. Pass through a gateway of soaring sandstone cliffs and, 0.4 mile from the last junction, reach the head of Red Rock Canyon and a trail map.

The last hike segment follows wide Red Rock Canyon Trail (also described in this book) down the canyon for 1.3 miles to the trailhead at the eastern end of the main parking lot. The scenic trail follows a closed road. Sandstone cliffs line the valley sides above the trail. Broad meadows broken by Gambel oak thickets and tall cottonwood trees fill the canyon floor. The sandstone cliffs in Red Rock Canyon are popular with local rock climbers, who find over 100 vertical adventures on its sunny slabs and faces. The canyon is also a great spot for wildlife watching on quiet days. Look for grazing deer, bobcats, red foxes, and occasional black bears in the canyon.

The trail descends along the east side of the canyon and after 0.8 mile reaches a pavilion built on the site of the old Bock house. Red Rock Canyon, after its quarry days were over, was acquired piecemeal over a twenty-year period by John G. Bock, who moved to Colorado from Philadelphia in 1923 to recuperate from tuberculosis. Bock built roads and trails and opened Roundup Stables, where he rented horses to tourists.

The original Bock house sat at the pavilion. After the site became a Colorado Springs parkland, the house was too dilapidated to restore so it was razed, and the pavilion was built using the original walls and building stone. Near the pavilion is a pond, which reflects mountains, sky, and red rock when it's filled with runoff, and seven interpretive signs about park history, natural history, and geology.

Continue north on the trail and pass by a gate to a trail junction. The closed road continues straight to the east parking area. Go left on the trail and hike down the west side of the canyon past the remains of another old quarry and the parking lot. Bend left and continue hiking past a freestyle biking course to the trail's end at the trailhead at the eastern side of the main parking lot. Portable toilets are at the trailhead.

Miles and Directions

0.0 Start from the trailhead at the far west end of the main parking lot (GPS: 38.853555, -104.881386) and follow Sand Canyon Trail southwest.

0.2 Reach the junction of Sand Canyon and Contemplative Trails on the south side of Bock Fin (GPS: 38.851352, -104.884387). Go right on the Contemplative Trail and hike south below sandstone hogbacks.

0.8 Climb timber stairs to the junction of the southern end of the Contemplative Trail and Sand Canyon Trail (GPS: 38.845263, -104.88856). Go south on the Roundup Trail from this junction.

1.3 Hike south for 0.5 mile to the junction of the Roundup and Mesa Trails (GPS: 38.840697, -104.890837). Go straight on the Roundup Trail.

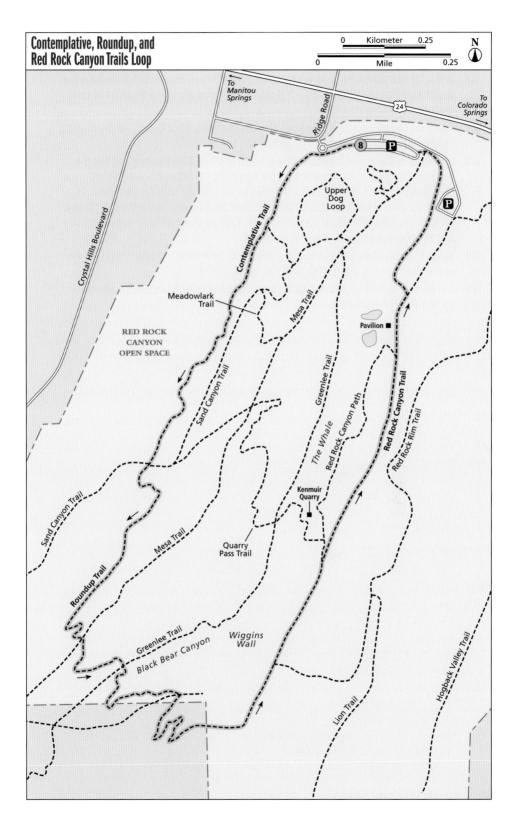

Contemplative, Roundup, and Red Rock Canyon Trails Loop

0   Kilometer   0.25

0   Mile   0.25

N

To Manitou Springs

Ridge Road

24

To Colorado Springs

8

P

P

Upper Dog Loop

Crystal Hills Boulevard

Contemplative Trail

Meadowlark Trail

RED ROCK CANYON OPEN SPACE

Mesa Trail

Pavilion ■

Sand Canyon Trail

Greenlee Trail

The Whale

Red Rock Canyon Path

Red Rock Canyon Trail

Red Rock Rim Trail

Sand Canyon Trail

Mesa Trail

Kenmuir Quarry ■

Quarry Pass Trail

Roundup Trail

Greenlee Trail

Black Bear Canyon

Wiggins Wall

Lion Trail

Hogback Valley Trail

1.5 Hike across a shallow canyon for 0.2 mile to the junction of the Roundup and Greenlee Trails (GPS: 38.840044, -104.889396). Continue straight on the Roundup Trail.

1.7 Hike 0.25 mile across the head of Black Bear Canyon to another junction of the Roundup and Mesa Trails (GPS: 38.839255, -104.887475). Go straight on the Roundup Trail and descend into a canyon.

2.1 Reach the end of the Roundup Trail and the start of the Red Rock Canyon Trail below a gap between sandstone hogbacks (GPS: 38.83832, -104.885426).

2.2 Hike north on the closed-road trail to the junction of the Red Rock Canyon Trail and the Red Rock Rim Trail, which comes in from the right (GPS: 38.840008, -104.884358). Continue straight down a long hill, then along the east side of Red Rock Canyon. After 0.25 mile reach the junction with Quarry Pass Trail (GPS: 38.843289, -104.882461). (***Option:*** Go left if you want to scramble up to the historic Kenmuir Quarry.) Continue straight down Red Rock Canyon another 0.4 mile to a pavilion.

3.0 Reach a junction past the pavilion and a gate (GPS: 38.849727, -104.879643). Go left on the main trail and descend the west side of the canyon.

3.3 End the hike at the east trailhead on the far eastern end of the main parking area (GPS: 38.853318, -104.879159).

9 Coyote Run Trail

This short, lollipop-loop hike in Cheyenne Mountain State Park, perfect for families with small kids, explores the foothills above the park visitor center, passing open meadows, scrub oak forests, and scattered ponderosa pines on open hillsides.

Start: West side of parking lot at park visitor center
Distance: 1.4-mile lollipop
Hiking time: 1 to 2 hours
Difficulty: Easy
Elevation gain: 130 feet
Trail surface: Singletrack dirt path
Seasons: Year-round
Schedule: Open daily for day-use only, 5 a.m. to 10 p.m.; recommended use is sunrise to sunset.

Other trail users: Mountain bikers
Canine compatibility: Dogs not permitted
Land status: Colorado state park land
Fees and permits: Daily fee to enter the park
Maps: USGS Cheyenne Mountain; Cheyenne Mountain State Park trail map at website
Trail contacts: Cheyenne Mountain State Park, 410 JL Ranch Heights, Colorado Springs 80926; (719) 576-2016; https://cpw.state.co.us/placestogo/Parks/cheyennemountain

Finding the trailhead: From I-25 on the south side of Colorado Springs, take the South Academy Boulevard exit 135 and drive west on South Academy past Pikes Peak Community College. Continue west to CO 115 and turn south on CO 115. Drive south on the divided four-lane highway to a stoplight. The park entrance is to your right, opposite Fort Carson Gate 1. Drive west on JL Ranch Heights Road to the park visitor center. Park in the visitor center lot and pay an entrance fee in the center. The trailhead is on the west side of the parking lot (GPS: 38.734987, -104.819761).

The Hike

The 1.4-mile-long Coyote Run Trail makes a fun loop hike for kids and families in the scrubby hills above the Cheyenne Mountain State Park visitor center. Before doing the hike, the visitor center is an educational stop, with lots of informative displays as well as books about the area's natural history. The easy-to-follow, singletrack trail has minimal elevation gain, gradual grades, plenty of rest stops, and great views. It's well marked with signposts at regular intervals as well as posts with GPS coordinates if you need to contact a ranger for help.

Start the hike on the west side of the parking lot at the visitor center, at 6,055 feet. The trailhead is between two benches right of a ramada with an interpretive display about trail etiquette. Hike west for 100 feet to a sign on the left that explains the park's web of life. Continue to a registration box on the right and sign in.

The trail heads west alongside a dry wash and through scrub oak thickets for about 0.1 mile to a Y junction with a trail sign in a garden of scattered granite boulders. This point is the start of the Coyote Run loop trail. Go left (south) to begin the loop hike.

Coyote Run Trail twists across hillsides covered with grass, scrub oak, and pines below Cheyenne Mountain.

The next 0.8-mile trail segment runs south, crossing the park road. The trail twists through a shallow wooded draw studded with boulders and shaded by oaks and pines. Several interpretive signs about park wildlife, including black bears, prairie dogs, and mountain lions, are scattered along the trail. The path reaches the park road at its turnoff to Limekiln Trailhead. Cross the road and pick up the trail again on its west side.

Past big granite boulders, swing across meadows on the northern edge of broad Limekiln Valley to a trail fork with a granite block in the fork. The next two left forks are 1.0-mile-long Zook Loop Trail, another pleasant hike. Take the right fork and stay on Coyote Run Trail. The trail bends north and gradually climbs, passing a sign about lizards, to a Y junction with Boulder Run Trail, which heads left.

Go right on Coyote Run Trail and hike past picnic tables to a building with restrooms and then a road. Follow small signs with arrows pointing the trail direction, and walk along the right (east) side of the building on a sidewalk. Cross the road at a crosswalk to the east side of the road and another building and small parking area for the picnic area. Cross the road to the left (north) and pick up Coyote Run Trail.

Hike north on the trail, dipping in and out of shallow rocky drainages, and after 1.1 miles reach a junction with Soaring Kestrel Trail just past a bench beneath a tall ponderosa pine. Keep right on the marked Coyote Run Trail.

The next trail section descends about 0.1 mile from the junction to the lower trail fork near the visitor center. The trail bends sharply right (south) and descends open stony terrain, passing a sign about rattlesnakes. Prairie rattlers do live at the park but are rarely seen. These warm rocky slopes, however, form an ideal habitat for rattlesnakes. It's more likely, however, that you will see a bull snake, which resembles a rattlesnake and often mimics a rattler's behavior by coiling up and making a rattling noise in its throat.

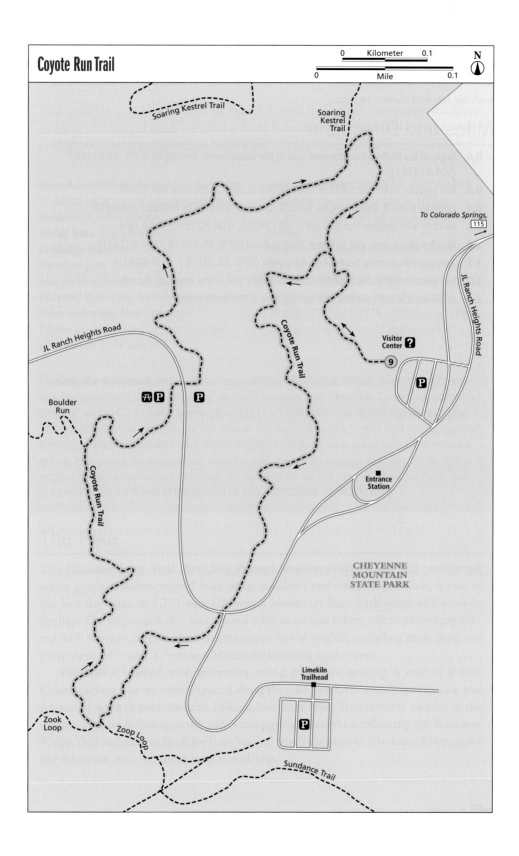

Coyote Run Trail

Soaring Kestrel Trail

Soaring Kestrel Trail

To Colorado Springs, 115

JL Ranch Heights Road

JL Ranch Heights Road

Visitor Center ❓

9

Coyote Run Trail

Boulder Run

🅿

Coyote Run Trail

Entrance Station

CHEYENNE MOUNTAIN STATE PARK

Zook Loop

Zoop Loop

Limekiln Trailhead

🅿

Sundance Trail

The Blackmer Loop Trail winds through meadows and oak groves below Cheyenne Mountain.

Cheyenne Mountain State Park offers 27 miles of hiking on twenty-one trails on wooded foothills below the sharp escarpment of rugged Cheyenne Mountain. The well-maintained trails, ranging in difficulty from easy to strenuous, are easily combined to create longer hikes. The trails are open to hikers and mountain bikers, but no horses or pets are allowed to protect both fragile ecosystems as well as the park's abundant wildlife. Smoking is not permitted on any of the trails. After doing these two hikes, consult the comprehensive park trail map, available at the visitor center or park website, to plan other hikes.

To reach the trailhead, drive up the park road from the visitor center and park at a large lot on the right side of the road at the campground visitor services area. From here you have two choices to reach the Blackmer Trailhead. The best and most scenic alternative is to follow the recommended 0.6-mile Raccoon Ridge Trail, which begins at the north side of the parking lot and spirals southwest past tent campsites to the park road and its junction with Boulder Run Trail.

Option: Park at the lot and hike 0.3 mile down the park road's shoulder to the same trail junction on the right. Look for the Boulder Run Trail and a marker on the right (west) side of the road and right of a concrete drain and locked gate. This reduces the total mileage of the hike by 0.6 mile.

From the start of Boulder Run Trail on the park road, follow the first trail segment on Boulder Run Trail for 0.1 mile west through groves of scrub oak and broad meadows to a Y-shaped junction at 6,408 feet on a south-facing hill—the start of the Blackmer Loop Trail. Both forks at the junction are for Blackmer Loop. Take the right trail fork to hike the loop in a counterclockwise direction. A park trail map sign is on the right side of the junction.

The trail slowly climbs as it swings through meadows flanked by scrub oak. Stop at a bench with a view to the east and read an interpretive sign that details the area's earliest inhabitants, including the Ute Indians. Past the bench the trail works southwest across open meadows. Keep an eye out for bull snakes in the tall grass by the trail's edge.

Past several large boulders the trail turns south and reaches a junction with Cougar's Shadow Trail below shady ponderosa pines. Keep straight or left on the main trail. Cougar's Shadow Trail, a 0.9-mile path, is an alternative to Blackmer here. This trail climbs southwest, then contours south and drops down to meet Blackmer farther south.

From the junction, the next Blackmer Trail section runs southwest for 0.9 mile to the southern Cougar's Shadow Trail junction. This segment offers great hiking, with the trail threading through boulder gardens, passing beneath stately ponderosa pines, and edging grassy glades rimmed with scrub oak as the trail slowly climbs to its high point. To the west towers the bulk of 9,565-foot Cheyenne Mountain above the forest. Several interpretive signs about bats, climate, and ponderosa pines are found along the way. At the ponderosa sign is a bench. Take a seat to admire a tall pine splitting a crack in a 10-foot-high granite boulder.

Past the high point, the trail dips down and meets Cougar's Shadow Trail in a wooded ravine. Go left (east) at this three-way junction.

The next Blackmer Loop Trail segment runs northeast for 1.4 miles, twisting down wooded slopes and following shallow draws filled with boulders. Occasional breaks in the trees allow views eastward to Fort Carson and the tawny prairie beyond. As the trail descends, the pine forest thins with scrub oak and meadows becoming prevalent. At the edge of a shallow valley, Blackmer reaches a three-way junction. A side trail heads right to join Zook and Medicine Wheel Trails. Stay left on the main trail. A trail map at the junction keeps you on course.

The final section of the Blackmer Loop climbs 0.8 mile from the junction back to the beginning of the loop and the end of Boulder Run Trail. The trail steadily

GREEN TIP:
Stay on established trails to avoid damaging vegetation and creating new social trails. Try to stay on durable surfaces that will be least affected by your passage, like rock, gravel, dry grasses, or snow.

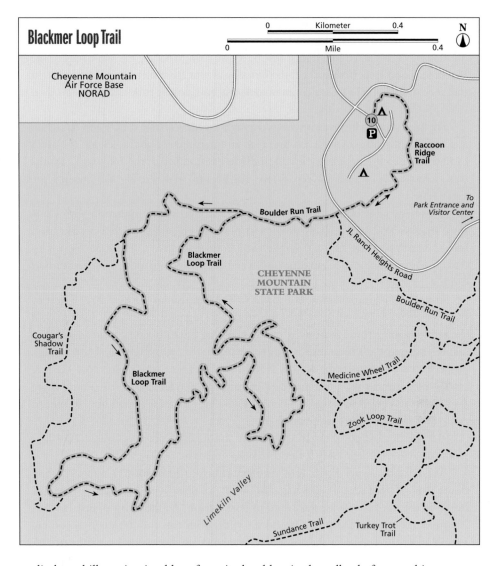

0   Kilometer   0.4

0   Mile   0.4

N

Cheyenne Mountain
Air Force Base
NORAD

10

P

Raccoon
Ridge
Trail

To
Park Entrance and
Visitor Center

Boulder Run Trail

JL Ranch Heights Road

Blackmer
Loop Trail

CHEYENNE
MOUNTAIN
STATE PARK

Boulder Run Trail

Cougar's
Shadow
Trail

Blackmer
Loop Trail

Medicine Wheel Trail

Zook Loop Trail

Limekiln Valley

Sundance Trail

Turkey Trot
Trail

climbs uphill, passing jumbles of granite boulders in the valley before reaching open meadows on a south-facing slope. An interpretive sign details the transition life zone that you're passing through, a species-rich ecosystem where the foothills scrubland meets the montane forest. Past the sign the trail edges across the hillside and meets the three-way junction that marks the start of the Blackmer Loop.

Go straight (east) on the main trail, which now becomes Boulder Run Trail. Hike 0.1 mile back to the park road, then cross the road and follow Raccoon Ridge Trail for 0.5 mile back to the parking lot.

Miles and Directions

0.0 Begin at the parking lot at the camper services building. Start from the north side of the lot on Raccoon Ridge Trail (GPS: 38.734896, -104.822126).

0.5 Junction of Raccoon Ridge Trail and park road. Cross road to Boulder Run Trail (GPS: 38.734753, -104.830736).

0.6 Y junction of Boulder Run Trail and the start of Blackmer Loop Trail (GPS: 38.735111, -104.832847). Go right on Blackmer.

0.9 Three-way junction with north end of Cougar's Shadow Trail. Go left.

1.8 Three-way junction with south end of Cougar's Shadow Trail. Go left.

3.2 Three-way junction with side trail to Zook and Medicine Wheel Trails (GPS: 38.731573, -104.831489). Keep straight or left.

4.0 Return to the Y junction with Boulder Run Trail and the start of the Blackmer Loop. Go straight.

4.1 Reach a parking area and the park road. Cross the road to start the final segment on Raccoon Ridge Trail. Go straight.

4.6 Arrive back at the trailhead, parking lot, and camper services building.

11 Aiken Canyon Trail

The Aiken Canyon Trail explores a pristine foothills ecosystem with grasslands, piñon-juniper woodlands, and ponderosa pine forests along the edge of the Front Range south of Colorado Springs.

Start: Turkey Creek Ranch Road trailhead west of CO 115
Distance: 3.8-mile lollipop
Hiking time: 3 to 5 hours
Difficulty: Moderate
Elevation gain: 400 feet
Trail surface: Singletrack dirt path
Seasons: Year-round
Schedule: Open daily dawn to dusk
Other trail users: Hikers only
Canine compatibility: Dogs not permitted

Land status: Area owned by Colorado State Land Board and leased by the Nature Conservancy
Fees and permits: None
Map: USGS Mt. Big Chief quad
Trail contact: The Nature Conservancy, 5398 Manhattan Circle, Boulder 80303; (303) 444-2950; www.nature.org/en-us/get-involved/how-to-help/places-we-protect/aiken-canyon-preserve/

Finding the trailhead: From Colorado Springs drive south on I-25 and take exit 135 for Academy Boulevard. Go west on Academy to CO 115. Turn south on CO 115 and drive 11.5 miles. At 0.1 mile past mile marker 32, turn right (west) onto Turkey Creek Ranch Road. Drive a couple hundred yards to the marked preserve parking area and trailhead on the right (GPS: 38.619942, -104.888297).

The Hike

The Aiken Canyon Trail explores the 1,621-acre Aiken Canyon Preserve, a unique and pristine foothills ecosystem along the mountain edge southwest of Colorado Springs. The main Aiken Canyon Trail covers 3.4 miles with a short (0.2-mile) out-and-back trail that climbs to a lookout point atop a hill. An option includes an 0.8-mile-long out-and-back spur trail that goes up the canyon until it peters out. Hike all three trails for a 5.8-mile-long loop. The hike described here includes the main trail and the short spur to the lookout for a total of 3.8 miles.

Aiken Canyon, a section of state land leased by the Nature Conservancy, lies along the southern edge of the Front Range below Pikes Peak. An unspoiled foothills ecosystem with a variety of habitats and plant communities, including tallgrass meadows, piñon-juniper woodlands, mixed coniferous woodlands with ponderosa pine, Douglas fir, and spruce, and shrublands composed of Gambel oak and mountain mahogany, blankets the canyon and surrounding hills. The preserve is also rich in wildlife, including mammals like black bears, mountain lions, mule deer, elk, squirrels, and foxes. Occasional reptiles like rattlesnakes and bullsnakes are also spotted.

With its diversity of habitats and plant communities, the canyon is well known as one of the best birdwatching spots along the Front Range, with more than one hundred bird species sighted here, including many migratory species. Many of the birds fly south to Central America in winter, then migrate north to breed and nest here in spring, the best birding season. These species include western tanagers, black-headed grosbeaks, and other migratory birds. The canyon itself is named for famed nineteenth-century ornithologist Charles Aiken, who surveyed the area in the 1870s.

The Aiken Canyon area is considered one of the best remaining examples of the southern Front Range foothills ecosystem, which has slowly vanished with suburban sprawl along the edge of the mountains north from Colorado Springs to Fort Collins. The Nature Conservancy signed a ninety-nine-year conservation lease with the State of Colorado in 1991 to manage and protect this unique area as well as educate the public. A straw-bale visitor center at the trailhead offers educational programs for students and visitors.

Begin the hike at a gravel parking lot on the right side of Turkey Creek Ranch Road just west of CO 115. Follow a wide, flat trail a few hundred feet to an information kiosk with four panels that explain and interpret the nature preserve. The left panel details what the Nature Conservancy is all about; the second panel talks about the partnership between the Conservancy and the army at Fort Carson east of the preserve; the third panel is about the trail and exploring the area; and the fourth panel, on the right, is about saving Colorado's grasslands.

Go left from the kiosk to the El Pomar Foundation Field Station, a visitor center that is sometimes open on weekends, and restrooms. The trail, however, goes right from the kiosk and heads east through tall grass, sage, and clumps of scrub oak. After a short distance you reach a trail sign that details the hike and warns you to stay on the trail to avoid damaging vegetation, disturbing wildlife, and affecting scientific research. The sign also lists the preserve rules: no pets, hunting, camping, or vehicles; no smoking or alcohol; and collecting plants, rocks, and animals is prohibited.

The trail goes left from the sign and reaches the first of several wooden interpretive plaques that explain the area's natural history, plant life, and animal inhabitants. After 0.2 mile the trail reaches a dry creek bed and follows it northwest toward the mountains, dipping in and out of the rocky bed and passing beneath scattered ponderosa pines, junipers, and piñon pines. Look for occasional cairns or stacks of rocks to stay on the trail, especially in spots where it might be washed out.

Eventually the trail leaves the wash and heads west up a gently sloping plain covered with tall grass, wildflowers, and a shrubland of Gambel or scrub oak and mountain mahogany. This shrubland is important habitat for wildlife, including mule deer, elk, coyotes, and lots of bird species. Look overhead for soaring raptors including Cooper's and sharp-shinned hawks, prairie falcons, and golden eagles, while turkeys forage in the underbrush. Keep an eye out on warm days for the occasional rattlesnake that might be sunning in the middle of the narrow trail.

As the trail slowly climbs, the shrubland gives way to a pygmy woodland of juniper and piñon pine, which again provides important habitat for wildlife. This pristine area has been practically undamaged and ungrazed since the early 1900s. The trail continues following the creek bed, which is occasionally a shallow braided stream after heavy thunderstorms. One trail section passes beneath towering ponderosa pines that line the wash. Finally, after 0.7 mile you reach a trail junction and the start of the hike's loop segment.

As you take the left fork, the trail heads northwest across a broad meadow and then dips across the creek bed, where water, forced above ground by bedrock, riffles over a rock bench. Continue hiking west above the south bank of the wash beneath a forest of tall ponderosa pines.

Red sandstone buttresses and cliffs rise above the trail on the sides of the narrowing canyon. The rock here is Fountain Formation sandstone, a rough conglomerate deposited some 200 million years ago on an outwash plain below an ancient mountain range. Farther west the trail passes through thin layers of limestone and dolomite before reaching the bedrock formation called Silver Plume quartz monzonite, a type of granite that forms the steep slopes and mountain peaks on the west side of the preserve.

The trail winds along the creek past the sandstone ramparts and then bends north and crosses a wide meadow. Continue north on the narrow trail, climbing up a steep ravine to a saddle, a large rounded boulder, and a signed junction with the Overlook Trail at 1.5 miles. Go right on the Overlook Trail and climb 0.2 mile to a scenic viewpoint atop a small, sharp peak with great views southeast across scrubby hills on Fort Carson. Retrace the trail back to the junction with the main trail.

From the junction, go right on the main trail and descend northward 0.1 mile to another trail junction on the south side of a broad grassy meadow. (**Option:** If you want a longer adventure hike, take the 0.8-mile spur Canyon Trail, which heads west up a narrowing canyon, crossing tree-fringed meadows and then following an intermittent creek. The narrow part of this canyon is cool and moist with tall Douglas firs shading the trail. At the end of the spur, you reach the remains of an old stone cabin and the turnaround point. Retrace your steps back to the main trail for an extra 1.6 miles of hiking. Turn left to return to the counterclockwise loop.)

At the main trail continue to hike to the northeast. The trail crosses a big meadow before bending east and following a creek, which often flows during wetter months. Tall ponderosa pines line the trail, providing welcome shade in summer. The trail crosses the creek four times, with the last crossing over a smooth bench of worn sandstone. At some rocky bluffs the trail bends south and leaves the creek, ascending on to a lush sloping plain covered with tall grass, yuccas, copses of scrub oak, and scattered junipers and piñon pine. The trail skirts the western edge of a big meadow against a

Ponderosa pines line an intermittent creek and the Aiken Canyon Trail. ▶

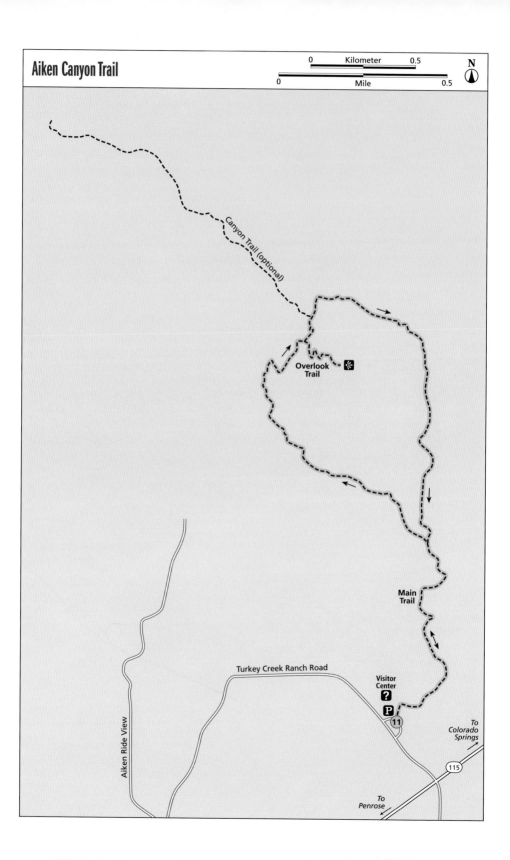

Aiken Canyon Trail

0   Kilometer   0.5

0   Mile   0.5

N

Canyon Trail (optional)

Overlook
Trail

Main
Trail

Turkey Creek Ranch Road

Visitor
Center

11

Aiken Ride View

115

To
Colorado
Springs

To
Penrose

rocky mountain before dipping through a small creek and reaching the Y junction and the end of the loop trail at 3.1 miles.

From the major trail junction, follow the trail for 0.7 mile back to the kiosk, trailhead, and parking area.

Miles and Directions

0.0 Parking lot and trailhead on the north side of Turkey Creek Ranch Road (GPS: 38.619942, -104.888297). After 200 feet you come to an information kiosk (GPS: 38.620467, -104.888119). Go left to the preserve visitor center. The hike goes right behind the kiosk on the trail.

0.2 Trail reaches a dry creek bed (GPS: 38.621049, -104.886381) and follows it northwest toward the mountains.

0.7 Trail junction and start of the hike's loop segment (GPS: 38.626692, -104.886868). Go left at the fork.

1.5 Junction with Overlook Trail at a saddle (GPS: 38.634267, -104.893014). Go right to hike 0.2 mile to the overlook at the top of a small peak, then return to this junction. Go north and downhill on the main trail.

2.0 Junction with canyon spur trail. (**Option:** Take the left spur trail for an optional 1.6-mile out-and-back hike up a wild and scenic canyon. Go left when you return to the main trail and hike northeast to a creek.)

3.1 Follow the loop counterclockwise to return to the Y junction with the main trail. Go left.

3.8 Reach the trailhead and parking area.

12 Ute Valley Park Loop

This easy loop hike with minimal elevation gain explores the forest and rocky bluffs at Ute Valley Park, a Colorado Springs city park on the northwest edge of the city below the Rampart Range.

Start: Trailhead at parking lot on south side of Vindicator Drive
Distance: 2.6-mile lollipop
Hiking time: 1 to 2 hours
Difficulty: Easy
Elevation gain: 120 feet
Trail surface: Single- and doubletrack dirt trail
Seasons: Year-round
Schedule: Open daily; May 1 to Oct 31, 5 a.m. to 11 p.m.; Nov 1 to Apr 30, 5 a.m. to 9 p.m.
Other trail users: Multiuse trail with runners and mountain bikers; watch for speeding rogue bikers on some trails.

Canine compatibility: Leashed dogs only. Pick up your dog's waste.
Land status: City of Colorado Springs City Park
Fees and permits: None. Colorado Springs city park rules apply.
Map: USGS Pikeview
Trail contact: Colorado Springs Parks, Recreation and Cultural Services, 1401 Recreation Way, Colorado Springs 80905-1975; (719) 385-5940; https://coloradosprings.gov/parks

Finding the trailhead: To reach Ute Valley Park from I-25, take the Woodmen Road exit 149 and turn west. Drive west on Woodmen Road, which turns into Rockrimmon Boulevard for 1.8 miles to Vindicator Drive. Turn right (west) on Vindicator and drive 0.8 mile. Turn left (south) into the parking lot (GPS: 38.924958, -104.857106). The trailhead is at the southeast corner of the lot. Additional weekend parking when the Vindicator lot is full is 0.1 mile east of the lot at Eagleview Middle School.

If the Vindicator parking lot is full, consider starting your hike from an alternative trailhead on Piñon Park Drive by Piñon Valley Park at the southwest corner of Ute Valley Park (GPS: 38.911270, -104.858178). Park on the street and hike uphill on a closed road from the trailhead to join the described hike.

The Hike

Ute Valley Park is a natural city park with craggy bluffs and over 10 miles of trails that explore its ridges, bluffs, and valleys among the suburbs of northwest Colorado Springs. This 538-acre Colorado Springs city park offers a quick hiking getaway with easy grades, wide trails, and plenty of privacy. Even if the parking lot is full on Vindicator Drive, Ute Valley Park has plenty of room to roam and hike among its high rocky ridges and wooded valleys.

A foothills ecosystem, with a mixed woodland of ponderosa pine, scrub oak, juniper, and piñon pine interspersed with wildflower-strewn meadows, covers Ute Valley

Evening light floods across Popes Bluffs, the high point of Ute Valley Park.

Park. The park's bare-bones landscape is composed of sandstone, with the main formation being a long hogback on the west side of the park.

When hiking, especially in summer, watch out for rattlesnakes. They're common here in the park. Keep an eye on dogs and children, especially if they're scrambling around on the rocks where rattlers are usually found. Other wildlife may include black bears, mountain lions, coyotes, and red foxes.

To start your Ute Valley hike, begin at the main trailhead at the southeast corner of the parking lot off Vindicator Drive. Hike southeast on a wide trail for 120 feet past a couple benches to a trail junction. Go right on the right trail and cross a boardwalk. Hike past a small pond lined with fuzzy cattails, then descend southwest on a double-track trail across a broad meadow in a valley. (**Option:** Go south from the parking area on a wide trail and join the above trail after 0.1 mile.)

At 0.2 mile there is a major Y-shaped trail junction at a ponderosa pine. Go left on singletrack Beaver Trail, marked with a "Hiking Only" sign. No mountain bikes are allowed on this next trail section. The right fork at the Y is Pine Ridge Trail, the return trail for this loop hike.

The next hike section, running on a good trail for 0.6 mile to the next trail junction, heads southeast across a broad sandstone bench through a sparse ponderosa pine and scrub oak woodland that is interrupted by short-grass meadows and spiky yucca. The trail gently rises up a hill and then begins a long, winding descent. A scenic cliff-rimmed canyon parallels the trail to the right.

As the trail descends, look for a narrow trail on the left just before the main trail drops into the wide main valley at 0.7 mile. Go left (east) on this side trail for 150 feet to a small sandstone arch that spans a trail. The unique window is 5 feet high and

6 feet wide. Follow the trail through the arch. Avoid climbing on top of the arch; it's fragile and already has a deep crack on one side and one in the middle of the span. After viewing the arch, return to the main trail and descend south into Popes Valley, a broad open valley blanketed with tall grass.

The wide trail bends southeast along the valley floor beside a deep arroyo carved by heavy runoff from summer thunderstorms. Follow the trail eastward until it divides at a Y junction marked with a trail sign. Go either right or left to avoid a dense thicket of scrub oak. The right trail (0.2 mile) dips across the edge of the arroyo and climbs back out, while the left trail (0.2 mile) passes the oaks and reaches another trail. Go either way to the next trail junction.

Go right at this junction on a doubletrack trail and cross the arroyo on a dirt-covered steel culvert. Continue straight ahead for 0.2 mile to a T-shaped trail junction at the forest edge on the south side of the valley. Go left (east) at this junction on the main trail and hike 100 feet to a Y-shaped trail junction. Angle right on sandy Bear Trail at 1.1 miles.

The next 0.25-mile segment heads south on Bear Trail, gently climbing a sandy double- to singletrack trail through an open ponderosa pine woodland. Stop and sniff the pines and decide if they smell like butterscotch or vanilla. Watch for mountain bikers on this segment. It's popular with pedal heads that sometimes fly down the trail without warning.

Partway up the hill an old road veers left. Stay on the narrow trail to the right. At 0.2 mile from the last junction (this is the halfway point, 1.1 miles from the trailhead), a side path heads west, but you'll continue straight on the main trail for another

A natural arch hides along the Beaver Trail in Ute Valley Park.

hundred feet to a major junction at 1.2 miles. Go right (west) here on Scrub Oak Path. Look for a trail marker at the junction.

The next 0.4-mile trail segment on Scrub Oak Path climbs west through ponderosa pines and scrub oaks, twisting through the trees and occasionally crossing bedrock. This singletrack trail segment is popular with mountain bikers. The trail emerges from the forest at an old road and a major trail junction at 1.7 miles east of the trailhead by Piñon Valley Park. Stop, catch your breath, and enjoy a great view of Pikes Peak here.

An alternate trailhead for this hike is found down the closed road at the end of Piñon Park Drive to the west of the junction. Along this old road are several large sandstone boulders and short cliffs, which are a popular bouldering area for local rock climbers.

Go right (north) at the trail junction for the last major hike segment on Pine Ridge Trail, which runs 0.6 mile north along the east side of a high hogback. The wide, rocky trail slowly climbs uphill. At a high point at 1.9 miles, scramble right across sandstone slabs and balanced boulders to a flat, rocky outcrop for good views east across Ute Valley Park. This is a perfect place to stop for a snack and drink of water before heading back to the main trail. Hummingbird Trail heads east from this junction.

Continue hiking north and slightly downhill on the straight, rocky trail, passing a couple more viewpoints of Popes Valley to the east. Then descend to a willow-lined ravine and an intermittent creek. Cross a small footbridge over the creek and ascend back to the first major trail junction with Beaver Trail at 2.4 miles. Keep right and follow the Bobcat Cutoff Trail 0.2 mile back to the parking lot and trailhead on Vindicator Drive.

You can combine this loop hike with other Ute Valley Park trails to create either longer or shorter loops. Consult the park hiking map for details. For extra credit you can also climb 6,730-foot Popes Bluffs, the park's high point on the northwest side of the park and almost directly west of the trailhead and parking lot. To climb the bluff, hike to the first trail junction, then head west across the valley on a trail to a steep social trail that climbs onto the hogback. Scramble north to the rocky summit and a great view west across Piñon Valley to the Rampart Range escarpment.

Miles and Directions

0.0 Trailhead is at the southeast side of the parking lot (GPS: 38.924958, -104.857106) on the south side of Vindicator Drive. Hike south on the Bobcat Cutoff Trail.

0.2 Reach the first trail junction (GPS: 38.922449, -104.858196). Go left on Beaver Trail.

0.7 A small natural arch is 150 feet to the left of the trail. Soon the trail splits in the bottom of the valley. Go either right or left around a scrub oak thicket.

0.8 Reach a trail junction (GPS: GPS: 38.916362, -104.851371). Go right across a culvert in the bottom of the valley. After about 500 feet come to another trail junction. Go left (east) down the valley. Do not go south on the narrow trail.

13 Templeton Trail

This loop trail offers an excellent tour through the colorful sandstone bluffs of Palmer Park in northeast Colorado Springs.

Start: Southeast corner of the Yucca and Mesa Trails parking area off Paseo Road. Ending trailhead is at north side of lot.
Distance: 4.0-mile loop
Hiking time: 2 to 3 hours
Difficulty: Easy
Elevation gain: Minimal
Trail surface: Singletrack dirt surface
Seasons: Year-round
Schedule: Open daily, dawn to dusk
Other trail users: Runners, mountain bikers

Canine compatibility: Leashed dogs only. Pick up your dog's waste.
Land status: City of Colorado Springs park
Fees and permits: None. All city park rules must be obeyed.
Maps: USGS Pikeview; downloadable park trail map from Colorado Springs Parks website
Trail contact: Colorado Springs Parks, Recreation and Cultural Services, 1401 Recreation Way, Colorado Springs, CO 80905-1975; (719) 385-5940; https://coloradosprings.gov/parks gov.com

Finding the trailhead: From I-25 take the Fillmore Street exit 145. Drive east on Fillmore Street, which becomes North Circle Drive beyond the Union Boulevard intersection, for 2.5 miles to Paseo Road. Take a left onto Paseo Road and drive 0.8 mile northwest past the Colorado Springs Country Club golf course. Drive through the gated park entrance on Paseo Road, drive to the top of a hill, and make a left turn toward Lazy Land and Ute Crest Picnic Area. Drive a short distance to a Y junction and go left to a parking area at the end of the road (GPS: 38.879888, -104.772355). The trailhead is at the southeast corner of the parking area.

Palmer Park also has an entry road from Academy Boulevard on the east. To reach the trailhead from the east, turn west on Maizeland Road from Academy Boulevard and drive 2 blocks. Turn right on Paseo Road and enter Palmer Park. Follow Paseo to a right turn to the trailhead.

The Hike

Palmer Park lies smack in the middle of Colorado Springs. This rock–rimmed natural area surrounded by city sprawl is an enclave of forest and grassland with grand vistas of Pikes Peak and the Front Range escarpment. More than 25 miles of trails are available for a quick hiking getaway. Palmer Park, one of the city's first public natural areas, was donated to the city in 1902 by William Jackson Palmer, the founder of Colorado Springs, a former Civil War general, Confederate prisoner of war, and a Medal of Honor recipient for his bravery in a cavalry battle at Red Hill, Alabama, in 1865. Besides hiking trails, Palmer Park also offers picnic grounds, baseball and soccer fields, a botanic reserve, and Grandview Overlook, one of the best viewpoints above Colorado Springs.

The 730-acre park has a variety of trails, including closed roads, constructed and maintained trails, and social trails. All of the main trails are signed with posts at junctions with arrows indicating which way to go. The Yucca and Mesa Trails on top of the north bluff are popular with walkers and dogs, while the better-maintained trails are used by mountain bikers and equestrians from Mark Reyner Stables on Paseo Road.

Palmer Park is composed of two flat-topped bluffs lined with rimrock cliffs, crumbling sandstone buttresses, fanciful hoodoos, and toadstool-shaped rocks tucked among the pines like primitive sculptures. The feldspar-rich sandstone and conglomerate, called Dawson arkose by geologists, has a rough granular texture and a hardness that ranges from crumbling rock with the consistency of brown sugar to hard compact stone that forms cliff bands as high as 80 feet.

The high headlands at Palmer Park, locally part of a range of hills called Austin Bluffs, are an isolated remnant of a large rock formation deposited by ancient streams and rivers flowing from the Pikes Peak massif during the late Cretaceous period some 65 million years ago. Nearby Pulpit Rock is composed of the same sandstone.

The 4-mile Templeton Trail is a great hike that circumnavigates the north bluff in the park, threading across flat sandstone benches above canyons, passing through stands of sturdy ponderosa pine and dense thickets of Gambel oak, and providing great views across downtown Colorado Springs to the abrupt mountain front.

Beginning at the Yucca Flats / Templeton Trailhead, Templeton Trail is easy to hike, with minimal elevation gain and loss. The trail roughly follows the 6,500-foot contour around the bluff. While it can be hiked in either direction, it is described here for hiking clockwise since the views are better and the trail is easier to follow. The first mile of the trail is the busiest as it's used by both hikers and mountain bikers. After rounding the southwest end of the bluff, the trail narrows and is usually deserted and quiet except for the din of traffic on Union Boulevard and Austin Bluffs Parkway in the valley below. Remember to bring water in summer since none is available; nor are there restrooms. Both are, however, found at the Edna Mae Bennett Trailhead on Paseo Road.

The trailhead is located at the southeast corner of the cul-de-sac parking lot. It might be hard to spot but head down the first trail left of some scrub oaks. The trail descends through yucca and stunted oaks and reaches a junction with a spur of the

AUSTIN BLUFFS

The bluffs and prairie northeast of Colorado Springs, whose downtown was a huddled cluster of buildings back in 1870, was originally part of a ranch owned by Matt France, who sold the property to sheep rancher Henry Austin in 1873. The area became known as Austin Bluffs. General William Jackson Palmer (1836-1909), founder of Colorado Springs, later purchased the property and donated it to the city as a public park in 1902.

Yucca Trail. Go right at the signed post and follow the trail west, contouring across a hillside high above Paseo Road and a shallow canyon.

After 0.4 mile you reach an overlook on a broad sandstone bench and a great view west across the bluffs toward the mountains. The trail bends north here, swings around a rocky draw, and at 0.5 mile reaches a junction with the Edna Mae Bennett Nature Trail, which it follows north for another 0.4 mile. The Bennett Trail goes south from the junction to its trailhead on Paseo Road.

After hiking through pines and along the rim rock, the trail passes a junction with the Yucca Trail at 0.7 mile and then another junction with the Bennett Trail, which descends to the left, at 0.8 mile. Keep right on the marked Templeton Trail and clamber up a boulder staircase. The trail, passing through ponderosa pines, dips across the top of a draw and contours west to a compact rock outcropping with a couple of pinnacles and a small arch at 1 mile. This is a good spot to scramble up for rock photos.

The trail heads southwest, following the rim edge and passing two spur trails that go right to the bluff-top Mesa Trail. At 1.4 miles there is a flat rock ledge that offers great views south across the city, and at 1.5 miles is the junction with the southern terminus of Mesa Trail. From here the hike becomes wilder and less popular.

Follow the Templeton Trail to the southern edge of the bluff and a fine view of 14,115-foot Pikes Peak. The trail descends rocky slopes on the southern bluff slope, passing beneath tawny cliff bands and scrambling over rounded boulders. At 1.9 miles the trail reaches the southwestern corner of the bluff and boulder pile.

The hike turns north here and for the next 0.5 mile winds through a forest of ponderosa pine and scrub oak. Cliffs, some as high as 80 feet, loom above the trail. The cliff tops are studded with stubby pinnacles and magical hoodoos. A housing development and busy Union Boulevard are west below the trail.

At 2.5 miles is an unmarked trail junction at the northwest corner of the bluff. You can go either right or left since they meet up 0.1 mile ahead. The left trail is more scenic, edging across steep north-facing slopes then scrambling up boulders to the next junction.

After 2.9 miles the trail bends slightly southeast above Lazy Land valley to the east and crosses bedrock to a viewpoint above a perfect 20-foot-high toadstool with a balanced rock summit. The trail goes west here, contouring above a wide draw. At 3.1 miles is the junction with the Lazy Land Trail, which descends east to a group picnic area. Continue straight and contour southeast around the draw, passing a couple junctions with spur trails that go right onto the mesa top to the Mesa and Yucca Trails.

The marked junction with Palmer Point Trail is reached at 3.5 miles. Go right, uphill, and in 0.4 mile you reach the Yucca Trail, an old closed road on the bluff top. Turn left here and hike another 0.1 mile to the trailhead on the north side of the parking area and the end of our Templeton foot adventure.

◀ *A hiker passes below sandstone hoodoos on the Templeton Trail.*

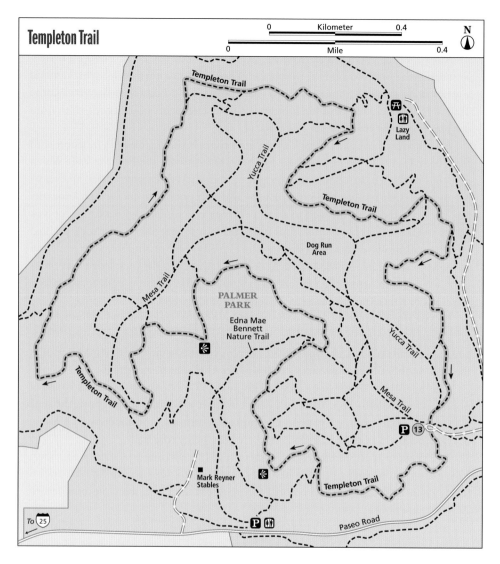

0   Kilometer   0.4

0   Mile   0.4

N

Miles and Directions

0.0   Trailhead on the southeast side of the parking area (GPS: 38.879841, -104.772265). Go south to a junction.

0.1   Junction of Templeton Trail and Yucca Trail. Go right at signed post.

0.4   Reach an overlook (GPS: 38.87848, -104.77572).

0.5   Junction with the Bennett Trail. Keep straight.

0.7   Junction with Yucca Trail spur. Keep straight.

0.8   Junction with Bennett Trail. Go right up stony trail (GPS: 38.88185, -104.77613).

1.0   Arch and hoodoos (GPS: 38.88282, -104.77698).

1.2   Junction with the Mesa Trail.

1.4 Canyon Overlook (GPS: 38.88188, -104.77927).

1.5 Junction with Mesa Trail. Keep left.

1.7 Reach the south end of the bluff. Good views of Pikes Peak. Trail descends west below cliffs.

1.9 Trail reaches the southwest corner of the bluff and turns north along the western edge of the escarpment (GPS: 38.88110, -104.78448).

2.5 Trail junction (GPS: 38.88735, -104.77987). Go left (*Option:* Or right since the trails meet up 0.1 mile northeast).

2.6 Reach the northwest corner of the bluff. The trail bends east here and goes through pine woods above Austin Bluffs Parkway.

2.9 Trail bends south above the shallow Lazy Land valley to the east. After a few hundred feet, stop on the rim rock and admire a perfect 20-foot-high toadstool with a balanced rock summit (GPS: 38.88682, -104.77470).

3.1 Junction with the Lazy Land Trail. Continue west and contour around the head of a draw.

3.2 Junction with Mesa Trail. Keep straight on main trail.

3.4 Junction with Yucca Trail, which goes up left. Continue straight.

3.5 Junction with Palmer Point Trail (GPS: 38.88457, -104.77168). Go up right.

3.9 Reach the Yucca Trail, a wide closed road, and go left (south) toward the parking area.

4.0 End the hike at the north side of the parking lot (GPS: 38.8800, -104.77233).

plateau rises above the trail. After 0.3 mile you reach another three-way trail junction. Yucca Trail goes left. Keep straight on the Bennett Trail. Continue hiking south and then southeast. As the trail contours onto sunny south-facing slopes, the forest thins out and more views open up. Look for spectacular scenic vistas of downtown Colorado Springs to the southwest and Pikes Peak, lifting its bulky snow-covered shoulders above the lower forested mountains.

As you hike, keep alert for birds, including magpies, ravens, hawks, chickadees, pygmy nuthatches, and towhees. Palmer Park is a prolific birdwatching area with good habitat. Few animals besides birds are seen here, however, since the city has engulfed the park. But you might spot squirrels, rabbits, red foxes, coyotes, and an occasional rattlesnake.

After skirting along the edge of North Cañon, the trail reaches its high point. Stop here to enjoy the spacious views from a rocky overlook. Pale cliffs spill down the steep slope below while the city spreads west to the mountain front. The trail heads southeast and begins a gentle descent as it switchbacks and traverses the hillside. After dipping across a shallow ravine, the trail bends south and reaches a fork. Templeton Trail goes left, while the Bennett Trail heads right. Take the right fork and descend the stony trail to a short scrambling section on bedrock.

A pastel-painted sandstone outcrop and amphitheater soon appear to your left, making an excellent opportunity to catch a rest and have a drink of water. Enjoy the scenic view from a broad ledge below cliffs and peer into an interesting shelter cave to the left. The small, dark cave corkscrews up into the cliff, forming a unique chamber that kids love to explore. This sandstone formation, deposited by ancient streams that flowed from the Rocky Mountains, has a rough, granular texture with a variety of rock sizes, from sand grains to fist-size cobbles. The sandstone formation, called Dawson arkose by geologists, is relatively soft and erodes quickly.

From the trail at the north end of the amphitheater, make a sharp right hairpin turn to stay on the Bennett Trail. Look carefully so you don't miss the trail and end up in the brush below. The trail rapidly descends stone stairs and steep grades in a ravine, before leveling out at the base of a craggy white bluff at a three-way trail junction. Do you recognize the junction? You should, as this is where the Edna Mae Bennett Trail splits. Take the left fork and easily walk 400 feet back to the trailhead, restrooms, and parking lot.

For extra credit, take more hikes in the park. Palmer Park boasts an extensive system of trails (check out the detailed map at the parking area) as well as other recreational opportunities, including mountain biking and nature study, to round out a full day outside. The park, donated to Colorado Springs by its founder, General William Jackson Palmer, in 1902, offers over 25 miles of multiuse trails. The Civilian Conservation Corps built 14 miles of the trails in the mid-1930s.

Pikes Peak towers beyond a cliffed overlook along the ▶
Edna Mae Bennett Nature Trail.

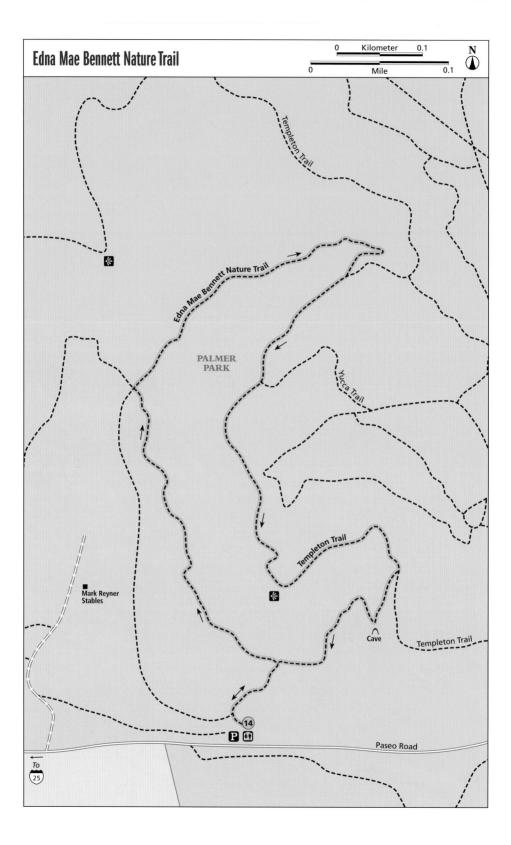

Edna Mae Bennett Nature Trail

Templeton Trail

Edna Mae Bennett Nature Trail

PALMER PARK

Yucca Trail

Templeton Trail

Mark Reyner Stables

Templeton Trail

Cave

14

Paseo Road

To 25

Kilometer
0   0.1

Mile
0   0.1

N

Miles and Directions

0.0 Start at the trailhead at the North Cañon parking lot (GPS: 38.877803, -104.777684).

0.1 Reach the Bennett Trail loop junction (GPS: 38.878215, -104.777156). Go left. You will return on the right-hand trail.

0.6 Reach a four-way junction at an old parking area (GPS: 38.880792, -104.778793). Go right at the northeast corner of the lot past an interpretative sign about Edna Mae Bennett.

1.2 Reach a trail junction with the Templeton Trail (GPS: 38.88185, -104.77613). Go straight on the marked trail.

1.7 Reach the high point above North Cañon and a viewpoint to the west.

2.1 Reach a trail junction. Keep right.

2.2 A rocky amphitheater and cave are to the left of the trail.

2.5 Reach the first trail junction and the start of the Bennett Trail loop. Go left downhill to the trailhead.

2.6 Arrive back at the trailhead and parking lot.

15 Pulpit Rock Trail

This short out-and-back hike leads to the summit of Pulpit Rock, a white-cliffed rampart in Austin Bluffs Open Space that overlooks northern Colorado Springs and offers spacious views of the city and the mountains to the west.

Start: Pulpit Rock Trailhead on east side of North Nevada Avenue
Distance: 2.1 miles out and back
Hiking time: 1 to 2 hours
Difficulty: Easy
Elevation gain: 490 feet
Trail surface: Single- and doubletrack dirt trail
Seasons: Year-round
Schedule: Open daily; May 1 to Nov 1, 5 a.m. to 11 p.m.; Nov 2 to Apr 30, 5 a.m. to 9 p.m.
Other trail users: Runners, mountain bikers
Canine compatibility: Leashed dogs only

Land status: City of Colorado Springs Austin Bluffs Open Space
Fees and permits: None
Map: USGS Pikeview
Trail contact: Colorado Springs Parks, Recreation and Cultural Services, 1401 Recreation Way, Colorado Springs 80905-1975; (719) 385-5940; https://coloradosprings.gov/parks
Special considerations: Carry water. No restrooms at trailhead. Watch for rattlesnakes in summer. Use caution on summit because of abrupt drop-offs and lightning danger during summer thunderstorms.

Finding the trailhead: From I-25 in northern Colorado Springs, take exit 148 from either the north or south. Drive southeast from the interstate on North Nevada Avenue and make the first left or east turn onto North Nevada Avenue (confusing, but North Nevada ends at I-25 while the continuation is a frontage road on the east side of the interstate). Drive north beside I-25 on North Nevada Avenue for 0.6 mile and turn right (east) into a large parking area and the trailhead (GPS: 38.918591, -104.813850).) The parking lot is south of a utilities substation.

The Hike

Pulpit Rock, a gleaming castle lined with white sandstone ramparts, dominates the northern part of Colorado Springs and rises directly above I-25, the main north–south thoroughfare through the city. The rocky 6,610-foot summit, reached by a 1-mile hike, offers spectacular views of upper Monument Creek Valley as well as the steep mountain front and 14,115-foot Pikes Peak to the west. The hike, following the main trail and then a couple of social trails, is mostly easy with a final steep scramble up a loose-rock trail to the summit block.

Pulpit Rock lies in 585-acre Austin Bluffs Open Space, a Colorado Springs parkland that also includes University Park and Austin Bluffs Open Spaces to the southeast. This area protects a wide swath of bluffs, mesas, and valleys east of North Nevada Avenue, forming important wildlife habitat within the city, a valuable scenic and natural area, and a buffer from encroaching development.

Wildflowers cover a meadow below Pulpit Rock, a Colorado Springs landmark.

The area is dominated by native plant communities, including grasslands, mixed shrubs, and scattered ponderosa pine on the cooler north-facing slopes. The tallgrass community on the lower slopes, with big bluestem and prairie sand-reed grasses, is considered significant by the Colorado Natural Heritage Program since it is relatively uncommon. The native shrublands are covered with copses of Gambel oak and skunkbrush, while the deep drainage that the trail initially crosses is filled with shady cottonwoods and Siberian elms, an intrusive species.

The open space also provides a refuge for both large and small mammals as well as birds commonly found in the foothills of the Front Range a few miles to the west. Mule deer graze in meadows while raccoons and skunks live in the wooded valleys. Nomadic big mammals like black bears, mountain lions, and bobcats sometimes roam through the area, but it is too small for them to inhabit. Keep an eye out for rattlesnakes, which live among the rocky outcrops.

Begin the hike at the Pulpit Rock Trailhead on North Nevada Avenue next to a utilities substation on the north side of the parking lot. Pass through a metal portal and follow a wide dirt trail southeast for a couple hundred feet to the first trail junction at a tall metal tower. Go right on the main trail and descend into a wide valley. Tall cottonwoods shade the east side of the trail while a fence on the west separates the open-space park from commercial development.

Cross a low concrete bridge over a dry wash and follow the trail up the south side of the valley to the second trail junction at a wide switchback. Go right on the main trail. Another trail heads left up the valley from the junction. Continue south into another shallow valley. Pulpit Rock rises directly to the south. After 0.6 mile the trail emerges onto a broad bench northwest of Pulpit Rock. Look for an obvious social trail that splits east here.

Hike east up the trail through grass and sage toward Pulpit Rock. After a few hundred feet it intersects another social trail. Go left on this singletrack trail and hike northeast and east, passing above a low cliff band, to the last trail junction. Go right on a good singletrack trail and hike uphill toward Pulpit Rock.

This last trail segment slowly steepens and becomes loose and rocky as it crosses clay slopes. The final trail section ends at a 40-foot-high cliff band. Scramble up left to the final obstacle, fractured bedrock that forms Pulpit Rock's summit. Look for the easiest passage up through the cliffs, making a few climbing moves onto the small, airy summit. Be extremely careful up here since there is a 90-foot vertical drop on the south and west sides of the summit. This is not a good place to bring small children or klutzy adults.

The summit views are simply spectacular, with much of Colorado Springs spreading below you and the high mountains rising beyond. The vista is breathtaking at sunrise, when rosy light spreads across the mountains and valley below, and at sunset as the sun dips behind Pikes Peak.

Pulpit Rock, besides being an enclave for wildlife and a local landmark, also offers a fascinating geological story. The rocky outcrops, hoodoos, and tall cliffs at the summit area are part of the Dawson Formation, deposited by energetic streams flowing off the rising Rocky Mountains, including the Rampart Range to the west, during the late Cretaceous period some 65 million years ago. This upper rock unit, usually called Dawson arkose, is a coarse white-and-gray sandstone laced with pebbled conglomerate.

The lower exposure of the Dawson Formation is a gray pebbly sandstone interbedded with claystone and siltstone deposited in swamps and along sluggish rivers. The trail up Pulpit Rock mostly traverses this soft, easily eroded facies, which forms the vegetated slopes below the caprock. While fossilized dinosaur bones have been

The upper cliffs of Pulpit Rock, composed of Dawson arkose, rise above I-25 and Monument Valley. ▶

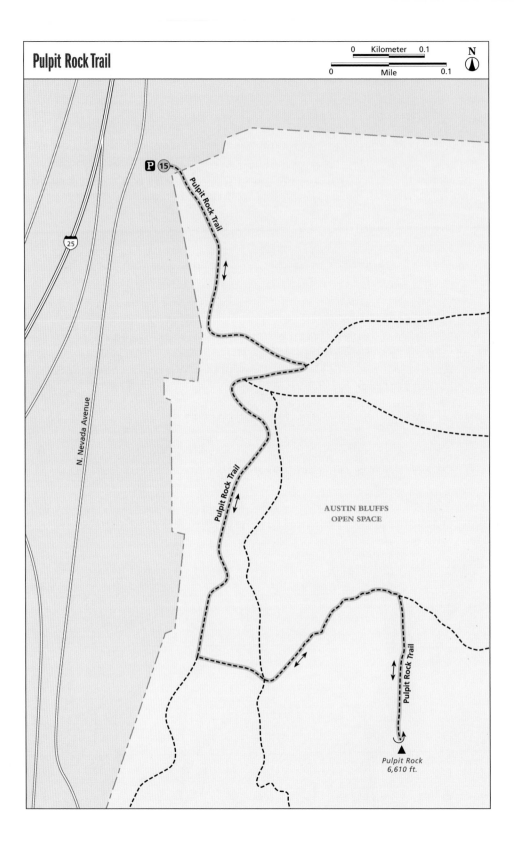

Pulpit Rock Trail

0   Kilometer   0.1

0   Mile   0.1

N

P 15

Pulpit Rock Trail

25

N. Nevada Avenue

Pulpit Rock Trail

AUSTIN BLUFFS
OPEN SPACE

Pulpit Rock Trail

Pulpit Rock
6,610 ft.

found in the Dawson Formation at other Colorado locales, none have been discovered around Pulpit Rock. A keen eye, however, can find ancient leaf imprints, plant material, petrified wood, and an occasional shark's tooth on the slopes below the rampart.

After enjoying the scenic views and meditating on Pulpit Rock's ancient history, head back to the parking lot by reversing your steps. Be careful descending the rock steps below the summit and the loose upper trail. If you want to shorten the hike, go straight at the first trail junction you reach instead of left, the way you came up. This other trail descends directly down to the main trail at a shallow valley.

Miles and Directions

0.0 Begin the hike at the parking lot and trailhead (GPS: 38.918591, -104.813850). After a couple hundred feet, reach the first trail junction at a large power pole. Go right and downhill on the main trail.

0.3 Second trail junction on the south side of a wide valley. Go right on main trail (GPS: 38.918209, -104.813398).

0.6 Third trail junction on the east side of the main trail. Go left (east) up a social trail toward Pulpit Rock (GPS: 38.912944, -104.813432).

0.7 Fourth trail junction. Go left on a good singletrack social trail and hike northeast (GPS: 38.912699, -104.812432).

1.0 Fifth trail junction at the intersection of two social trails. Go right on a good trail and hike uphill toward Pulpit Rock (GPS: 38.913641, -104.810348).

1.1 Scramble onto the summit of Pulpit Rock (GPS: 38.912254, -104.810339). Retrace your steps northward off the summit.

2.2 Arrive back at the trailhead and parking lot.

16 Spruce Mountain Trail

This wonderful hike climbs to the eastern end of Spruce Mountain's long summit and follows a loop trail through an open pine woodland to Windy Point, the high point, at the mountain's west end. It is a Douglas County Open Space parkland.

Start: Spruce Mountain Trailhead on Spruce Mountain Road / Douglas County Road 53 north of Palmer Lake
Distance: 5.3-mile double loop
Difficulty: Moderate
Elevation gain: 505 feet
Trail surface: Singletrack dirt
Seasons: Year-round. Winter is icy.
Schedule: Open daily, sunrise to sunset
Other trail users: Mountain bikers, runners, horses
Canine compatibility: Leashed dogs only
Land status: Douglas County public land
Fees and permits: None

Maps: USGS Larkspur; Douglas County Open Space map
Trail contact: Douglas County Division of Open Space and Natural Resources, 100 Third St., Castle Rock 80104; (303) 660-7495; www.douglas.co.us/dcoutdoors/openspace-properties/spruce-mountain-open-space-and-trail/
Special considerations: Bring water; none found along trail. Watch for rattlesnakes. Steep cliffs are found at the end of the trail and below the summit—keep an eye on children and watch your step. No horse trailers at the trailhead, park them at Spruce Meadows Trailhead on Noe Road to the northeast.

Finding the trailhead: From Colorado Springs drive north on I-25 past Monument. At the top of Monument Hill, take exit 163, turn left (west) on County Line Road, and drive a couple of miles to the north side of Palmer Lake. After crossing railroad tracks, the road dead-ends against Spruce Mountain Road / Douglas County Road 53. Turn right, drive 3.5 miles north, and make a left turn into the marked Spruce Mountain Open Space parking lot. The trailhead is at the west end of the parking lot (GPS: 39.167942, -104.875063). The trailhead address is: 13415 Spruce Mountain Road, Larkspur.

The Hike

The 5.3-mile-long Spruce Mountain Trail is a wonderful hike north of Palmer Lake and east of the Rampart Range, a low mountain range that runs from Ute Pass and the Garden of the Gods in Colorado Springs to the South Platte River at Waterton Canyon southwest of Denver. The singletrack trail climbs to the eastern end of Spruce Mountain's long mesa summit and then makes a long loop, first following the mountain's southern rim to its rocky 7,605-foot summit at the southwest end of the mesa before returning along its northern rim.

Spruce Mountain Trail offers easy hiking on a good singletrack and doubletrack dirt trail with gradual grades, open ponderosa pine and scrub oak woodlands, and spacious scenic views that stretch from Pikes Peak in the south to Longs Peak in the

Eagle Mountain and twin-summited Raspberry Butte rise north of Spruce Mountain.

north. The trail and mountain are on 932-acre Spruce Mountain Open Space land, a parkland that was purchased by Douglas County between 2000 and 2009 to protect it from development as a resort. A developer had proposed building a hotel on top of the mountain, a golf course on the rolling grassland below, and 180 luxury homes scattered across the property. Without that development, the parkland offers 8.5 miles of trails including Eagle Pass Trail, Eagle Ridge Trail, Eagle Pass Trail Cutoff, and part of the Spruce Meadows Trail. Check out the online map at the open space's website for details and directions for these other trails.

The hike begins from the Spruce Mountain Trailhead at the west end of a parking area on the west side of Spruce Mountain Road north of Palmer Lake. The only amenities at the trailhead are a bear-proof trash container and a portable toilet. Park only cars and trucks in the lot; no trailers or horse trailers. Remember to pack out your trash, keep your dog leashed, pick up your dog's waste, and stay on the trails—no shortcutting! Keep an eye out for mountain bikers and horseback riders on this multiuse trail.

At the trailhead, pass through a gate and walk 350 feet to the first trail junction. Go straight on the Spruce Mountain Trail and pass through a dense thicket of scrub oak. Continue hiking west up the slowly rising trail across open grassy meadows on the northern slope of Spruce Mountain. Eagle Mountain rises to the northwest, ringed by high sandstone cliffs like an ancient battlement. After 0.4 mile, go left at a trail junction signed Mountain Top Loop, on Spruce Mountain Trail. Eagle Pass Trail goes straight.

The singletrack trail bends left and contours up the steep north flank of Spruce Mountain. The damp north-facing slope is blanketed with a mixed forest of scrub or Gambel oak, ponderosa pine, Douglas fir, and spruce trees. After 0.2 mile of climbing, the trail reaches a junction with Oak Shortcut Trail on a slight knoll. Go right on the main trail.

The next 0.5 mile of trail is the toughest section of the hike. The trail switchbacks up the wooded east side of the mountain, passing beneath a jutting outcrop of Dawson arkose, a coarse sandstone, before crossing onto the cooler northern slope. After climbing 0.6 mile from the last junction or 1.2 miles from the trailhead, you reach Greenland Overlook, a lofty viewpoint that overlooks the rolling grasslands of Greenland Open Space. More good views are southwest toward 14,115-foot Pikes Peak, which rises beyond humpbacked Mount Herman.

The trail slowly climbs and passes onto the north side of Spruce Mountain's long cliff-rimmed summit and reaches Paddock's Point, a rocky viewpoint that looks north at 7,515-foot Eagle Mountain. Continue up the trail through dry pine woods to the Y junction for the 2.3-mile-long Mountain Top Loop, which follows the south rim out to Windy Point and then continues back along the north rim to this junction. Go left on the doubletrack trail. This junction is 1.6 miles from the trailhead.

Follow the wide trail for the next 0.8 mile along the airy south rim of Spruce Mountain to some strategically placed benches and picnic tables that make for good snack stops. The trail dips across broad ravines, climbs gentle slopes, and passes lots of rock-rimmed overlooks. None of these are fenced and all are dangerous, with vertical drops of 60 feet. Keep a close watch on small children. The cliff rim is soft and loose.

After hiking 2.8 miles from the trailhead, you reach Windy Point, the 7,605-foot high point of Spruce Mountain, on the far western edge of the summit plateau. This exposed overlook makes for a good water break and some marvelous scenic views. Look southwest toward the town of Palmer Lake cradled in a broad valley below and snowcapped Pikes Peak rising beyond. *Warning:* This overlook is very dangerous. Keep away from the cliff edge.

After resting and enjoying the view, begin your return hike on the next trail segment, which runs 0.4 mile northeast from Windy Point to a junction with the Service Road. Go right on the doubletrack loop trail for the described hike. (*Option:* A left turn on the Service Road descends 0.5 mile to Eagle Pass Trail, which you can follow back east for 1.8 miles along the base of the mountain to the trailhead.)

To complete the upper loop trail, keep right at the junction, and hike 0.7 mile along the wooded north rim of Spruce Mountain to the end of the loop at the Y junction. Go straight on the main trail. It is 1.4 miles from here to the trailhead and parking area. Retrace your steps back to Greenland Overlook, then down the switchbacks to Pine Junction.

Pikes Peak and Mount Herman rise beyond Windy Point at the western rim of Spruce Mountain. ▶

17 Inner Canyon–Lake Gulch Loop Trail

Two trails—Inner Canyon–Lake Gulch Loop Trail and Canyon View Nature Trail—explore the rim and inner canyon of Castlewood Canyon, an unusual state park on the high prairie north of Colorado Springs. The Inner Canyon–Lake Gulch Trail loops through the canyon, following Cherry Creek and winding among 25-million-year-old boulders.

Start: Trailhead at Bridge Canyon Overlook parking area on the right past the visitor center
Distance: 2.0-mile loop
Hiking time: 1 to 3 hours
Difficulty: Easy
Elevation gain: 200 feet
Trail surface: Dirt and paved
Seasons: Year-round. Summers can be hot, but shade is found. Winters can be cold and icy. In winter, snow may prohibit travel on the Inner Canyon Trail.
Schedule: Open daily sunrise to sunset. Gate at the east entrance opens at 8 a.m. Inbound gates are closed an hour before sunset, and both gates are locked at sunset.
Other trail users: Hikers only
Canine compatibility: Leashed dogs only
Land status: Colorado state park

Fees and permits: Entrance fee charged to enter the park. No permits required.
Map: USGS Castlewood Canyon; trail map available at visitor center and park website
Trail contact: Castlewood Canyon State Park, 2989 S. Highway 83, Franktown 80116; (303) 688-5242; https://cpw.state.co.us/placestogo/parks/CastlewoodCanyon
Other: Stay on designated trails. Mountain bikes are allowed only on park roads. Pets must be on a leash. Ground fires are prohibited. Gathering of artifacts, vegetation, and timber is prohibited. No camping. Drinking water, restrooms, books, and information are available at the park visitor center.
Special considerations: Carry water. Watch for rattlesnakes along the trail in summer.

Finding the trailhead: The easiest access from Colorado Springs and Denver to the canyon is by driving on I-25 to exit 184 in Castle Rock. Drive east for 9.3 miles on Founders Parkway/CO 86 to Franktown. Turn south at the crossroads onto CO 83 and drive 5 miles to the marked park visitor center turnoff. Turn right (west) and drive along the rim 0.5 mile to the visitor center. The Canyon View Nature Trail walk begins at the Bridge Canyon Overlook parking area just past the visitor center on the right (GPS: 39.329964, -104.737382).

To reach the Inner Canyon–Lake Gulch Loop Trail, continue on the road northwest from the visitor center to the large parking area at the road's end called Canyon Point (GPS: 39.333581, -104.744215). The trail begins on the north side of the lot.

The Hike

Cherry Creek springs from the rolling hills of the Palmer Divide, a forested ridge that separates the Platte and Arkansas watersheds between Denver and Colorado Springs. The creek twists northward through grasslands and cattle ranches for 15 miles before

Hikers cross a plank bridge over Cherry Creek on the Inner Canyon Trail.

slicing through cliff-lined Castlewood Canyon. Most of the 10-mile-long canyon, which lies southeast of Denver, is located within 2,621-acre Castlewood Canyon State Park.

The park preserves an environment more similar to that found in the Rocky Mountains 30 miles to the west than the surrounding prairie. With 19 inches of rainfall annually, the park harbors groves of ponderosa pine and Douglas fir on moist north-facing slopes. Quaking aspens, growing far below their normal 8,000- to 10,000-foot range, flourish in moist canyon draws. Grassy meadows, splotched with summer wildflowers, border the forest in the inner canyon, while twisted juniper and dense stands of scrub oak grow along the stony canyon rim.

Numerous hiking trails and walking paths lace this getaway of dense woodlands, tumbling water, and rough-hewn cliffs, offering hikers an opportunity to discover and explore Castlewood Canyon State Park's ecological diversity and unique scenery. Other visitor activities include picnicking beneath pines, climbing vertical cliffs, and observing the park's wildlife.

This book describes two of Castlewood's best walks. The Inner Canyon–Lake Gulch Loop Trail is a moderately rough trail that explores the canyon north of the park's visitor center. Canyon View Nature Trail, elsewhere in this guide, is a paved, wheelchair-accessible path that follows the west rim of the canyon.

Hikers should stay on the trails to avoid problems. Loose rock is found on the cliff bands and climbing the rocks should be left to experienced rock climbers with proper equipment. Beehives and wasp nests are found in cavities and cracks on the cliffs. Mosquitoes can be a problem in summer; carry bug juice to ward them off.

Rattlesnakes abound in the canyon and are sometimes found on the trails. To avoid rattler encounters during the warmer months, do not bushwhack off the trail.

To hike the Inner Canyon–Lake Gulch Loop Trail, begin at the large parking area for Canyon Point at the end of the park road by picnic pavilions. Restrooms and drinking fountains (not open in winter) are here. Find the trailhead for the Inner Canyon Trail on the north side of the lot. Also find a large sign for Canyon View Nature Trail with a map of the lower canyon and park facilities.

Walk north on the paved trail, dropping slightly downhill toward the canyon rim. Scattered ponderosa pines and junipers dot the rim along with groves of scrub oak and open meadows. Picnic tables are found near the rim.

At the canyon rim, the paved path intersects the marked Inner Canyon Trail. Follow the Inner Canyon Trail straight ahead. The narrow, gravel Inner trail drops steeply downhill, winding through cliff bands and tall scrub oaks. Watch your footing on the steep sections, particularly if any ice or snow is present. Trekking poles and micro-spikes are helpful in winter.

The trail emerges onto the boulder-strewn floor of Castlewood Canyon and crosses gurgling Cherry Creek on a wooden plank bridge to the creek's north bank. Head northwest above the creek for about 0.75 mile, passing many large, lichen-covered boulders and plunging through a dense scrub oak forest. The moist north-facing slopes on the opposite side of the canyon are thick with tall spruces, Douglas firs, and ponderosa pines.

Stop along the way and look at one of the immense boulders beside the trail that tumbled from the cliff rim above. The canyon's 25-million-year-old rock, called Castle Rock conglomerate, stretches along the east and west rims. The concrete-hard rock, deposited in an ancient river, is coarsely studded with volcanic pebbles and cobbles that jut out at odd angles.

The trail heads northwest and the canyon slowly deepens. At the mouth of the Inner Canyon, the trail intersects Lake Gulch Trail. This 0.9-mile trail heads south and southeast back to the walk's start.

The Inner Canyon Trail continues 0.2 mile northwest to the old dam ruins where it joins the Creek Bottom and Rim Rock Trails. Pick up a park map at the visitor center for information on these trails.

Take a left on Lake Gulch Trail, drop down to the creek, and cross via a wooden plank bridge. Follow the trail on the gravelly bank above the creek to a gravel bench, then along a bench that trends left around a forested headland to the western side of the hill.

The trail gradually ascends uphill, passing scrub oaks and scattered pines. To the west, a broad grassy valley is dotted with grazing cattle and a couple of ranch houses and barns. Snowcapped mountains in the Front Range tower beyond the valley's western rim.

A jumble of worn boulders line Cherry Creek in Castlewood Canyon. ▶

Inner Canyon–Lake Gulch Loop Trail

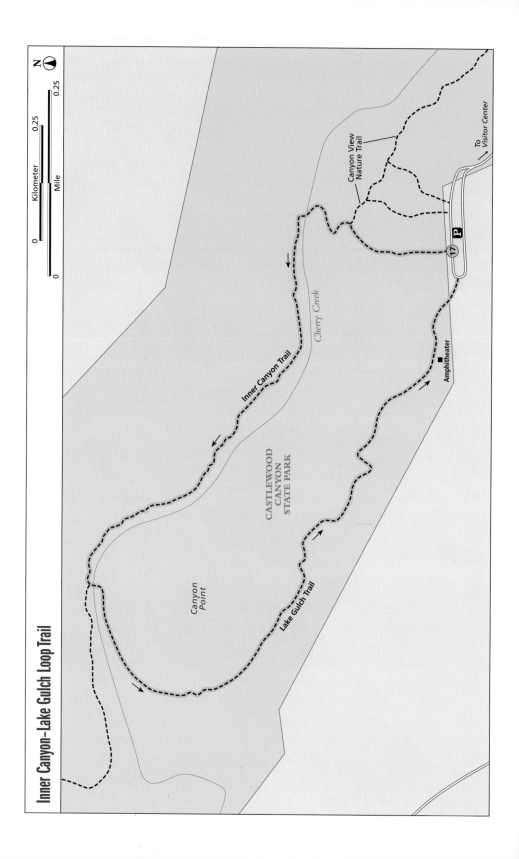

This valley was once part of a large lake formed by a downstream dam to the northwest where the canyon constricts. The earthen and stone dam, built in 1890, was used for flood control, irrigation, and recreation. The year after it was built, a panel of state engineers examined leakage in the dam and determined that the "dam has been built by irresponsible contractors under inadequate supervision." The dam's foundation, erected on a natural spring, was slowly weakened until the night of August 3, 1933, when a heavy rainstorm caused the dam to burst, sending a 30-foot cascade of water surging downstream toward Denver. The flood killed two people, caused over $1 million in damage, and excavated a deep channel through Castlewood's lower canyon. The ruins of the dam still straddle the canyon narrows below the Inner Canyon Trail.

Once the trail reaches the rimrock, it enters a ponderosa pine forest. Stop and sniff the rough bark. The pine has a distinctive smell similar to butterscotch or vanilla. Also note the trees where the bark has been gnawed or girdled by porcupines in search of the sweet inner bark during cold winters when other food is buried beneath snow.

Follow the trail southeast along flat ground to the picnic pavilions, parking area, and the hike's end point. Restrooms and a drinking fountain, which operate only in warmer months, are found here.

Miles and Directions

0.0 Begin at the Inner Canyon Trailhead on the north side of the parking area at the end of the park access road (GPS: 39.333588, -104.744206). Walk north on the paved path toward the canyon.

0.1 Reach a junction with the Inner Canyon Trail and Canyon View Nature Trail (GPS: 39.335296, -104.743589). Go straight on Inner Canyon Trail and descend into the canyon.

0.2 Cross the creek on a plank bridge and go west on the trail.

1.0 Reach a junction in the lower Inner Canyon with the Lake Gulch Trail (GPS: 39.339861, -104.752681). Go left on Lake Gulch Trail, crossing the creek and climbing the western slope of a cliff-rimmed mesa.

1.7 At a junction with the Amphitheatre Trail (GPS: 39.334287, -104.747319), continue straight on the main trail.

2.0 End at the trailhead on the west side of the parking lot and just east of restrooms and picnic pavilions (GPS: 39.333371, -104.74479).

18 Canyon View Nature Trail

The Canyon View Nature Trail is an out-and-back, wheelchair-accessible paved trail that explores the rim of Castlewood Canyon, an unusual state park on the high prairie north of Colorado Springs.

Start: Trailhead at Bridge Canyon Overlook parking area past the visitor center on the right

Distance: 2.1 miles out and back

Hiking time: About 1 hour

Difficulty: Easy

Elevation gain: About 70 feet

Trail surface: Paved

Seasons: Year-round. Summers can be hot, but shade is found. Winters can be cold and icy.

Schedule: Open daily sunrise to sunset. Gate at the east entrance opens at 8 a.m. Inbound gates are closed an hour before sunset, and both gates are locked at sunset.

Other trail users: Hikers only

Canine compatibility: Leashed dogs only

Land status: Colorado state park

Fees and permits: Entrance fee charged to enter the park. No permits required.

Map: USGS Castlewood Canyon trail map available at visitor center and park website

Trail contact: Castlewood Canyon State Park, 2989 S. Highway 83, Franktown 80116; (303) 688-5242; https://cpw.state.co.us/placestogo/parks/CastlewoodCanyon

Other: Stay on designated trails. Mountain bikes are only allowed on park roads. Pets must be on a leash. Ground fires are prohibited. Gathering of artifacts, vegetation, and timber is prohibited.

Special considerations: Carry water. Watch for rattlesnakes along the trail in summer. Drinking water, restrooms, books, and information are available at the park visitor center.

Finding the trailhead: The easiest access from Colorado Springs and Denver to the canyon is by driving on I-25 to exit 184 in Castle Rock. Drive east for 9.3 miles on Founders Parkway/CO 86 to Franktown. Turn south at the crossroads onto CO 83 and drive 5 miles to the marked park visitor-center turnoff. Turn right (west) and drive along the rim 0.5 mile to the visitor center. The Canyon View Nature Trail walk begins at the Bridge Canyon Overlook parking area just past the visitor center on the right (GPS: 39.329964, -104.737382).

The Hike

Visitors with physical challenges or those with small children and strollers will enjoy walking on Canyon View Nature Trail, a paved 0.7 mile (one-way) trail that traverses the west rim of Castlewood Canyon. The round-trip hike described here totals 2.1 miles if you hike to all the overlooks once (but be aware not all are wheelchair accessible). The trail offers marvelous views into the canyon from a series of rim-edge viewpoints.

A hiker follows the paved Canyon View Nature Trail along the rim of Castlewood Canyon. ▶

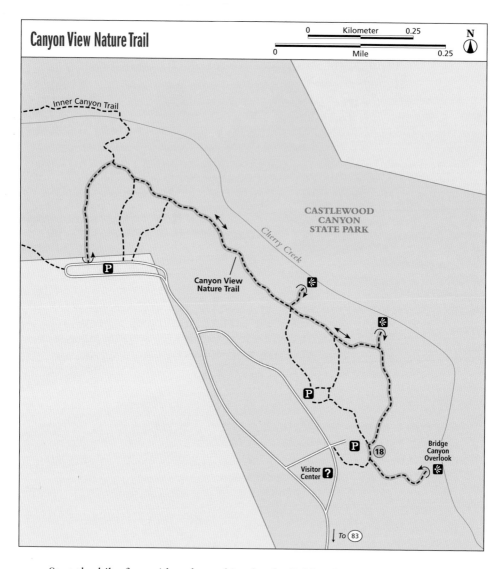

0   Kilometer   0.25   N

0   Mile   0.25

Inner Canyon Trail

CASTLEWOOD
CANYON
STATE PARK

Cherry Creek

Canyon View
Nature Trail

Bridge
Canyon
Overlook

Visitor
Center

To 83

Start the hike from either the parking lot for Bridge Canyon Overlook just east of the visitor center. (**Option:** Or start from the large parking area at the end of the park road where the Inner Canyon Trail begins.)

From the parking lot near the visitor center, hike 0.1 mile down a paved trail to Bridge Canyon Overlook. This viewpoint, which is not entirely wheelchair accessible, offers a great view into the lush canyon below and of the nearby concrete highway bridge. The historic Cherry Creek Bridge, sometimes called the "Bridge to Nowhere," arches gracefully over Castlewood Canyon. The bridge, built in 1948, spans 232 feet across the canyon. Retrace your steps 0.1 mile back to the parking area and follow the marked trail northwest along the canyon rim—taking advantage of two more viewpoints—to the start of the Inner Canyon Trail after 1.2 miles.

From here hike south on the paved trail up a slight uphill grade to the parking area and restrooms at the northwest terminus of the park road and the end of the nature trail. To return to your vehicle at the parking lot by the visitor center, retrace your steps back to the lot by following the paved nature trail for 0.7 mile. (*Option:* Follow a bike path alongside the road back for 0.4 mile to your car.) But I say: take the trail—the scenery looks better the second time anyway!

Miles and Directions

0.0 Begin at the parking lot on the east side of the park visitor center. Locate the trailhead on the far-right side of the parking lot (GPS: 39.329964, -104.737382).

0.1 Hike east on the paved trail to Bridge Canyon Overlook (GPS: 39.329751, -104.735921).

0.2 After retracing your steps, return to the first trailhead and parking lot. From the parking lot, walk to the middle trailhead for Canyon View Nature Trail (GPS: 39.330228, -104.737426) and hike northwest on the paved trail.

0.4 Hike to a trail junction (GPS: 39.332238, -104.737104). Go right for a couple hundred feet to an overlook. Return to the main trail and go right.

0.6 Reach a four-way trail junction (GPS: 39.332691, -104.73931). Go right for a couple hundred feet to an overlook, then return back to the junction and go right.

1.0 Reach trail junction, keep straight.

1.1 Reach trail junction, keep straight.

1.2 Reach junction with Inner Canyon Trail (GPS: 39.335296, -104.743588); go left toward parking lot and restrooms.

1.4 End of the trail at the north side of the parking lot at the end of the park road (GPS: 39.333588, -104.744206). Return to the trailhead via the paved path.

2.1 Arrive back at the trailhead.

The Mountains

Pikes Peak, a 14,115-foot-high sentinel of granite and snow, dominates Colorado Springs as well as the surrounding area, dictating not only its fickle climate but also its diverse natural history. The Pikes Peak massif as well as lower mountain ranges, including the Rampart Range and the Tarryall Range, are laced with numerous excellent trails that offer four seasons of high-mountain adventure. Intrepid hikers can tackle strenuous hikes up the Mount Manitou Incline Trail and Blodgett Peak as well as the Devils Playground Trail to the airy summit of Pikes Peak, while easier hikes scale lower peaks, explore wooded valleys, discover waterfalls and clear cascading streams, recall the area's colorful gold-mining history, and follow hidden canyons filled with wildlife and birdsong.

The summit ridge of Gray Back Peak offers expansive views of the southern Front Range (hike 22).

19 Mount Cutler Trail

The easy Mount Cutler Trail gently climbs through a ponderosa pine and Douglas fir forest in North Cheyenne Cañon Park to the rounded summit of 7,220-foot Mount Cutler. The well-maintained and popular trail offers a leisurely hike with panoramic views of Colorado Springs, the Broadmoor Hotel, and the distant prairie.

Start: Mount Cutler Trailhead on North Cheyenne Cañon Road
Distance: 1.8 miles out and back
Hiking time: 1 to 2 hours
Difficulty: Easy. Trail is mostly uphill but features gentle grades.
Elevation gain: 367 feet
Trail surface: Wide, singletrack dirt trail
Seasons: Year-round. Apr through Nov is best. Lower section of trail is icy in winter.
Schedule: Open daily; May 1 to Oct 31, 5 a.m. to 10 p.m.; Nov 1 to Apr 30, 5 a.m. to 9 p.m.
Other trail users: Runners. No mountain biking.
Canine compatibility: Leashed dogs only
Land status: North Cheyenne Cañon Park, a Colorado Springs city park

Fees and permits: None
Map: USGS Manitou Springs; park map available at park website.
Trail contact: Colorado Springs Parks, Recreation and Cultural Services, 1401 Recreation Way, Colorado Springs 80905-1975; (719) 385-5940; https://coloradosprings.gov/page/north-cheyenne-canon
Special considerations: Stay on designated trail. Don't shortcut and cause erosion on steep slopes below the trail. Cliffs and drop-offs are on the upper trail; watch children along cliff edges. Trail can be icy in winter; use caution and bring trekking poles and micro-spikes. Bring water in summer; none is available along the trail or at the trailhead.

Finding the trailhead: From I-25 take the Nevada Avenue / CO 115 exit 140 B. Drive south on South Nevada Avenue / CO 115 for about a mile and turn right (west) onto Cheyenne Road. Follow Cheyenne Road for 2.6 miles to its end at Cheyenne Boulevard. If you approach via Cheyenne Boulevard, stay right on Cheyenne Boulevard at this intersection. Go left (west) on Cheyenne Boulevard for 0.1 mile to a Y intersection. Go right, through an open gate into North Cheyenne Cañon Park. Drive 1.4 miles up the park road to the Mount Cutler Trailhead on the left (GPS: 38.791798, -104.887155).

The Hike

Serene, peaceful, and seemingly remote, North Cheyenne Cañon Park is one of Colorado Springs' best hidden gems. The city park, tucked against the southwest side of the city, is a spectacular canyon lined with soaring granite cliffs and steep slopes wooded with ponderosa pine and Douglas fir. Just beyond charming residential districts, a winding road climbs west into the canyon, which is also one of the city's oldest parklands.

The Colorado Springs skyline lies beyond towering granite cliffs in North Cheyenne Cañon.

The 1.8-mile round-trip hike up Mount Cutler is the easiest and most accessible summit climb in the Pikes Peak region. The easy trail makes a great introduction to local peak-bagging for kids as well as for visitors. Expect great views across North and South Cheyenne Cañons, an easy grade with a modest elevation gain of 367 feet, peaceful pine and fir woods, and airy exposure above cliffs on the last section.

Be careful and watch children as you hike along the exposed trail above South Cheyenne Cañon below the main summit and if you make the short hike out to the east summit, which perches high above dangerous, vertical cliffs. Some of the footing is on loose, slippery gravel scattered atop the granite bedrock.

Mount Cutler offers stunning panoramic views from its rounded summit with dark forests spilling down steep mountainsides, the North and South Cheyenne Creek drainages, towering granite formations, and tumbling Seven Falls, as well as vistas of Colorado Springs and the high plains to the east. The wide trail climbs steadily but is an easy ascent, with a thrilling touch of exposure as you traverse the west- and south-facing shoulders of the mountain.

Begin at 6,797 feet from the parking lot and trailhead on the south side of the park road in North Cheyenne Cañon and hike up a broad, well-used path through an evergreen forest that provides welcome shade in summer. The trail gently climbs and after 0.25 mile reaches an overlook with views of distant downtown Colorado Springs.

The trail continues climbing, crossing steep slopes littered with fallen trees, many killed by a spruce budworm epidemic spreading through Colorado's forests. The larva of the western spruce budworm, a type of moth endemic to Colorado, feed on new growth on white and Douglas fir trees, which compose about 60 percent of the forest in North Cheyenne Cañon. The feeding larva weaken the trees, making them susceptible to bark beetles, which will kill them. The city forester annually sprays the area with common bacteria that kill the larva if they feed on impacted plants.

The trail flattens out briefly beneath a squat rock tower, then bends through a gully and climbs again, reaching an overlook at 0.4 mile. An excellent view opens across the cliff-lined canyon to the urban sprawl of Colorado Springs.

Reach a saddle that separates North and South Cheyenne Cañons at 0.5 mile. The Mount Muscoco Trail heads right here. This excellent trail, rerouted and improved in 2015, climbs 1.8 miles to the rocky summit of 8,020-foot Mount Muscoco to the west. Keep straight ahead on the well-trod path for Mount Cutler. The trail traverses onto the dry southwest side of the mountain. Sparse pines cling to rocky soil on the steep mountainside below. The narrow trail edges across an exposed slope, with cliffs and drop-offs to your right. Keep your children in check here.

As you hike, look down right from the trail and you'll glimpse Seven Falls cascading over seven granite benches on the opposite side of South Cheyenne Cañon. The tumbling 181-foot waterfall, encased in a cliffed box canyon, has been a pay-to-play tourist attraction since naturalist James Hull bought it in 1882. A long-time Colorado Springs tradition was viewing the falls and canyon bathed in sparkling Christmas lights. The Broadmoor Hotel purchased Seven Falls in 2014 and turned it into a private Eden for hotel guests with luxury restaurants, a shuttle from the hotel, and a zipline filled with whooping visitors.

NORTH CHEYENNE CAÑON

North Cheyenne Cañon has long been a coveted and revered Colorado Springs city park. In the 1870s the canyon was a popular excursion, with visitors following a rough wagon road up the canyon to view several spectacular waterfalls, picnic by the rushing creek, and admire summer wildflowers. The area, owned by the Colorado College Land Company, was, however, closed on Sundays in 1882, leading to public outcry. The entrance gate was torn down by zealous citizens, speeches were made, and words were written by local notables like writer Helen Hunt Jackson to keep the canyon open, so the City of Colorado Springs purchased 640 acres in 1885 and made it into a park.

General William Jackson Palmer, Civil War veteran and founder of Colorado Springs, donated another 480 acres in 1907 and paid for the construction of a carriage road up the canyon and over High Drive, picnic areas and a pavilion, and several trails including the Mount Cutler Trail. Automobiles were first allowed into the park in 1917, although strict guidelines for driving up and down the canyon were enforced because the road was a single lane for most of its distance.

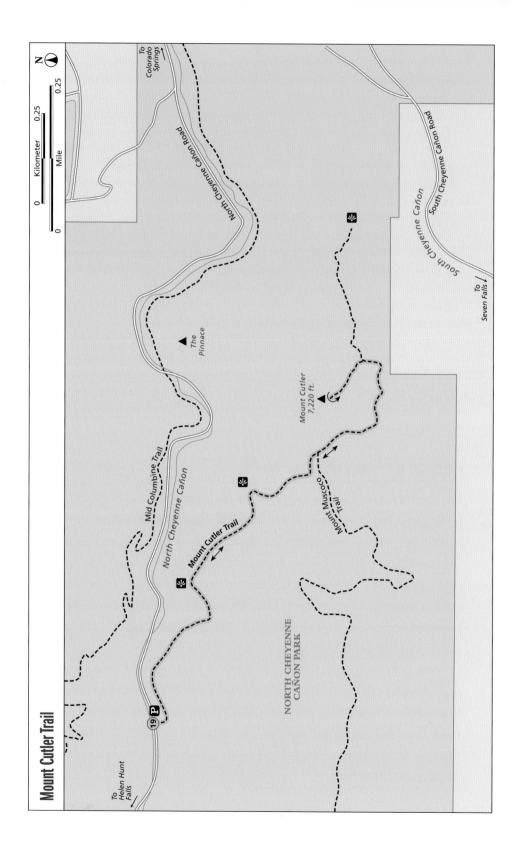

Mount Cutler Trail

N

Kilometer
0   0.25

Mile
0   0.25

To
Colorado
Springs

North Cheyenne Cañon Road

The Pinnace

Mid Columbine Trail

North Cheyenne Cañon

Mount Cutler
7,220 ft.

Mount Muscoco Trail

South Cheyenne Cañon

South Cheyenne Cañon Road

To
Seven Falls

Mount Cutler Trail

NORTH CHEYENNE
CAÑON PARK

19 P

To
Helen Hunt
Falls

The trail continues spiraling upward onto Cutler's south slope, passing a trail marker at a switchback at 0.8 mile. Keep left and scramble up the final trail section to 7,220-foot Mount Cutler's broad rounded summit at 1 mile. The summit offers 360-degree views, with the city and vast plains spreading east to the distant horizon, and the monumental peaks of the Front Range looming to the west. Sit on a shady bench for a well-earned snack and gaze north into North Cheyenne Cañon. The mountain as well as Cutler Hall, the first building erected at Colorado College in 1880, honors Henry Cutler, a Massachusetts philanthropist who contributed substantial sums to the college in the late nineteenth century and "saved the college from extinction."

Option: For extra credit on your way down, go left (east) from the main trail south of the summit on one of two narrow trails. A short distance east of the main path, these two trails join together. Follow the trail another 0.25 mile east to Cutler's lower summit. This lofty perch, surrounded by airy cliffs, offers superb views of Colorado Springs and the Broadmoor Hotel below. To return to the trailhead from Mount Cutler's summit, follow the trail back down.

It's all downhill now, and the views are just as good as when you're hiking up.

Miles and Directions

0.0   Start at the trailhead on the south side of the park road (GPS: 38.791798, -104.887155).

0.25 Arrive at an overlook with view of downtown 0.25 mile from the trailhead.

0.4   Reach an overlook with views across the canyon toward downtown Colorado Springs.

0.5   Trail reaches a saddle west of Mount Cutler's summit and junction with Mount Muscoco Trail. Continue southeast on trail across the southern flank of the mountain above South Cheyenne Cañon.

0.9   Keep left at every junction to reach the summit of Mount Cutler (GPS: 38.78780, -104.8774). Turn around to retrace your steps to the trailhead.

1.8   Arrive back at the trailhead.

20 The Columbine Trail

The Columbine Trail is an 8.6-mile out-and-back hike from the Starsmore Visitor and Nature Center at its eastern entrance to Helen Hunt Falls in North Cheyenne Cañon Park. The trail, accessed by three different trailheads, makes a fine day hike with spectacular scenery, soaring rock formations, and one of the area's best waterfalls.

Start: Starsmore Visitor and Nature Center on North Cheyenne Cañon Road at canyon entrance

Distance: 8.6 miles out and back

Hiking time: 2 to 5 hours

Difficulty: Moderate. Trail is gentle for the first mile then slowly climbs uphill with gentle grades.

Elevation gain: 1,005 feet total

Trail surface: Singletrack dirt trail

Seasons: Year-round. Apr through Nov is best. Parts of the trail may be icy in winter.

Schedule: Open daily, May 1 to Oct 31, 5 a.m. to 11 p.m.; Nov 1 to Apr 30, 5 a.m. to 9 p.m.

Other trail users: Trail runners. Mountain bikers sometimes use it for a descent from the upper canyon. Open to horses, which are rarely seen.

Canine compatibility: Leashed dogs only

Land status: North Cheyenne Cañon Park, owned by City of Colorado Springs

Fees and permits: None

Map: USGS Manitou Springs; park map available at park website.

Trail contact: Colorado Springs Parks, Recreation and Cultural Services, 1401 Recreation Way, Colorado Springs 80905-1975; (719) 385-5940; https://coloradosprings.gov/page/north-cheyenne-canon

Special considerations: Stay on the designated trail. Don't shortcut and cause erosion on steep gravel slopes below the trail. Trail can be icy in winter; use caution and bring trekking poles and micro-spikes as needed. Bring water in summer; none is available along the trail.

Finding the trailhead: From I-25 take the Nevada Avenue / CO 115 exit 140B). Drive south on South Nevada Avenue / CO 115 for about a mile and turn right (west) onto Cheyenne Road. Follow Cheyenne Road for 2.6 miles to its end at Cheyenne Boulevard. If you approach via Cheyenne Boulevard, stay right on Cheyenne Boulevard at this intersection. Go left (west) on Cheyenne Boulevard for 0.1 mile to a Y intersection. Go left toward Seven Falls and park immediately to the left in a large parking lot. The trail begins across the road at the Starsmore Visitor and Nature Center (GPS: 38.790943, -104.865078).)

The Hike

The Columbine Trail is an out-and-back hike that ascends North Cheyenne Cañon for 4.3 miles from the Starsmore Visitor and Nature Center at its eastern entrance to its western terminus on the road before Helen Hunt Falls and the Helen Hunt Falls Visitor Center. The trail, accessed by three different trailheads, makes a great day hike with spectacular mountain scenery, soaring rock formations, trickling North Cheyenne Creek, moist wooded vales, and one of the best waterfalls in the Pikes Peak region. The hike, with gentle grades and well-maintained gravel surface, is ideal for

Mount Muscoco towers above a viewpoint along the Columbine Trail.

families as well as anyone wanting a casual hiking getaway. The trail naturally divides into three segments: Lower Columbine, Middle Columbine, and Upper Columbine.

North Cheyenne Creek, beginning at Stratton Reservoir below the rounded summit of 12,367-foot Mount Almagre, the second-highest mountain in the Pikes Peak region, drains east down a steep canyon before emptying through the southwest part of Colorado Springs and joining Fountain Creek by I-25. The Columbine Trail, entirely within 1,277-acre North Cheyenne Cañon Park, a Colorado Springs city park, threads up the lower part of the canyon from its mouth below Mount Cutler to Helen Hunt Falls.

Lower North Cheyenne Cañon is a narrow gorge carved through pink Pikes Peak granite by the rushing creek. In the lower canyon, North Cheyenne Creek makes three wide, looping meanders below Mount Cutler. Above soar rocky precipices, split by seams, ledges, and sheltered alcoves. In winter, snow and rivulets of ice cling to the cliffs, while summer exposes carpets of moss and yellow lichen-covered walls.

North Cheyenne Cañon was a popular tourist destination in the early days of Colorado Springs in the 1880s and 1890s. Locals brought eastern visitors to the canyon by carriage to marvel at the granite skyscrapers and the tumbling creek of clear water. One writer praised the canyon in an 1893 travel brochure: "This canyon abounds in beautiful waterfalls and cascades.... Beautiful, picturesque, grand, and in places awe-inspiring, are these stupendous gorges, awakening deepest emotions in all beholders." The Columbine Trail was built in 1934 by a crew of unemployed men; a blacksmith sharpened as many as one hundred picks a day to hew the trail out of the granite hillsides. The

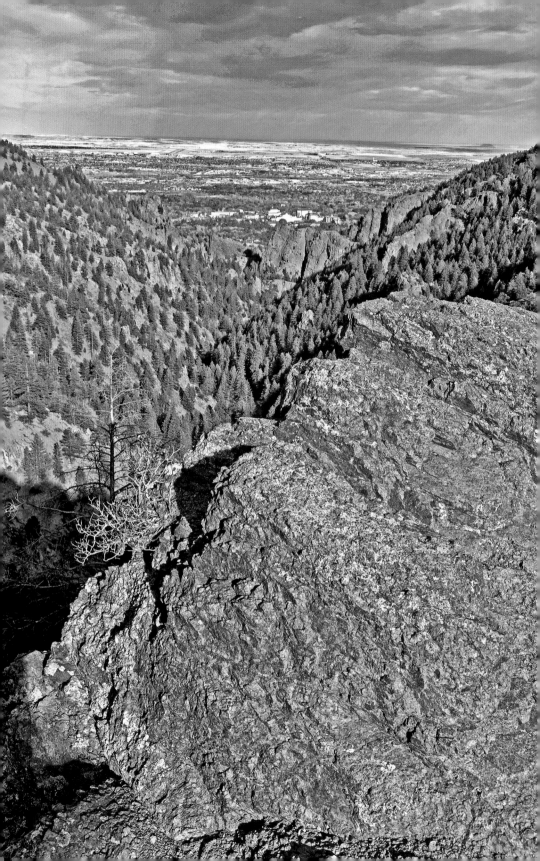

HELEN HUNT JACKSON

Helen Hunt, called the "greatest poet in America" by Ralph Waldo Emerson, emigrated from New England to Colorado Springs in 1873 for the dry salubrious air. Two years later she married local banker William Sharpless Jackson, but instead of socializing, Helen explored the Pikes Peak region. Over the next few years, she wrote seven books as well as many articles and poems, many about Colorado Springs, which she described as "a town lying due east of the great mountains and west of the sun."

In 1879 Helen Hunt Jackson left the Springs for the eastern United States with the mission of improving the government's treatment of Native Americans. She wrote *A Century of Dishonor* in 1881 and then her famed novel *Ramona*, a tragic story about a native girl living in California that has been reprinted more than 300 times. She died August 12, 1885, and was buried at Inspiration Point above Seven Falls in South Cheyenne Cañon, a site she dearly loved. Her family later had her reinterred at Evergreen Cemetery in downtown Colorado Springs.

The Columbine Trail has three trailheads. The Lower Columbine Trailhead is at Starsmore Visitor and Nature Center at the east entrance to the canyon. This is where most hikers start and is where the described hike begins. The Middle Columbine Trailhead is at the north side of the road about 1.2 miles west of Starsmore. This is a good spot to begin the upper trail for a shorter hike. The Upper Columbine Trailhead is a pullout on the switchback just above Helen Hunt Falls. It's better to park at the roadside parking area at the falls and walk 400 feet on the road's shoulder to the trailhead.

The Columbine Trail starts behind the Starsmore Visitor and Nature Center, where a sign marks the trailhead. Walk past the sign on a wide trail, pass through an open gate, and turn left. The trail gently climbs uphill on slopes above North Cheyenne Creek through an open forest of ponderosa pine, Douglas fir, and Gambel or scrub oak before dropping down alongside the trickling creek. Hike west on the trail, which widens to an old closed road, passing beneath a gateway of towering granite cliffs that hem in the lower canyon below Mount Cutler. Rappel Rock, a vertical 100-foot-high cliff, looms directly over the trail.

After 0.5 mile the trail passes some picnic tables by the creek and reaches an old stone bridge, closed with a chain, and a parking area on the opposite side of the bridge. The trail takes a sharp left here and follows a series of tight switchbacks uphill before leveling out. The Pinnacle, a popular granite formation for rock climbers, towers above the trail here. Hike beneath Pinnacle Slab, a low-angle cliff that rises directly above the trail, and continue up the canyon past a boulder that overhangs the trail to

Looking down North Cheyenne Cañon to the Broadmoor Hotel and Colorado Springs from the Columbine Trail

Graduation Boulder. This roadside block of granite, sitting by the road below the trail, is a popular spot for local climbers to do boulder problems.

The Columbine Trail spirals around the Pinnacle, which lifts tall dark cliffs overhead. The sound of the creek filters up through a shady spruce-and-fir forest, part of the canyon's unique White Fir Botanical Reserve. After a mile of hiking, the trail reaches another stone bridge and crosses it to the road. Cross at a designated crosswalk and then follow the trail on the opposite side of the creek, with great views of the West Face of the Pinnacle and a high row of cliffs lining Mount Cutler's north flank. Reach the Middle Columbine Trailhead and a gravel parking area after 1.2 miles.

The Columbine Trail continues west from the middle trailhead, which is at a sign on the west side of the parking lot. Many hikers drive to this trailhead to hike the upper trail section. The 3.1-mile-long upper trail gains lots of elevation along the north side of the canyon and offers spacious views into the canyon and east toward Colorado Springs.

Begin the Upper Columbine Trail from the middle trailhead on the west side of the parking lot below stubby Longfellow Pinnacle. The trail gently climbs switchbacks across gravel slopes shaded by scattered pines, gaining elevation and leaving the road and creek far below. After passing below the Nose, a craggy cliff perched directly above the trail, continue to a switchback above for a great view down canyon to The Pinnacle and its slabby west face.

The gravel trail continues climbing and then leaves the main canyon and enters a shallow side draw filled with wildflowers in summer and shaded by tall spruce and fir trees and a leafy understory of Gambel oak, skunkbrush, and Rocky Mountain maple trees. Look for columbines, the Colorado state flower, blooming in this moist vale in June and July. After 0.25 mile of level hiking, the trail bends sharply left at its junction with Spring Creek Trail and after crossing a trickling creek (only in springtime) fed by Columbine Spring. Go right on Spring Creek Trail for 0.2 mile to the Gold Camp Road if you desire. The Columbine Trail goes left; follow a trail sign.

After leaving Spring Creek Canyon, the trail begins steadily rising across steep south-facing slopes high above the narrow canyon floor. A couple of good overlooks offer views into the canyon. Look for two hidden waterfalls—Bridal Veil and Phantom Falls—alongside the twisting road far below. The trail continues west, threading over gravel slopes about 150 feet below the Gold Camp Road.

The dirt Gold Camp Road follows the old rail bed of the Cripple Creek District Railroad, affectionately called "The Short Line," a narrow-gauge railroad that twisted over 30 miles from a mill at Old Colorado City to the twin towns of Cripple Creek and Victor from 1901 to 1920. The railroad, hauling both passengers and gold ore to and from the "world's richest gold camp," passed through nine tunnels and climbed on an average 3.8 percent grade, making it one of the steepest railroads in the world at that time. After its last train in May 1920, a Colorado Springs businessman bought the railroad, tore up the tracks, and turned it into the toll Gold Camp Road. You can still drive most of the narrow road except for a closed 7-mile-long section from the top of North Cheyenne Cañon Road to St. Peters Dome. The road offers gorgeous

Columbine Trail

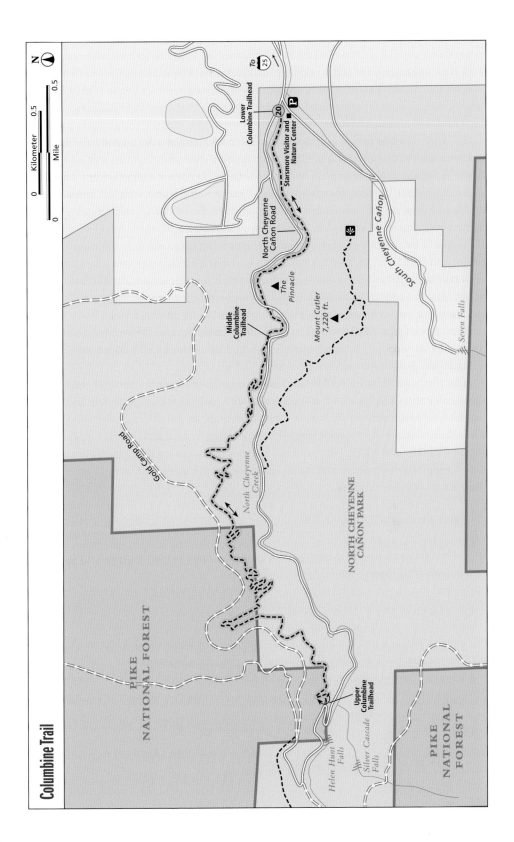

N

0   Kilometer   0.5

0   Mile   0.5

To (25)

Lower Columbine Trailhead

P

Starsmore Visitor and Nature Center

North Cheyenne Cañon Road

The Pinnacle

Middle Columbine Trailhead

Mount Cutler 7,220 ft.

South Cheyenne Cañon

Seven Falls

NORTH CHEYENNE CAÑON PARK

Gold Camp Road

North Cheyenne Creek

PIKE NATIONAL FOREST

Upper Columbine Trailhead

Helen Hunt Falls

Silver Cascade Falls

PIKE NATIONAL FOREST

views that are still the same as those seen by President Teddy Roosevelt, who called it, in typical theatrical fashion, a trip that "bankrupts the English language." For more information about the Gold Camp Road and other scenic drives in the Pikes Peak region, consult *Scenic Driving Colorado* by Stewart M. Green from FalconGuides.

The Columbine Trail levels out and contours across gravelly slopes with great vistas of Mount Muscoco, Stove Mountain, and Mount Rosa. Eventually the trail reaches a high ridgeline and a trail junction. A short spur trail runs 100 yards north to the Gold Camp Road. Jog left on the Columbine Trail from the marked junction and walk another 100 feet. The trail descends right onto steep slopes. Before dropping down, however, go left on another short spur and hike out to a couple marvelous rocky points that yield spectacular views down the canyon.

Descend on a series of switchbacks and then follow the trail as it contours east before climbing over another ridgeline. The trail descends into a deep canyon filled with tall fir and spruce trees, offering welcome shade on sunny days. Past the bottom of the canyon and a rocky talus slope, the Columbine Trail climbs steadily out of the canyon on its western side, eventually swinging onto a broad gravel ridge. Then the trail gently descends to the western trailhead and trail's end on a switchback of the paved park road above Helen Hunt Falls and the Helen Hunt Falls Visitor Center, at 4.3 miles from the trailhead by Starsmore.

If you've shuttled a car to the falls parking area, carefully walk down the narrow shoulder of the paved road for 400 feet to your vehicle as well as restrooms. If you haven't seen Helen Hunt Falls before, take a short walk up a trail to a bridge above it. The falls are usually alive and kicking with whitewater in May and June. If you didn't shuttle a car and are hiking out and back, turn around at the trailhead and follow the Columbine Trail back to one of the lower trailheads. It's usually a fast and easy hike since it's mostly downhill.

Miles and Directions

0.0 Start at the trailhead behind Starsmore Visitor and Nature Center at the mouth of North Cheyenne Cañon (GPS: 38.790943, -104.865078). Hike west on the good trail on slopes south of the creek.

1.2 Reach the Middle Trailhead for the Columbine Trail (GPS: 38.791668, -104.879321).

1.9 Reach Spring Creek Canyon (GPS: 38.794977, -104.886334).

2.6 Overlook down the canyon to the south of the trail (GPS: 38.791936, -104.893852).

4.3 End of the trail at a switchback just before Helen Hunt Falls (GPS: 38.788813, -104.901598). Turn around here to return eastward to the trailhead.

8.6 Arrive back at the trailhead at Starsmore Visitor and Nature Center.

Option: A shorter easy hike, perfect for families and seniors, begins at the Lower Columbine Trailhead at Starsmore Visitor and Nature Center and heads west for 1.1 miles to the Middle Columbine Trailhead, where you turn around and return for a pleasant 2.2-mile hike through the rugged lower canyon. This lower trail section, following the tumbling creek below towering granite cliffs, offers dramatic views.

21 St. Mary's Falls Trail

The St. Mary's Falls Trail is a scenic out-and-back hike that follows the old Gold Camp Road Trail before cutting up scenic Buffalo Canyon to a cascading waterfall perched on Stove Mountain above North Cheyenne Cañon. It's a fine half-day hike with great views, moderate grades, and one of the area's best waterfalls.

Start: Powell Trailhead at the top of North Cheyenne Cañon Road above Helen Hunt Falls
Distance: 6.4 miles out and back
Hiking time: 3 to 5 hours
Difficulty: Moderate
Elevation gain: 1,490 feet
Trail surface: Closed gravel road and single-track dirt trail
Seasons: Year-round. Apr through June are the best months to see the waterfall. Watch for snow and ice in winter.
Schedule: Open daily
Other trail users: Mountain bikers

Canine compatibility: Dogs allowed
Land status: Pike National Forest; USDA Forest Service public land
Fees and permits: None
Map: USGS Manitou Springs
Trail contact: Pike National Forest, Pikes Peak Ranger District, 601 S. Weber St., Colorado Springs 80903; (719) 636-1602; www.fs.usda .gov/psicc; https://coloradosprings.gov/page/ north-cheyenne-canon
Special considerations: Camping is allowed along the trail, but you must be 300 feet from any water.

Finding the trailhead: From I-25 take exit 140 A or B for South Nevada Avenue. Drive south on South Nevada Avenue for 0.4 mile, turn right (west) on West Cheyenne Road, and drive 2.8 miles to the junction of North Cheyenne Cañon Road (right) and South Cheyenne Cañon Road (left). Go right on North Cheyenne Cañon Road and drive 3.2 miles up the winding paved road, passing Helen Hunt Falls at 2.6 miles. Continue up to the Powell Trailhead at a large parking area at the junction of North Cheyenne Cañon Road, Gold Camp Road, and closed High Drive, and park. The trailhead is on the west side of the parking lot at a metal gate across the closed Gold Camp Road (GPS: 38.790816, -104.904178).

The Hike

The 6.4-mile round-trip hike to St. Mary's Falls follows two trails and is a popular and excellent excursion. It follows the closed section of the Gold Camp Road in North Cheyenne Cañon before heading up Buffalo Canyon to a lovely waterfall that tumbles down a steep granite slab. The hike is best done in spring when snowmelt swells the waterfall.

Begin the hike at a large parking area and the Powell Trailhead at the top of North Cheyenne Cañon Road where it intersects the Gold Camp Road and High Drive, a closed road that climbs north to the Bear Creek drainage. The lower Gold Camp Road ends at this parking area and the hike follows the closed section of the road west. The trailhead is a large metal gate on the west side of the parking lot.

Hike for 1.2 miles on the closed Gold Camp Road. This first easy hike section follows a doubletrack gravel roadbed, formerly the rail bed of the old Short Line Railroad in the early twentieth century The old road gradually gains elevation as it heads west on the north side of the deep canyon. After 0.7 mile the trail makes a wide 180-degree bend to the left and crosses North Cheyenne Creek and the junction with Seven Bridges Trail (#622), which goes west up the narrow floor of the canyon to Undine Falls and Jones Park.

Continue east on the old Gold Camp Road Trail for 0.5 mile after the bend. The wide trail continues to gain elevation on the south side of the canyon and eventually reaches closed railroad Tunnel #3. The trail leaves the Gold Camp Road here, climbs over the top of the tunnel, and then descends its east side, passing above Silver Cascade Slab, an east-facing granite cliff laced with climbing routes.

Tunnel #3 was closed in 1987 because of vandalism and its imminent collapse from rotting timbers, with both ends of the tunnel shuttered with heavy iron fencing. The tunnel, along with two other tunnels on Lower Gold Camp Road, are spooky sites that have gained traction among ghost hunters. The tunnels lie along the old rail bed of the Colorado Springs and Cripple Creek Railroad, a twisting 31-mile line that ran between the two cities from 1901 to 1920. Later the tracks were torn up and it was turned into a scenic road that passed through seven tunnels, their ceilings still black with locomotive soot. Some fanciful accounts note the sounds of giggling children in Tunnel #3's darkness, while others say they felt tugs on their clothes or were slapped. Outside they saw small handprints in dust on their cars. The story goes that the tunnel had collapsed on a school bus, killing several children. The only problem with this tall tale is that the tunnel never collapsed on a bus and no children ever died in the tunnel. The only ghosts in the tunnel were those that made a fire inside the tunnel in 2005, probably to keep warm, that destroyed the remaining wooden supports. Just past the east side of the closed tunnel and after 1.2 miles, the trail reaches Buffalo Creek and the trailhead for the St. Mary's Falls Trail (#370) at 7,700 feet. This major trail junction can be easily missed if you aren't paying close attention. After passing the tunnel, look for tumbling Buffalo Creek on your right and a metal trail sign, which can be hard to spot. This is where the 1.6-mile-long trail to St. Mary's Falls begins (GPS: 38.785765, -104.906579).

Go south on the singletrack St. Mary's Falls Trail up wide Buffalo Canyon. The trail follows Buffalo Creek, passing through a shady forest of pine, spruce, fir, and quaking aspen. The trail and canyon make a gradual bend to the left and begin gaining elevation. Just north of a low saddle, the trail reaches a junction with a short path that passes over the saddle to the south and drops down a short distance to the Gold Camp Road below.

Keep right at this obscure junction and continue up the trail, gradually gaining elevation in Buffalo Canyon. The creek riffles over boulders and plunges over numerous short waterfalls left of the trail. When the trail reaches the first major switchback,

Buffalo Creek tumbles down granite slabs, forming St. Mary's Falls, at the end of the hike.

take a left turn on a short path that leads to a pleasant cascading waterfall. Here the creek slides down a bedrock slab.

Back on the main trail, go right after the first switchback and cross a steep hillside to the next switchback, which takes the trail left. After a short distance reach a major trail junction with a metal directional sign. Go left on the trail for 500 feet to the base of St. Mary's Falls at 8,880 feet. The water sweeps down a wide trough of slabby granite, splashing and dashing for over 60 feet. At the base are some halved logs for crossing boulders when the creek is running high with snowmelt. There is also a metal plaque on a dead tree commemorating Eamon Murphy, who died in 2008 scrambling up 9,782-foot Stove Mountain, the rock-rimmed peak that towers south of the falls. The best time to view the falls is in May when plenty of water feeds it from melting snow on Mount Rosa to the west. Usually it's a mere trickle by midsummer.

Option: A right turn at the trail junction leads up a series of switchbacks on the steep mountainside for 0.2 mile to the top of St. Mary's Falls. Here are more great views down Buffalo Canyon to sprawling Colorado Springs. Be careful at the top falls because it's easy to slip on slick water-polished granite as well as loose gravel lying on bedrock. The trail continues west from the top of St. Mary's Falls, continuing up Buffalo Canyon and then climbing to the summit of 11,499-foot Mount Rosa, another 3 miles from the top of the falls.

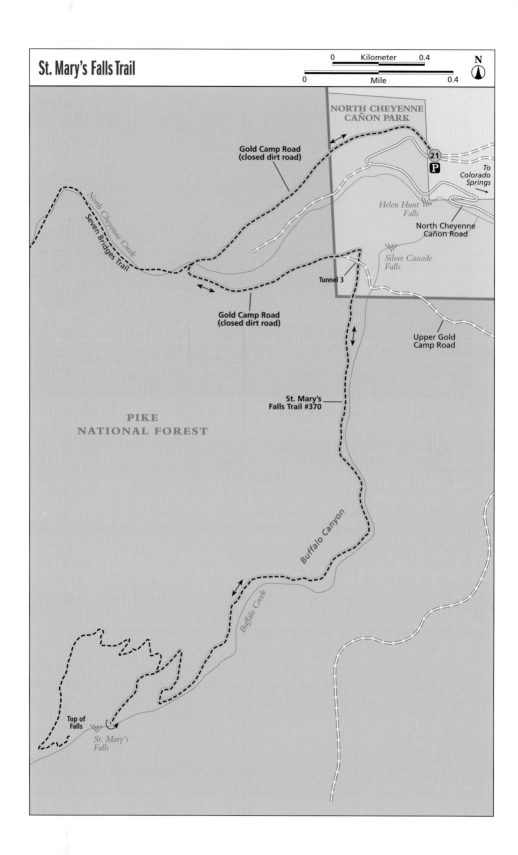

St. Mary's Falls Trail

NORTH CHEYENNE
CAÑON PARK

Gold Camp Road
(closed dirt road)

21
P

To
Colorado
Springs

Helen Hunt
Falls

North Cheyenne
Cañon Road

North Cheyenne Creek

Seven Bridges Trail

Silver Cascade
Falls

Tunnel 3

Gold Camp Road
(closed dirt road)

Upper Gold
Camp Road

PIKE
NATIONAL FOREST

St. Mary's
Falls Trail #370

Buffalo Canyon

Buffalo Creek

Top of
Falls

St. Mary's
Falls

Your hike, however, ends at the falls. After enjoying the sound and spray of falling water, turn around and hike back down the trail to the road and then back along the old Gold Camp Road to the trailhead and your car.

Miles and Directions

0.0 Powell Trailhead at end of North Cheyenne Cañon Road and its junction with Gold Camp Road and High Drive (GPS: 38.790816, -104.904178). Hike west from the parking lot on the closed section of Gold Camp Road.

0.7 Reach Seven Bridges Trail, which goes right up North Cheyenne Cañon (GPS: 38.786593, -104.914598). Stay on the closed-road Gold Camp Road Trail and hike east on the south side of the canyon.

1.2 After hiking over closed Tunnel #3, the trail reaches Buffalo Creek and the signed trailhead for St. Mary's Falls Trail (GPS: 38.785734, -104.906613). Go right (south) on the single-track trail into Buffalo Canyon. Pay attention at this junction so that you don't continue hiking east on the road; it's easy to miss the right turn.

1.5 Reach a trail junction. The left fork goes south over a low saddle and drops down to Gold Camp Road. Keep right on the main trail up Buffalo Canyon.

3.2 Reach the base of St. Mary's Falls (GPS: 38.770870, -104.918409). (**Option:** If you continue up the trail to the top of the falls, go back to the junction and left. Hike for 0.2 mile to a viewpoint above the falls [GPS: 38.7706440, -104.9199320]).

5.2 Return down St. Mary's Falls Trail to Gold Camp Road and go left on the closed road.

6.4 Arrive back at the trailhead and parking area.

22 Gray Back Peak Trail

This trail ends with wide views from the summit of 9,288-foot Gray Back Peak on the southern edge of the Pikes Peak massif. The off-the-beaten-track hike offers moderate grades, is family friendly, and travels through pine, spruce, and aspen forest, providing solitude and a wilderness experience.

Start: Gray Back Peak Trailhead on FR 371

Distance: 3.8 miles out and back

Hiking time: 2.5 to 3 hours

Difficulty: Moderate

Elevation gain: 538 feet

Trail surface: Singletrack dirt path

Seasons: Year-round. Apr through Nov is best. Trail can be icy and snow-covered in winter.

Schedule: Open daily

Other trail users: Horses on first section of trail. Occasional mountain bikers.

Canine compatibility: Dogs allowed

Land status: Pike National Forest

Fees and permits: None

Map: USGS Mount Big Chief quad

Trail contact: Pike National Forest, Pikes Peak Ranger District, 601 S. Weber St., Colorado Springs 80903; (719) 636-1602; www.fs.usda .gov/psicc

Special considerations: Bring water; none is available on the trail. Get off the summit during thunderstorms.

Finding the trailhead: From I-25 take the Circle Drive exit 138 and drive west on Circle Drive, which becomes Lake Avenue at its junction with CO 115. Continue west on Lake Avenue until it dead-ends at the Broadmoor Hotel. Turn right on Lake Circle and drive 0.25 mile to a roundabout. Turn left at the roundabout on Mesa Avenue and follow it around the west side of the Broadmoor Hotel and golf course. At a four-way intersection, go left on El Pomar Road and drive up it to an angling right turn onto Old Stage Road (left fork goes to Cheyenne Mountain Zoo). Follow the steep paved road until it turns to gravel at a sharp switchback. Continue up the twisting gravel road for about 6 miles to FR 371 at a sign for Emerald Valley Ranch. Turn left on FR 371 and drive 0.3 mile on the narrow road to a saddle. Park in a sloping parking area on the left that fits three vehicles (GPS: 38.731456, -104.906634). Use caution driving on Old Stage Road as it's steep, often busy with traffic, dusty, and can be muddy, icy, and slippery.

The Hike

The Gray Back Peak Trail offers a marvelous backcountry hike that climbs to the rocky summit of 9,288-foot Gray Back Peak, a high peak on the southeast edge of the Pikes Peak massif. The summit yields great views of Emerald Valley to the west, bulky Cheyenne Mountain to the northeast, and the brown plains below, stretching east toward Kansas. The gravel trail has moderate grades and is easy to follow. The first half of the trail is often used by horses from The Ranch at Emerald Valley, part of the Broadmoor Hotel complex, so it is worn and eroded in places.

The Wicked Cliffs form a vertical bastion on the west side of Gray Back Peak. ▶

23 Emerald Valley Pipeline Trail

The Pipeline Trail follows the old pipeline that carried water from Penrose-Rosemount Reservoir to the Broadmoor Hotel along the north side of Emerald Valley, a hidden valley on the south side of the Pikes Peak massif. The pleasant out-and-back hike passes through evergreen forest and grassy meadows with minimal elevation gain.

Start: Parking area on right side of FR 371 off Old Stage Road
Distance: 5.8 miles out and back
Hiking time: 2 to 3 hours
Difficulty: Moderate
Elevation gain: 175 feet total
Trail surface: Singletrack dirt trail
Seasons: Year-round. Apr through Nov is best. The trail may be icy in winter.
Other trail users: Mountain bikers, horseback riders
Canine compatibility: Leashed dogs only

Land status: Pike National Forest; USDA Forest Service public land
Fees and permits: None
Schedule: Open daily
Map: USGS Mount Big Chief
Trail contact: Pike National Forest, Pikes Peak Ranger District, 601 S. Weber St., Colorado Springs 80903; (719) 636-1602; www.fs.usda .gov/psicc
Special considerations: Stay on the designated trail. Trail can be icy in winter; use caution and wear micro-spikes as needed.

Finding the trailhead: From I-25 take the Circle Drive exit 138 and drive west on Circle Drive, which becomes Lake Avenue at its junction with CO 115. Continue west on Lake Avenue until it dead-ends at a roundabout at the Broadmoor Hotel. Turn right on Lake Circle and drive 0.25 mile to a roundabout. Turn left on Mesa Avenue and follow it around the west side of the Broadmoor Hotel and golf course. At a four-way intersection, go left on El Pomar Road and drive to an angling right turn onto Old Stage Road. Follow the steep paved road until it turns to gravel at a sharp switchback. Continue up the twisting gravel road for 6.25 miles to FR 371 at a sign for Emerald Valley Ranch. Turn left on FR 371 and drive 0.3 mile on the narrow road to a saddle (parking for Gray Back Peak Trail). Park in a small area on the right just past the saddle. The trailhead is 0.1 mile down the road on the right (GPS: 38.730733, -104.908160). Use caution driving on Old Stage Road as it's steep, often busy with traffic, dusty, and can be muddy, icy, and slippery.

The Hike

The Pipeline Trail, sometimes called Emerald Valley Trail so it's not confused with another Pipeline Trail in North Cheyenne Cañon, is one of the best unknown hikes in the Pikes Peak region. The trail is close to the city, and the trailhead is relatively easy to reach from the Old Stage Road on the south side of the Pikes Peak massif.

The trail follows an old pipeline, so it has minimal elevation gain. The singletrack path is generally wide and easy to follow as it threads across steep dry drainages and open wooded slopes on the northern edge of broad Emerald Valley. It's a perfect

The Pipeline Trail passes beneath towering granite cliffs on the southern slope of San Luis Peak.

family hike on a summer afternoon when wildflowers dapple meadows or in early October when golden aspens blaze across mountain slopes.

To access the trailhead and hike, drive up the dirt Old Stage Road, a rough road that accesses the Broadmoor Stables, The Ranch at Emerald Valley, and the Gold Camp Road, which continues west to Cripple Creek. The road is sometimes busy, can be steep in places, and may be a rough washboard. Take your time driving and watch for cars on blind corners. The road is usually snowpacked and icy in winter; a four-wheel-drive vehicle is recommended in winter conditions.

Begin the hike by walking 0.1 mile down the dirt road from the parking area to the trailhead at 8,618 feet altitude on the right. Look for an exposed 10-inch metal pipe—the pipeline—in the trail. If you walk down the road to The Ranch at Emerald Valley, a Broadmoor Hotel property, you've gone too far.

The historic Emerald Valley Ranch area below the Pipeline Trail was the site of a sawmill in the late 1800s and then it was an Episcopal retreat and Girl Scout camp before Spencer Penrose, founder of the Broadmoor, bought the property and used it as Camp Vigil for his friends. Later the ranch belonged to the City of Colorado Springs and was used by groups like the YMCA and the Boy Scouts. It was turned into a dude ranch in 1946 until the Broadmoor bought it in 2011 and turned it into an exclusive retreat with expensive cabins.

Hike west on the mostly level trail alongside an old pipeline. The pipeline, which delivered water from Penrose-Rosemount Reservoir to the Broadmoor Hotel below, was built around 1920. Just past the trailhead the trail swings by the wooden ruins of an old mine. Continue another 0.3 mile to a trail junction at Little Fountain Creek. Keep straight on the Pipeline Trail. This area around Cather Springs does have some private property so stay on the trail to avoid trespassing.

The right turn off the Pipeline Trail follows a rough path for 0.5 mile up the steep draw to Bear Trap Ranch and on to Mount Vigil, the prominent peak above that's ringed by tall granite cliffs. Some historians believe that this draw was descended by Lieutenant Zebulon Pike and his band of merry men when they retreated down to the prairie after failing to climb his namesake mountain in late November 1806.

The hike continues west on the Pipeline Trail, dipping through shallow dry drainages and edging across steep gravel slopes. Broken granite cliffs loom above the trail. A stone wall composed of jumbled moss-covered boulders borders the pipeline and trail in places. Douglas fir and Engelmann spruce fill cool, shady vales while ponderosa pines spread across sunny well-drained slopes.

Emerald Valley, drained by an unnamed tributary of Little Fountain Creek, is bounded on the north by a high ridge of rocky peaks. Mount Vigil, an unranked 10,073-foot peak girded by cliffs, anchors the eastern edge of the ridge. In the middle of the ridge are 10,433-foot San Luis Peak and 10,450-foot McKinley Peak, while 10,490-foot Knight's Peak anchors the west end above Penrose-Rosemount Reservoir.

After 1.8 miles, as the valley begins narrowing, the trail crosses a stone bridge and at 2.4 miles intersects FR 371 (which may be closed), a rough road that runs west up the valley from the ranch, at the site of the old Emerald Valley Boys Camp. Little remains of the camp except a stone fireplace from a now-vanished building and several foundations. Continue west on the trail, now following the four-wheel-drive road west up the valley.

The valley floor opens, with grassy meadows and groves of quaking aspen along a trickling creek. After 2.9 miles the trail reaches several beaver ponds. This is the turnaround point for this out-and-back hike. (**Option:** It is possible to continue hiking west up the old road, which eventually becomes a rough trail that passes over a saddle southwest of Knight's Peak, descends into East Beaver Creek's valley, and then climbs back northwest to the Gold Camp Road by the reservoir.) But for your trip, return to the trailhead and your vehicle by following the trail back east, making a 5.8-mile round-trip hike.

Miles and Directions

0.0 Park at a lot on the right side of FR 371. Walk down the road to the trailhead (GPS: 38.731474, -104.906631).

The Beaver Creek Trail traverses below tall cliffs in a rugged canyon carved by Beaver Creek.

colorful sign that introduces you to Beaver Creek State Wildlife Area and includes a map.

The 2,228-acre state wildlife area, lying mostly within the wilderness study area, is a long, thin property along West Beaver Creek from Skaguay Reservoir (9,206 feet) near Victor to the parking area at the lower mouth of Beaver Creek (5,720 feet).

Follow the right fork of Beaver Creek Trail across a meadow on the right side of the valley, then ascend a stony hill on the wide trail to a sloping meadow studded with junipers and piñon pines. The trail passes under a rustic gateway of old juniper logs and descends to the wilderness study area boundary, marked by a sign at a mile.

Continue down the trail into stony Trail Gulch and a trail junction above the trickling creek. This is the start of the Beaver Creek Loop. The Beaver Creek Trail coming up from the creek to the left is the way you will return to this point. A sign here points west to "Beaver Creek" and south to "Parking Lot." Go right on the Trail Gulch Trail and head northeast into a V-shaped canyon. This next hike segment up Trail Gulch Trail is just over a mile long and gains over 400 feet to the junction with the Powerline Trail, the hike's third leg. The trail follows the cliff-lined canyon northeast, threading along the narrow canyon floor. The lower part of the canyon is dry and rocky with scattered piñon pines, junipers, and tall cottonwoods that shade

Horses graze in a meadow in Beaver Creek's lower canyon.

the creek. During wet seasons or after rain, you make as many as 20 creek crossings depending on the water level as the trail gently climbs north up the canyon. Eventually the canyon loses the cliffs and begins to widen.

The singletrack trail crosses meadows filled with wavering grass, passes through open ponderosa pine woods, and after 2 miles reaches a junction with the Powerline Trail that's marked by a small cairn and a sign. This is a good place to sit down and have a sip of water and snack. The next hike segment up the Powerline Trail climbs over 1,000 feet in 1.7 miles to the hike's high point. Beyond the junction, Trail Gulch Trail continues up the canyon a few more miles to Rosemount Reservoir and the Gold Camp Road.

Go left at the junction on Powerline Trail. The narrow gravel trail quickly gains elevation, switching back and forth on a blunt ridge. After a steep 0.5 mile, you can catch a breather at a good viewpoint that looks north up Trail Gulch. Continue up the trail to the top of the first summit, a rocky outcrop that gives a view down Trail Gulch to the parking lot and your vehicle to the south. Beyond stretch the wooded Wet Mountains and the ragged snowcapped Sangre de Cristo Mountains.

After 3.7 miles the trail reaches the high point, an open spot on a narrow ridge. If you want a close look at an old power-line pole erected some one hundred years ago, go right up the ridge a hundred yards to the double-trunked pole with two cross-beams. Broken glass insulators are on the ground below the power line. The power line once ran from the Skaguay Power Plant up upper West Beaver Creek. The plant produced electric power from 1901 until 1965 when a flash flood destroyed most of the plant's infrastructure. Besides supplying electricity to Cripple Creek and Victor mines, the power plant also provided power to Cañon City and Pueblo. The power line that its namesake trail follows ran southeast to Pueblo.

From the ridgeline and high point, the narrow trail descends a steep mile, losing some 1,200 feet, to East Beaver Creek. The trail makes a series of wide switchbacks down the steep west side of the ridge, crossing gravel slopes dense with scrub oak thickets and a mixed woodland of ponderosa pine and Douglas fir on the shady north-facing mountainsides.

Eventually the slope eases and the trail easily descends a draw, passing a small waterfall, until it reaches a trail junction marked with a cairn. This is the end of the Powerline Trail. Just below are the remains of an old prospector's cabin and an over-look above East Beaver Creek. This is a good stopping point for a snack. You can scramble down to the creek to the right here if you want. The confluence of East and West Beaver Creeks and their deep canyons is a few hundred feet downstream.

The next 2 miles of the hike, following the Beaver Creek Trail, is simply spec-tacular, with soaring granite cliffs decorating the mountainsides and the roaring creek dashing through the walled canyon below the trail. At the trail junction go left (south) on Beaver Creek Trail from the Powerline Trail. The trail climbs through fir and scrub oak, then edges across steep dry slopes covered with cacti and grass above cliffs that drop down to the inner canyon and the creek.

The trail dips across dry ravines and rolls across hillsides before descending to Beaver Creek. The trail parallels the creek, crossing rounded boulders before climbing back up slopes above the cliff-lined creek in the lower canyon. After 5.5 miles the trail reaches a 100-foot-high cliff that blocks progress. The creek bends right beneath the right side of the cliff, forming a deep pool.

In dry conditions you can traverse the rock face above the pool, making a few tenuous climbing moves to finish. Don't attempt it, however, if the water is high or you're unsure of your footing since a fall would be dangerous. Instead, look for a crossing farther upstream where the creek is shallower and wider. If the creek is full in springtime, be sure to find a sturdy pole to lean against in the current when you cross.

Past the crossing, the trail climbs onto a flat ridge and crosses a short-grass meadow spiked with cholla cacti. It then edges shelf-like across a steep slope that drops directly down to the creek below and finishes by descending into lower Trail Gulch. Scramble up the south side of the canyon to the junction at the beginning of the loop at 6 miles. Go right (south) at the wooden sign that says, "Parking Lot" and continue on the Beaver Creek Trail.

The last trail section retraces your original footsteps from the trail junction for 1 mile back to your vehicle in the parking lot.

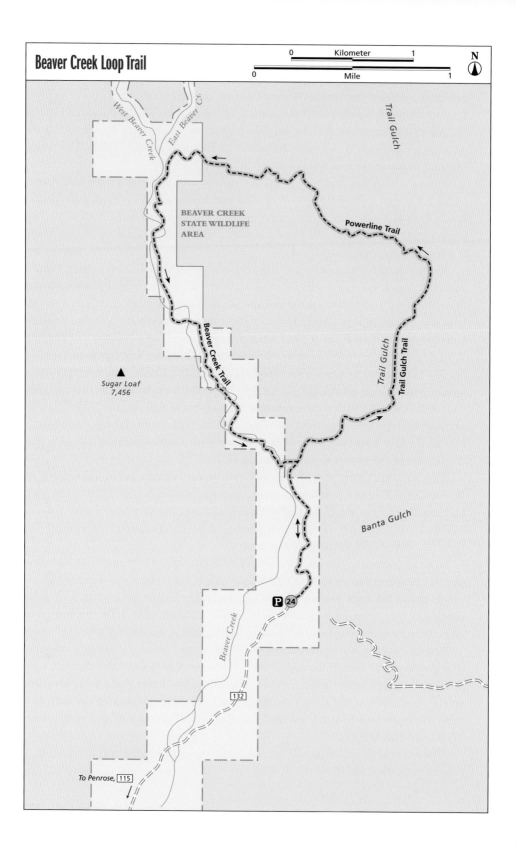

Beaver Creek Loop Trail

0   Kilometer   1

0   Mile   1

N

West Beaver Creek

East Beaver Ck.

Trail Gulch

BEAVER CREEK
STATE WILDLIFE
AREA

Powerline Trail

▲ Sugar Loaf
7,456

Beaver Creek Trail

Trail Gulch

Trail Gulch Trail

Banta Gulch

Beaver Creek

P 24

132

To Penrose, 115

Miles and Directions

0.0 Start at the trailhead on the east side of the parking area (GPS: 38.570727, -105.012000) and hike east on a closed road. After about 500 feet, reach a fork in the closed road. Go left (GPS: 38.571896, -105.010555).

0.5 Reach another major fork. Go right on the wide Beaver Creek Trail (GPS: 38.573824, -105.01125). The left fork follows the creek north.

0.9 Boundary of the Beaver Creek Wilderness Study Area.

1.0 Reach the beginning of the loop section at the junction of the Beaver Creek Trail, which goes left up the canyon, and Trail Gulch Trail (GPS: 38.57980, -105.01167) to the right. Go right and head northeast up Trail Gulch Trail.

2.0 Reach the junction with Powerline Trail (GPS: 38.59245, -105.00043). Go left on Powerline Trail and climb steeply uphill.

3.7 Trail reaches the top of a ridgeline and the high point of the hike (GPS: 38.59776, -105.01090).

4.7 Descend steeply down west-facing slopes and reach the bottom of the trail and the junction with Beaver Creek Trail (GPS: 38.59966, -105.02203). Go left on Beaver Creek Trail on slopes above and along the east side of Beaver Creek.

6.0 Reach the junction with Trail Gulch Trail and the end of the hike's loop. Go right on Beaver Creek Trail and follow back to the trailhead.

7.0 End the hike at the trailhead and parking area.

25 Red Mountain Trail

The Red Mountain Trail climbs 800 feet from Ruxton Avenue on the west side of Manitou Springs to the 7,361-foot-high summit of Red Mountain, a spur peak that rises above the picturesque town. The hike follows a good trail with easy grades to the ruins of an abandoned incline railway and summit house and offers spectacular views of Manitou, Ute Pass, Garden of the Gods, and Pikes Peak.

Start: Iron Springs Trailhead for Intemann Trail in Manitou Springs
Distance: 3.0 miles out and back
Hiking time: 1 to 2 hours
Difficulty: Moderate
Elevation gain: 800 feet
Trail surface: Double- and singletrack dirt
Seasons: Year-round but best hiking is Mar through Nov. Icy in winter.
Schedule: Open daily

Other trail users: Mountain bikers on lower Intemann Trail; runners
Canine compatibility: Dogs allowed
Fees and permits: None
Map: USGS Manitou Springs
Trail contact: Manitou Springs Chamber of Commerce and Visitors Bureau, 354 Manitou Ave., Manitou Springs 80829; (719) 685-5089; manitousprings.org

Finding the trailhead: From Colorado Springs drive west on US 24 and exit onto Manitou Avenue. This is the first Manitou exit on US 24. Drive west on Manitou Avenue to a roundabout and turn left onto Ruxton Avenue, following signs for the Pikes Peak Cog Railway. Follow Ruxton until it splits into a one-way road to the Cog Railway depot and a one-way street back to Manitou Avenue. Follow the right road to the depot and make a U-turn left onto the return one-way street. Find a place to park here or along the right side of Ruxton Avenue. The Iron Springs Trailhead for Intemann Trail is on the right before Ruxton becomes two-way (GPS: 38.857289, -104.927498).

Parking is limited; on busy days and weekends, park free at 10 Old Man's Trail and ride the Manitou Springs Free Shuttle (Route #33) from Memorial Park. Pickup point is the east end of the park. Shuttle operates 7 days a week from 6 a.m. to 8 p.m. with 20-minute waits and 10-minute waits on Saturday and Sunday from 10 a.m. to 8 p.m. https://manitousprings.org/manitou-free-shuttle/

The Hike

Red Mountain, an unranked peak rising above Manitou Springs' south side, offers a great hike to a lofty lookout and views of Manitou. Despite the mountain's steep slopes, the singletrack trail wends to the peak's 7,361-foot summit with gentle grades that switchback across the steepest slopes. Besides fun hiking and great views, Red

Pikes Peak and Engelmann Canyon lie west of Red Mountain's summit. ▶

THE RED MOUNTAIN INCLINE RAILWAY

An incline railway, or funicular, ran up the steep north side of Red Mountain to a summit house perched on its granite summit. The Red Mountain Scenic Railway was built in the first eight months of 1912 and opened in late summer. Tickets cost 50 cents round-trip and 25 cents for children. The incline, however, was extremely steep, making it too scary for many riders. Some riders actually refused to ride the incline down, preferring instead to safely hike down from the summit pavilion.

The incline brochure extolled the pleasures of a trip up Red Mountain: "This very experience is for you, yes—and with thrills, yes, but with absolute safety, comfort and pleasure.... Unlimited stopover at summit, free pavilion, picnic grounds, 'hike' trips, music, dancing, etc. See the beautiful sunset from the mountaintop." Sounds like fun! The railway, however, only lasted a few years before closing down.

Mountain also offers a surprise ending—the abandoned concrete foundations of an old restaurant, casino, and summit house of an incline railway that, like neighboring Mount Manitou Incline, once carried tourists to the top.

Begin your Red Mountain adventure at the Iron Springs Trailhead for the Paul Intemann Trail next to Ruxton Avenue below the Pikes Peak Cog Railway station and the Iron Springs Chateau. After finding a parking spot on either Ruxton Avenue or Iron Springs Road, which can be a problem during the busy summer tourist season, or taking the free shuttle from Memorial Park, hike east on a trail along the south side of Ruxton Creek past Iron Springs, a mineral spring under a pavilion on the north bank of the creek. Continue down the trail to Spring Street and turn right.

Walk up the dirt road to a gate and pass onto the Intemann Trail. The first 0.5-mile segment of this hike follows the Intemann Trail, an incomplete trail that contours east above Manitou Springs to the Section 16 Trail above the Gold Camp Road. The trail is named for Paul Intemann, a Manitou Springs city planner who envisioned a network of trails above Manitou. He died in a car accident in New Mexico in 1986.

Follow the trail, a closed road that doubles as a fire road, up a draw, around a blunt ridge, and up a broad vale toward a couple of power poles. Look to the right before the poles for a sign marking the start of the Red Mountain Trail. This 1-mile spur trail, built by volunteers in 1999 and 2001, is on a swath of Manitou Springs Open Space land.

Turn right (south) and hike up the Red Mountain Trail, which slowly climbs southwest in a mixed conifer forest of ponderosa pine and Douglas fir left of a steep ravine. Follow the switchbacking trail up the steep slope until it swings left and climbs to a saddle on a wooded ridgeline. This is the official end of the trail but not the hike.

Go left at the saddle and continue up the rocky trail, which threads above the steep eastern flank of Red Mountain. After gaining 50 more feet of elevation, the trail ends on the mountain's flat summit.

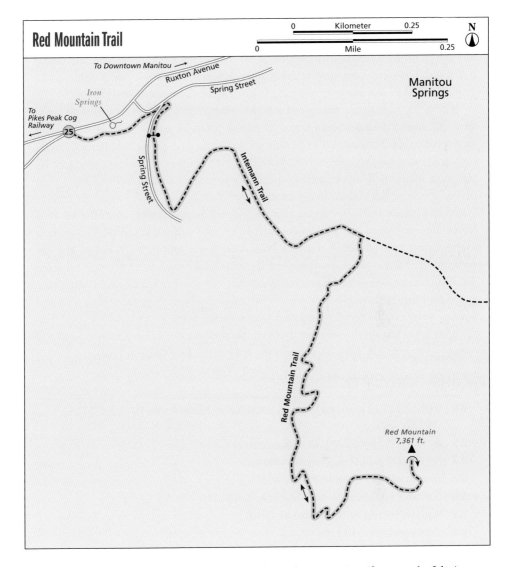

0   Kilometer   0.25

0   Mile   0.25

N

To Downtown Manitou

Ruxton Avenue

Spring Street

Iron
Springs

To
Pikes Peak Cog
Railway

25

Spring Street

Intemann Trail

Manitou
Springs

Red Mountain Trail

Red Mountain
7,361 ft.

The spacious summit of 7,361-foot-high Red Mountain offers wonderful views. Below nestles Manitou Springs, with houses lining its hilly roads. The distant sounds of traffic, barking dogs, and music filter upward. To the east rise the red rocks at Garden of the Gods, and beyond spreads Colorado Springs and the distant prairie horizon. The westward view is spectacular. Pikes Peak rears high above. Lower are the pinnacles Gog and Magog perched on a wooded ridge on the north slope of Cameron Cone.

The top of Red Mountain, however, is not just about great views. If you look around, you'll see the concrete foundations of several buildings erected here in the early twentieth century. The Red Mountain Incline Railway, which competed with the nearby Mount Manitou Incline Railway, ferried visitors up the mountain's steep northeast face. The lower concrete footings mark where the railway ended, and visitors disembarked. The upper foundations are the site of a restaurant, bar, and dance hall where both live music and whiskey flowed. Some even say it was a casino and a gentleman's club, a polite way of saying it was a brothel, but that's just rumor.

Before the railway, the summit of Red Mountain was a gravesite. In the late nineteenth century, Manitou Springs was a healing place for tuberculosis patients who journeyed west for dry air and its healing mineral springs. A young lady named Emma Crawford came for the cure in 1889 but died on December 4, 1891, at the age of 19. She once hiked to Red Mountain's summit, where she had a vision and left a scarf tied on a tree by her chosen burial plot.

After Emma's death, her fiancé and twelve pallbearers carried her coffin up Red Mountain and buried her on the summit. In 1912 the coffin was moved to the south so the incline summit house could be built. After heavy rain in 1929, Emma and her coffin washed down the mountain's east slope, spilling her remains. She was reburied in a Manitou cemetery, but many locals say that her ghost still stalks Red Mountain, and some claim to have glimpsed the Victorian-clad specter. Every October Manitou Springs hosts a coffin race in her honor and remembrance.

After brooding on the summit about all this melancholic history, turn around and retrace your steps 1.5 miles back down the trail to the Iron Springs Trailhead.

Miles and Directions

0.0 Trailhead for Paul Intemann Memorial Nature Trail on Ruxton Avenue (GPS: 38.857289, -104.927498).

0.1 Junction with Spring Street. Go right.

0.2 Junction with road. Go right on Intemann Trail.

0.5 Junction with Red Mountain Trail. Go right.

1.5 Summit of Red Mountain (GPS: 38.8514, -104.9212).

2.5 Return to junction with Intemann Trail. Go left.

3.0 Arrive back at the trailhead.

26 Mount Manitou Incline Trail

The 0.9-mile Mount Manitou Incline Trail, rising directly above Manitou Springs along the abandoned route of a 1907 incline railway, is one of the most popular hikes in the Pikes Peak region. The trail goes straight up the steep mountainside, gaining 2,000 feet in less than a mile with an average grade of 41 percent and a maximum grade of 68 percent. The trail, usually just called the Incline, offers a strenuous sustained uphill hike to the top of the grade below the summit of 9,250-foot Rocky Mountain and then returns 3.2 miles down gradual grades on Barr Trail to the trailhead for a 4.5-mile loop hike.

Start: Trailhead at north side of Pikes Peak Cog Railway parking lot on west side of Manitou Springs

Distance: 4.5-mile loop

Hiking time: 1.5 to 3 hours

Difficulty: Very strenuous. Do not attempt this trail if you are overweight or have heart or other health problems. It is advisable to consult your doctor before hiking the Incline Trail.

Elevation gain: 2,011 feet. Starting elevation is 6,574 feet. Ending elevation is 8,585 feet.

Trail surface: Gravel and loose gravel with railroad-tie steps

Seasons: Year-round

Other trail users: Hikers only

Canine compatibility: Dogs not permitted. Dog waste has been a serious problem on the trail.

Land status: Owned by three different entities. The lower 25 percent is owned by the City of Colorado Springs / Colorado Springs Utilities. The middle 50 percent is owned by the Manitou and Pikes Peak Railway. The upper 25 percent is public land in Pike National Forest.

Fees and permits: None

Schedule: Open daily except during events like the Pikes Peak Marathon in August. Apr 1–Oct 31: 6 a.m. to 8 p.m.; Nov 1–Mar 31: 6 a.m. to 6 p.m.

Map: USGS Manitou Springs

Trail contact: Pike National Forest, Pikes Peak Ranger District, 601 S. Weber St., Colorado Springs 80903; (719) 636-1602; www.fs.usda.gov/psicc. Manitou Incline, www.manitouincline.com/

Special considerations: Use Incline Trail at your own risk. No pets. Practice No Trace ethic; trash cans at the trailhead. The Incline Trail is recommended for uphill use only to avoid downhill accidents and trail crowding. Parking is limited in the area. Park at Memorial Park in Manitou and take the free shuttle to the trailhead.

Finding the trailhead: To reach the Incline Trailhead from I-25, take the Cimarron Street / US 24 exit 141 and drive west on US 24 for 5.4 miles to the first Manitou Springs exit. The exit ramp circles down to Manitou Avenue. Go west on Manitou Avenue for 1.4 miles, following signs for "Cog Railway." At a roundabout at the junction of Manitou Avenue and Ruxton Avenue, go west on Ruxton and drive 0.7 mile to the cog railway depot.

Parking is difficult. All parking near the Incline is by fee only. Park at the Barr Trailhead farther up in Ruxton; in legal parking spaces on Ruxton Avenue; at Iron Springs Chateau Melodrama lot; or at a Manitou Springs public parking lot where you can take a free shuttle to the Incline Trailhead. The trailhead is on the north side of the Cog Railway parking lot (GPS: 38.856934,

-104.931457). Do not park in the Cog Railway lot. It is reserved for cog patrons only, and illegally parked vehicles will be towed.

Parking is limited; on busy days and weekends, park free at 10 Old Man's Trail and ride the Manitou Springs Free Shuttle (Route #33) from Memorial Park. Pickup point is the east end of the park. Shuttle operates 7 days a week from 6 a.m. to 8 p.m. with 20-minute waits and 10-minute waits on Saturday and Sunday from 10 a.m. to 8 p.m. https://manitousprings.org/manitou-free-shuttle/

The Hike

The Mount Manitou Incline Trail, which actually ascends 9,250-foot Rocky Mountain, is an almost mile-long trail that climbs straight up the mountainside above Manitou Springs for 2,011 feet with an average grade of 41 percent; a short, steep section of 68 percent; and 2,744 timber steps. The trail, often called the Incline or the Manitou Incline, is one of the most popular trails in the Pikes Peak region, with 350,000 to 500,000 hikers annually.

It's recommended that, after you reach the top of the Incline Trail, you descend 3.2 miles down Barr Trail for a 4.5-mile round-trip hike. Descending the Manitou Incline is not only dangerous because of loose gravel footing and occasional rusted pieces of metal, but also because it creates traffic jams and disturbs uphill hikers. The Master Plan for the Incline includes a descent trail on the mountain slope north of the Incline with several bailout points to alleviate foot traffic and erosion from thousands of Incline hikers on historic Barr Trail, a 13-mile trail from Manitou Springs to the summit of 14,115-foot Pikes Peak. The proposed 5-mile descent trail awaits funding and approval from the different land management agencies.

The Incline is often used as a cardio workout by local athletes, including Olympians training at the US Olympic Training Center in Colorado Springs, as well as local soldiers and cadets. The current uphill record belongs to triathlete Mark Fretta, who ran up it in 16 minutes, 42 seconds, while Olympic short-track speed-skating gold medalist Apolo Ohno did it in 17 minutes, 45 seconds. The verified satellite-tracked record belongs to Joseph Gray, who ran the course in 17 minutes, 45 seconds in 2015. Most hikers do the ascent in 40 to 50 minutes, although many take over 2 hours to reach the top.

Use caution before attempting to hike the Incline Trail. A sign at the beginning of the trail reads: "WARNING: This is an EXTREME TRAIL. Consult with your doctor before adding the Incline to your exercise routine. If you need medical attention on the Incline, it could take First Responders over an hour to get to you."

The Mount Manitou Incline Trail began as an incline railway, or funicular, in 1907, that allowed access to a small hydroelectric plant and water pipes at the mountaintop, providing water to Manitou Springs below. The steep railroad and its stunning

The Mount Manitou Incline Trail follows a straight-up path on the old grade of an incline railway. ▶

Pikes Peak lifts broad shoulders above the rocky summit of Cascade Mountain.

Cascade Mountain, with 296 feet of prominence, is an unranked summit that offers great views for the intrepid hiker. Bulky Pikes Peak towers above its boulder-strewn summit, while the stream of traffic on US 24 in Ute Pass is a distant hum below. Heizer Trail and Cascade Mountain offer a private wild experience. Don't plan on seeing anyone else on this backcountry hiking gem.

The Heizer Trail is a great workout trail for runners, comparable with the first part of Barr Trail up Mount Manitou. The trail's steady uphill grade offers few spots to catch your breath without stopping. The good news is that after you reach the summit, it's a fast downhill run back to the trailhead. Few mountain bikers use Heizer Trail due to its steepness and occasional sections of gravel.

The Heizer Trailhead is located at the top end of steep Anemone Hill Road on the south side of Cascade just west of US 24. Park by a sign that says "Snow Plow Turn Around" if it is not winter. If no parking is available, it is best to park down in the bottom of the valley by a small park and hike up the road to the trailhead.

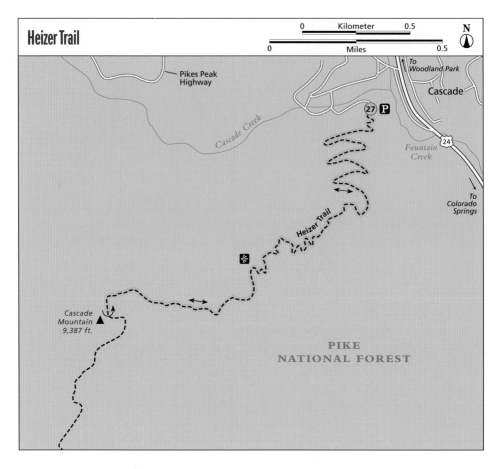

The Heizer Trail begins quickly climbing, following a series of wide switchbacks up steep mountain slopes. There are plenty of scenic points for rest stops, with dramatic views up the pass to the slowly turning Ferris wheel at Santa's Workshop and the Pikes Peak Highway. This first trail section has moderate grades with a good gravel surface. It can, however, be icy and slippery in winter since it doesn't get much sunshine.

After about a mile the trail reaches a group of large granite boulders, swings onto the sunny east flank of the mountain, and passes through dense thickets of Gambel oak. Above here the trail features more switchbacks with steeper grades and occasional patches of slippery gravel.

After a couple of miles, the trail moves back onto the shaded north slopes and reaches a lofty vantage point above tall cliffs. This is a great stop for resting and drinking some needed liquid refreshment. The Pikes Peak Highway crosses slopes across the broad canyon below the overlook.

The trail continues up the mountain, but the grade lessens. Eventually it reaches a clump of tall boulders surrounded by a forest of quaking aspens, firs, and spruces.

The high point of Cascade Mountain is atop one of those granite boulders west of the trail. If you are a true highpointer and need to tag the mountain's summit so you can say you actually reached the highest point, then you have to do a rock climbing problem up the boulder. It's best to have a short rope, especially for getting down off the summit.

While you are up there, enjoy great views with the rocky northeast flank of Pikes Peak dominating the vista. (*Option:* The trail continues south from here, gently descending into a shallow valley. Look for a sign that points the way to Trail 703. If you want a longer trail adventure, follow orange ribbons on trees to join that trail and continue hiking south to Barr Trail.)

To return to the trailhead in Cascade, simply follow the Heizer Trail back down the mountain. Take your time on the steep sections since the gravel can be slippery and you don't want to fall.

Miles and Directions

0.0 Begin at the trailhead on Anemone Hill Road (GPS: 38.895249, -104.972694).

2.8 Rocky summit of Cascade Mountain is reached by scrambling (GPS: 38.8883, -104.9853).

5.6 Arrive back at the trailhead.

28 Catamount Trail

The Catamount Trail is an out-and-back hike that begins in Green Mountain Falls, follows a road through a residential area to Catamount Falls, then switchbacks through open woods to the Garden of Eden, a hidden valley. The hike ends below South Catamount Reservoir on the north slope of Pikes Peak before returning to Green Mountain Falls.

Start: Junction of Ute Pass Avenue and Belvidere Avenue in Green Mountain Falls
Distance: 6.4 miles out and back
Hiking time: 2 to 4 hours round-trip
Difficulty: Moderate
Elevation gain: 1,400 feet
Trail surface: Paved road to closed dirt road to singletrack dirt trail
Seasons: Year-round. The trail has snow and ice in winter. Bring micro-spikes and trekking poles.
Schedule: Open daily
Other trail users: Mountain bikes and horses are allowed but rarely seen on the rocky trail.
Canine compatibility: Leashed dogs only

Land status: Green Mountain Falls and Pike National Forest
Fees and permits: None
Map: USGS Woodland Park
Trail contact: Town of Green Mountain Falls, www.gmfco.us. Also Pike National Forest, Pikes Peak Ranger District, 601 S. Weber St., Colorado Springs 80903; (719) 636-1602; www.fs.usda.gov/psicc
Other: Parking for the hike is along Ute Pass Avenue in Green Mountain Falls. There is no public parking on either of the two streets that access the start of the trail. Illegally parked cars may be towed.

Finding the trailhead: From downtown Colorado Springs and I-25, take the Cimarron Street / US 24 exit #141 off I-25. Drive west on US 24 for 15.5 miles to the second Green Mountain Falls exit. Go left across the westbound lanes of US 24 and follow Ute Pass Avenue southwest for 0.7 mile into the town of Green Mountain Falls. Park on Lake Street to the left on the north side of a small lake (GPS: 38.933954, -105.014739) or in one of several roadside parking lots along the east side of Ute Pass Avenue north of Lake Street. The trailhead is the junction of Ute Pass Avenue and Belvidere Avenue a couple of blocks north of Lake Street (GPS: 38.935728, -105.017427).

The Hike

The popular Catamount Trail is one of the Pikes Peak region's hiking gems. The 6.4-mile out-and-back hike from Green Mountain Falls in Ute Pass to South Catamount Reservoir off the Pikes Peak Highway offers a well-maintained trail, waterfalls and cascades, granite cliffs and boulders, and a gorgeous hidden valley filled with tall grass and birdsong on summer afternoons. The hike, despite ascending steep slopes, has an amenable grade and is easily completed in 4 hours. The trail, creek, and waterfall are named for the elusive catamount, another name for the mountain lions that inhabit Colorado.

Catamount Trail crosses meadows below granite cliffs in the Garden of Eden.

Two roads—Belvidere and Hondo Avenues—allow access from Ute Pass Avenue to the beginning of Catamount Trail on a closed dirt road that leads to a waterworks building below Catamount Falls and the actual trailhead for Catamount Trail. Both Belvidere and Hondo, however, have no public parking; only residents are allowed to park along the streets. There is no parking at the gated end of either street; violators will find their cars towed. To reach the trail, park at the Gazebo Lake on Lake Street or in one of several roadside parking areas on the east side of Ute Pass Avenue north of Lake Street. The roads were closed for hiker parking after years of cars clogging the narrow streets, blocking driveways, and parking along the streets below the gates.

The hike starts at the junction of Ute Pass Avenue, the main street through Green Mountain Falls, and Belvidere Avenue, which goes left (west) from Ute Pass Avenue on the north end of town. After parking your vehicle on Lake Street or at one of the lots on the east side of Ute Pass Avenue, walk north to the road junction and the unofficial trailhead for the hike.

Walk west up paved Ute Pass Avenue, passing rustic cabins and residences along gurgling Catamount Creek, for 0.7 mile until the road ends at the forest on the town's edge and a gated dirt road. Houses of note along the narrow, quiet street include the 1889 House of Seven Gables at the junction of Belvidere and Ute Pass Avenues; the

Willomere House, built in 1888 for early settler George Howard; the first log house in Green Mountain Falls, built in 1887; and at the end of the road, the Hummingbird, a small house built by a groom for his bride. He was tragically killed in a railroad accident before the wedding.

Belvidere Avenue dead-ends at a gate that blocks a dirt road that goes left (south) up to a waterworks area and Catamount Falls. Go around the left side of the gate and hike up the road for 0.3 mile to the start of the Catamount Trail, a bridge over the creek, and a small tumbling waterfall, the lowest of a series of falls that makes up Catamount Falls. The lowest falls are seen from a bridge over the creek, while the rest of Catamount Falls is seen from Catamount Trail. A mile to the south is Crystal Falls on Crystal Creek, which again is several small falls that cascade over boulders. For more information on both falls, read *Hiking Waterfalls in Colorado* (FalconGuides, 2013).

After a mile of walking, you reach the official trailhead for the Catamount Trail at the north side of the wooden bridge over the creek. A weathered sign marks the trailhead. Follow the blue dots nailed to trees to stay on the path at important junctions. There are two options to reach the Garden of Eden, a verdant hidden valley above the falls and behind the ridge above the trail. The old trail steeply follows the creek into the valley, while the described and preferred route follows a trail built between 1990 and 2000 up the mountainside north of the falls. This route, with lots of switchbacks, gradually gains elevation, is easy to follow, and offers two short trails to scenic overlooks.

From the trailhead and road, scramble up the steep stony trail. Take care stepping on water-worn cobbles in the trail. A junction, marked by a post with two small signs, one yellow and one blue, is reached after a couple hundred feet. Go right on the blue dot trail and pass beneath Dome Rock, a 100-foot-high cliff.

Option: Take a left turn on the yellow dot trail. This follows the old trail up to the Garden of Eden as well as offers access to upper Catamount Falls and the Thomas Trail, which traverses south from Catamount Creek across steep slopes to Crystal Falls before dropping down Boulder Street to Ute Pass Avenue and the lake in Green Mountain Falls. This alternative loop hike is almost 3 miles long if you hike from town to falls and back.

Catamount Trail heads north, gently climbing through a forest of spruce and fir while switchbacking up the steep mountainside. Partway up, a side trail traverses 300 feet south to rocky Town Overlook, a viewpoint above Green Mountain Falls. Return to the main blue-dot trail and continue hiking upward. The trail gains over 700 feet from the road to a gravel saddle at 8,850 feet on a high ridge. Another short trail, marked with light-blue dots, goes southeast for 400 feet to Valley Overlook and more great views of Green Mountain Falls nestled in the valley below.

The trail gently descends 100 feet into the eastern end of the Garden of Eden, a moist hidden valley filled with wildflowers, honeybees, and birdsong in summer. Broken granite cliffs hem in the valley on the north while a dense woodland of Engelmann spruce and Douglas fir blanket the cooler south side. The long ridge on

GREEN MOUNTAIN FALLS AND CATAMOUNT TRAIL

The town of Green Mountain Falls was named in December 1887 by William J. Foster for the waterfalls on Catamount Creek as well as Crystal Falls to the south. The area was previously part of a ranch owned by George Howard, who settled here in 1881. Foster bought the valley from Howard in 1887 with the intention of making a resort town beside the Colorado Midland Railroad, which was built up Ute Pass at that time. In 1888, streets were platted, the lake was excavated, a gazebo was built on a small island, and over one hundred tent cabins, rented for $4 to $7 a week, were erected for summer guests escaping the lowland heat.

The following year a couple of hotels, the seventy-room Green Mountain Falls Hotel and Lakeside Hotel, opened, and a train depot made the town an official stop. The town, incorporated in 1890, flourished as a lakeside resort. The Catamount Trail was built back in those early days for vacationers—men in suits and bowler hats and women in Victorian hoop skirts—to hike up to the falls for a picnic and game of cards. Many also hiked beyond the falls to the summit of Mount Rebecca.

Now the vacation cabins have been converted to year-round residences, and Green Mountain Falls, with 640 residents, has lapsed into a quiet reverie as a Colorado Springs bedroom community. The network of trails that connected the town to the waterfalls and mountains was ill-defined and fell into disrepair, especially the popular trail alongside Catamount Falls. The steep trail became a mess of slick boulders and a hike to the valley beyond required balance and sturdy shoes. By the late 1980s, after several hiking injuries and rescues, a town committee decided to build a better trail. Work began in 1990 on a new Catamount Trail, which, instead of following the creek, angled up slopes to the north. The trail, with twenty-two switchbacks and 770 feet of elevation gain, was finished in 2000 after ten years of work done by hundreds of volunteers. Much of the work was completed in 1997.

the south is 9,461-foot Mount Rebecca. Towering ponderosa pines grow alongside the trail as it threads west alongside willow-lined Catamount Creek.

The valley slowly pinches down as it bends southwest. The trail crosses the creek, climbs over some big boulders, and passes through a maze of fallen trees. Farther along, the creek tumbles over granite blocks, forming small waterfalls and noisy cascades. Continue hiking along the rocky trail above the creek until it passes through a broken fence and makes a sharp right turn to a gravel road and a small diversion dam. Walk up the road for 100 yards to a utility road at about 9,000 feet that provides access to the South and North Catamount Reservoirs' dams. This is the end of the hike. From here you turn around and retrace the trail back to your car parked down on Ute Pass Avenue.

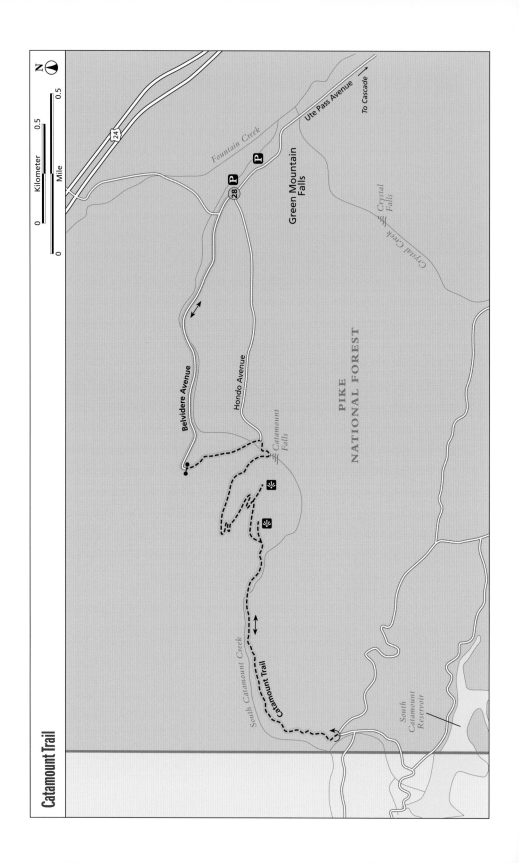

Catamount Trail

N

Kilometer
0   0.5

Mile
0   0.5

24

Fountain Creek

P

P

28

Green Mountain Falls

Ute Pass Avenue

To Cascade

Crystal Falls

Crystal Creek

Belvidere Avenue

Hondo Avenue

Catamount Falls

PIKE NATIONAL FOREST

South Catamount Creek

Catamount Trail

South Catamount Reservoir

Miles and Directions

0.0 Trailhead on the east side of Ute Pass Avenue in Green Mountain Falls (GPS: 38.935728, -105.017427).

0.7 Gate at the west end of Belvidere Road (GPS: 38.937259, -105.03131). Go left through the gate and up the closed dirt road.

1.0 Reach the junction of Catamount Trail and the dirt road (GPS: 38.93394, -105.02989). Go right on the trail past a couple of small waterfalls.

1.1 Hike a short distance up the trail to a junction (GPS: 38.93330, -105.03018). Go right on Catamount Trail. A left turn follows the old trail up steep slopes alongside the creek.

1.6 Junction with overlook trail (GPS: 38.93409, -105.03292). Go left to the first overlook, then return to the main trail and continue uphill.

1.8 Reach the top of a ridge (GPS: 38.93398, -105.03541). Go left to the upper overlook (purple blazes), then return to the trail. Go left (west) and descend into the upper valley.

3.2 Turnaround point of the hike at the utility road (GPS: 38.930752, -105.045846).

6.4 Arrive back at the trailhead.

Option: To extend the hike to the lakes and get a view of Pikes Peak, take the right fork of the service road, then the middle fork, and follow it up South Catamount Creek for 0.3 mile. Finish by climbing up the road between the rock rubble dam and spillway to the top of the dam at 9,225 feet. South Catamount Reservoir along with neighboring North Catamount Reservoir and Crystal Reservoir compose the 2,267-acre North Slope Recreation Area, a Colorado Springs watershed area managed for outdoor recreation. Most folks come to fish in the high lakes, catching brook, rainbow, and cutthroat trout as well as lake trout up to 30 inches long. There is also picnicking but no water sports, wading, or swimming in the city water supply. The area offers more than 15 miles of hiking on nine trails.

29 Raspberry Mountain Trail

Raspberry Mountain Trail, following an old closed road and then a singletrack trail, is a wonderful out-and-back hike to the summit of a high mountain northwest of Pikes Peak. Raspberry Mountain offers great views of Pikes Peak, the Crags, the Continental Divide, and a dozen fourteeners (14,000-foot peaks).

Start: Parking area on north side of CR 62

Distance: 5.8 miles out and back

Hiking time: 3 to 4 hours

Difficulty: Moderate

Elevation gain: 1,155 feet from trailhead to summit; 1,350 feet total elevation gain

Trail surface: Double- and singletrack dirt trail

Seasons: Year-round. Apr through Nov is best. This is a good winter hike, but the trail may be icy or the snow deep enough for snowshoes. Use caution and wear micro-spikes as needed.

Schedule: Open daily

Other trail users: Mountain bikers, horseback riders

Canine compatibility: Leashed dogs only

Land status: Pike National Forest, USDA Forest Service public land

Fees and permits: None

Map: USGS Divide and Woodland Park quads

Trail contact: Pike National Forest, Pikes Peak Ranger District, 601 S. Weber St., Colorado Springs 80903; (719) 636-1602; www.fs.usda .gov/psicc

Finding the trailhead: Drive west from Colorado Springs and I-25 on US 24 to Divide. Turn left (south) on CO 67 toward Cripple Creek. Continue south for 4.25 miles, passing the Mueller State Park entrance, to a left turn on Teller County Road 62 (GPS: 38.879986, -105.157162). This is signed "Rocky Mountain Camp" and "Crags Campground." Drive east on the dirt road for 1.2 miles to a small parking area on the left just before a sharp right turn in a valley (GPS: 38.890543, -105.144635). The trailhead is on the north side of the parking lot.

The Hike

Raspberry Mountain, a 10,605-foot humpbacked mountain rising northwest of Pikes Peak, is reached by a moderate 2.9-mile trail (making it a 5.8 out-and-back hike) that follows an old road as well as a singletrack trail to its rocky summit. The bulky mountain, studded with granite cliffs and blanketed with dense forest, is the easiest high mountain to climb in the Colorado Springs area. It offers not only fun hiking along a quiet trail but also marvelous 360-degree summit views, including the northwest flank of Pikes Peak to distant views of the Sangre de Cristo Range, Mosquito Range, Sawatch Range, Tarryall Range, and the Mount Evans massif in the Front Range.

The Raspberry Mountain Trail is a good hike for all seasons. Wildflowers and tall grass fill meadows in summer, while golden groves of quaking aspen color hillsides in late September. Winter brings snow, making it a great trail for snowshoeing and, if there is enough snow, cross-country skiing. Granite boulders on the mountain's upper

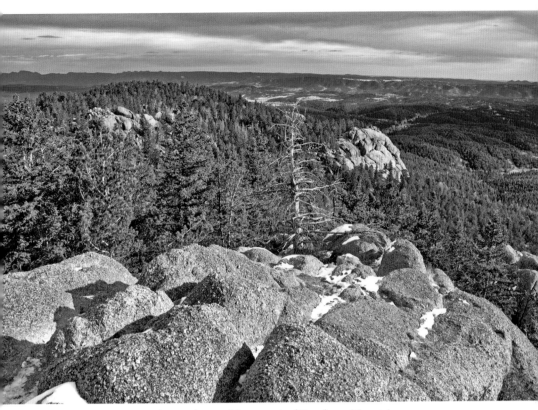

The Rampart Range lies northeast of the summit of Raspberry Mountain.

reaches appeal to boulderers so bring a pair of rock shoes for an hour-long session of fun climbing if you're a climber.

The trailhead is on Teller County Road 62 just over a mile east of CO 67. The dirt road is passable to passenger cars but may be icy in winter. The road continues southeast to Crags Campground and the trailhead for the Crags Trail and the Devils Playground Trail up the northwest flank of Pikes Peak.

Begin the hike at the 9,450-foot trailhead on the north side of the small parking area. Head north up an old road on the left side of a draw filled with meadows and aspen groves. The trail follows the road up a series of switchbacks, gradually gaining elevation until after 0.6 mile it reaches the top of a broad forested ridge at 9,700 feet.

Hike northeast along the ridge, passing power lines and the foundation of an old house. The easy trail gently rises, passing a bench for rests and scenic views on the right at 1 mile, and bends east. After reaching a high point, it begins a short descent. Look northeast for a view of Raspberry Mountain, also named Sleeping Giant. The trail begins climbing again, following the edge of a rutted, closed road through a thick forest of fir and spruce. It finally reaches another high point on the ridge, then descends steeply north and becomes a singletrack trail at 2.2 miles.

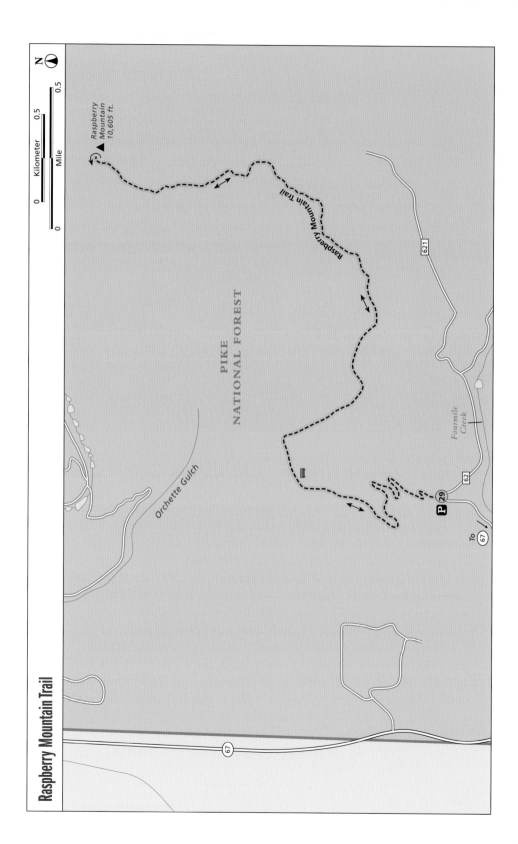

Raspberry Mountain Trail

▲ Raspberry Mountain 10,605 ft.

Raspberry Mountain Trail

PIKE NATIONAL FOREST

Orchette Gulch

Fourmile Creek

621

62

P 29

To 67

67

N

Kilometer 0 0.5

Mile 0 0.5

The trail climbs gravel and boulder-strewn slopes until it reaches a level shoulder on the south side of Raspberry Mountain. The final ascent keeps left up the western slopes below the summit. Avoid going directly up large boulders to the top. Instead, from the shoulder hike left and pass the right side of a giant overhanging boulder. The trail scrambles up rocky terrain until it reaches a final short cliff band on the north side of the mountain. Scramble up a granite groove and then clamber over rounded boulders to the open rocky summit and, after 2.9 miles, the end of the trail.

Raspberry Mountain's 10,605-foot summit is a wonderful place to take a break and enjoy the foot-earned views. Pikes Peak looms to the southeast, with views from the Crags, a wonderland of rock formations, to rounded tundra-clad slopes above timberline. To the east lie Catamount Reservoir and the lower Rampart Range. When you face west, the panorama is simply staggering. The long, ragged ridge of the Sangre de Cristo Mountains stretches against the southwest horizon. The Sawatch and Mosquito Ranges run across the western horizon, while the rugged Tarryall Range and Mount Evans rise to the northwest. On a clear day, look north for 100 miles to flat-topped 14,265-foot Longs Peak in Rocky Mountain National Park.

After enjoying the wide views, pack up and retrace your steps down the trail to the parking area. Use caution when descending the upper trail in winter since it is usually snow covered and the boulders may be icy. Use trekking poles and wear micro-spikes on your shoes for traction in winter.

Miles and Directions

0.0   Start at the trailhead (GPS: 38.890543, -105.144635) on the north side of a small parking area on the left side of the access road. Hike north up an old road, which switchbacks up an east-facing slope.

0.6   Reach the top of the switchbacks on the closed road and the crest of a broad ridge. Continue northeast past power lines.

1.0   A bench is on the right (south) side of the trail at the top of a wooded draw.

2.2   After topping the ridge, descend the old road, which becomes a steep singletrack trail (GPS: 38.898965, -105.124471).

2.8   The trail reaches the south shoulder of the mountain. Keep left, passing beneath the right side of a big boulder. Climb the rocky trail up the west side of the peak to a final scramble on the north side.

2.9   Reach the rocky summit of Raspberry Mountain (GPS: 38.9071, -105.1244). Turn around here to retrace your steps.

5.8   Arrive back at the trailhead and parking lot.

30 Crags Trail

The Crags Trail is an out-and-back hike that follows a broad valley filled with grassy meadows and wildflowers. It continues along trickling Fourmile Creek to a scenic overlook on the northern shoulder of Pikes Peak.

Start: Crags Trailhead on Teller County Road 62
Distance: 5.0 miles out and back
Hiking time: 2 to 3 hours
Difficulty: Moderate
Elevation gain: 760 feet (from 10,040 feet at the start to 10,800 feet at the end)
Trail surface: Singletrack dirt trail
Seasons: Apr through Oct. Winters are snowy. Bring skis or snowshoes.
Schedule: Open daily
Other trail users: Mountain bikers
Canine compatibility: Leashed dogs only
Land status: Pike National Forest, USDA Forest Service public land
Fees and permits: None

Maps: USGS Pikes Peak and Woodland Park
Trail contacts: Pike National Forest, Pikes Peak Ranger District, 601 S. Weber St., Colorado Springs 80903; (719) 636-1602; www.fs.usda .gov/psicc
Special considerations: While this trail is relatively easy, its high elevation could lead to altitude sickness including headache and nausea. If you develop symptoms of altitude sickness, the best cure is to descend to a lower elevation. On summer afternoons watch for thunderstorms accompanied by lightning. Carry a raincoat and retreat to your car if you see approaching bad weather. Drinking water is available at the campground.

Finding the trailhead: From Colorado Springs take the Cimarron Street / US 24 exit 141 from I-25. Follow US 24 west for about 24 miles up Ute Pass and through Woodland Park to the town of Divide. Turn left (south) on CO 67 and drive 4.3 miles south to a left (east) turn onto Teller County Road 62, marked with a Crags Campground sign. Follow the dirt road through the Rocky Mountain Mennonite Camp for 3.2 miles to the Crags Campground on the left. Park on the right in a large parking lot surrounded by a split-rail fence (GPS: 38.873759, -105.123988). The trailhead is next to the restrooms across the road. (**Option:** Hike up the road through the campground to the Crags Trailhead at its east end.)

The Hike

The Crags Trail (Forest Service Trail #664) on the northwest flank of Pikes Peak may be the perfect summer hike in the Colorado Springs region. The trail slowly ascends gentle grades in a lush subalpine valley along Fourmile Creek, which originates on the north slope of 14,115-foot Pikes Peak and eventually empties into the Arkansas River near Cañon City to the south.

The hike, rambling below granite cliffs and dark forested mountainsides, offers all the views of a mountain ascent, but your thighs and lungs won't feel the burn like climbing a real fourteener (14,000-foot peak). Expect not only scenic views but also crisp mountain air, wildflower-strewn meadows, and plentiful wildlife, including deer and elk.

From the trailhead by the restrooms on the east side of Teller County Road 62, the Crags Trail crosses Fourmile Creek and the most difficult part of the hike begins. The trail switchbacks up a steep hillside, quickly gaining elevation before leveling off above the Crags Campground. Curve southeast around a hillside and drop down to a trail junction at 0.6 mile. Keep to the left, minding the trail marker for the Crags, and begin hiking alongside tumbling Fourmile Creek.

The trail passes through a jumbled boulder field before opening onto a broad grassy expanse. The trail heads east up the narrowing valley and reaches a wider meadow. The creek makes wide meanders across the valley floor, its banks densely lined with willows. Outcroppings of granite line the hillside to the left. Groves of aspen trees shade the trail while tall Engelmann spruce and subalpine

Columbines, the Colorado state flower, bloom along the Crags Trail.

fir trees stand sentinel-like along the edge of the meadow. Pangborn's Pinnacle, a pointed granite dome, towers above the broad valley to the east.

The Crags Trail briefly jogs to the left, climbing higher before dropping back into the meadow. The trail splits just before a large granite dome on the left. Keep to the right-hand track with the cliff on your left. The trail then tracks across the edge of a swampy marshland before stepping back to solid ground.

The bare northwest shoulder of Pikes Peak, Colorado's thirtieth-highest mountain, looms to the right. Tall cliffs and crags dot the steep forested slopes above the valley. As the valley narrows, the trail passes a cliff to the right. The shady north side

1806: PIKE ATTEMPTS THE PEAK

Lieutenant Zebulon Pike led a detachment of fifteen men to explore the southern boundary of the newly acquired Louisiana Purchase in 1806. The valiant expedition, exploring unmapped and unknown territory, attempted to climb what Pike called "Grand Peak" in late November. Pike and three of his men, clad in summer clothes, failed in snow and cold, turning back after climbing one of the smaller mountains southeast of the great peak, possibly Mount Rosa. The lieutenant famously wrote in his journal that the mountain would never be climbed, but a close examination of the text reveals that he thought it was impossible in the 22°F temperatures and waist-deep snow that his party encountered.

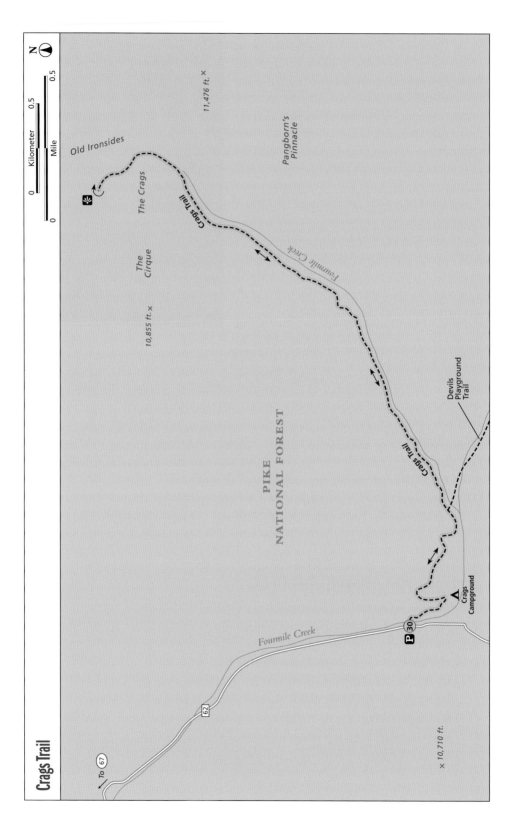

Crags Trail

N

Kilometer
0   0.5   0.5

Mile
0

PIKE
NATIONAL FOREST

Old Ironsides

11,476 ft. ×

Pangborn's
Pinnacle

The Crags

The Cirque

10,855 ft. ×

Crags Trail

Fourmile Creek

Crags Trail

Devils
Playground
Trail

Crags
Campground

30

P

Fourmile Creek

62

To 67

× 10,710 ft.

of the cliff makes an excellent rest stop on bedrock slabs. Sit down and enjoy the trickle of the creek and take in the valley up which you just hiked. This is also a good turnaround point since the next 0.5-mile trail segment gains lots of elevation and is heavily wooded.

Continue hiking up a wooded canyon on the rustic trail, then climb a steep gully. Keep an eye on the trail since it can be easy to lose as it switches back and forth over tree roots and lumpy boulders. Eventually the trail reaches a high saddle at 2.3 miles.

The trail goes left here and scrambles to a small summit at 10,800 feet with a big view across Pikes Peak's northern slopes and the trail's end point at 2.5 miles. This is a great place to linger and enjoy breathtaking expansive views. To the east is the cliffed backside of a huge granite buttress called Old Ironsides; farther east twists the Pikes Peak Highway, a couple reservoirs at the North Slope Recreation Area, and the flat top of the Rampart Range. On a clear day you can even see the distant prairie horizon. Also check out the ancient weathered limber pines that inhabit this windswept ridge.

To return, retrace the trail for 2.5 miles back to the trailhead. Remember to stay on the trail as you descend the wooded gully below the saddle.

Miles and Directions

0.0 Start from the trailhead (GPS: 38.873633, -105.123719) on the east side of CR 62 and opposite the parking area.

0.6 Junction with trail from Crags Campground. Continue straight (east).

1.4 Reach the west side of a wide valley. Trail heads east along the north edge of the willows and meandering creek.

2.0 Junction with trail that goes left to the Cirque. Continue straight on the main trail.

2.3 Reach a high saddle. Go left up a gravelly ridge.

2.5 End of trail at a viewpoint (GPS: 38.888471, -105.097989).

5.0 Arrive back at the trailhead.

31 Devils Playground Trail

The Devils Playground Trail is the standard hiking route up Pikes Peak. The 13.8-mile round-trip hike up the northwest side of the Peak is easily done in a day by competent, fit hikers and offers spectacular views, fun hiking, and a diverse variety of terrain and ecosystems.

Start: Crags Trailhead on east side of Teller County Road 62

Distance: 13.8 miles out and back

Hiking time: 10 to 14 hours

Difficulty: Strenuous. Class 2 with mostly trail hiking but some scrambling up a boulder field below the summit.

Elevation gain: 4,100 feet

Trail surface: Singletrack dirt trail with some doubletrack trail in places

Seasons: Year-round

Other trail users: Runners

Canine compatibility: Dogs allowed

Land status: Pike National Forest, USDA Forest Service public land

Fees and permits: None

Schedule: Open daily

Map: USGS Woodland Park and Pikes Peak quads

Trail contact: Pikes Peak Ranger District, 601 S. Weber St., Colorado Springs 80903; (719) 636-1602; www.fs.usda.gov/psicc

Other considerations: Camping is allowed along the trail. Campsites must be 300 feet from all water sources. The upper half of the hike parallels the Pikes Peak Highway. A $500 fee per person will be charged if a hiker or tourist requests rescue, recovery, or assistance from the Pikes Peak Highway staff after hours. This is the minimum charge based on circumstances. The Pikes Peak staff will only transport in emergency situations or for safety. Fees are payable at the time of transport. Transport during normal hours is $20 per person. After-hours transport after the highway is closed and if staff is still on location is $100 per person. Call the Pikes Peak Highway at (719) 385-7325.

Finding the trailhead: From Colorado Springs drive west on US 24 up Ute Pass to Woodland Park and then on to Divide. Turn south in Divide on CO 67 and drive 4.1 miles. Just past the Mueller State Park turnoff on the right, look for a left turn onto dirt Teller County Road 62, marked with a small sign for Crags Campground. Follow the dirt road east and south, passing through a Mennonite camp, for 3.2 miles to a large marked parking lot on the right and a trailhead on the left. Park in the lot (GPS: 38.873759, -105.123988). The turnoff for the Crags Campground is 0.1 mile farther south on the left side of the road.

The Hike

The 6.9-mile-long (one-way) Devils Playground Trail, climbing the northwest side of 14,115-foot Pikes Peak, is an excellent hike up one of America's most famous mountains and the thirtieth-highest mountain in Colorado. The trail is hiked round-trip in a day, generally easy to follow, and much shorter than 13.0-mile Barr Trail up the east side of the mountain. Devils Playground Trail is considered the standard hiking route on Pikes Peak.

Pikes Peak, the historic landmark of the Rocky Mountains and the biggest skyscraper in Colorado Springs, stands east of the main bulk of the Colorado Rockies. This huge, conspicuous mountain dominates the Front Range landscape like no other. Rising abruptly from the high plains, Pikes Peak is easily seen from over 100 miles away. Its distinctive silhouette is glimpsed from north of Denver and from far out on the undulating eastern prairie, where its snowcapped countenance appears like a distant mirage. Standing apart from other high mountains, Pikes Peak was a symbol and beacon for prospectors and pioneers journeying westward in the 1850s "Pikes Peak or Bust" gold rush.

The bulky mountain that explorer Zebulon Pike and his band of merry men could not climb on a snowy November day in 1806 now has more people reach its airy summit—via trail, highway, and cog railroad—than any other high mountain in North America and probably the world, except for Mount Fuji in Japan.

Every August thousands of runners gather in Manitou Springs to race up Barr Trail to the summit, doing the ascent only, while the next day hundreds run up and down the Peak for a grueling 26-mile marathon. Race cars negotiate the curving loops of the Pikes Peak Highway in an annual Race to the Clouds. On New Year's Eve members of a local group, the Ad-a-Man Club, trudge through snow to set off midnight fireworks from the summit.

While it is easy to drive in comfort to the summit on the Pikes Peak Highway or to take the cog railroad, the most satisfying and exhilarating way to get there is on foot. Because of its easy access, fame, and Front Range dominance, more hikers reach Pikes Peak's summit than any other 14,000-foot peak in Colorado.

A lot of prospective hikers ascend the mountain on the 13.0-mile-long Barr Trail, which begins in Manitou Springs and climbs the eastern side of the mountain. Barr Trail is, despite its easy grades and well-manicured surface, a difficult trail to both ascend and descend in a grueling 26-mile round-trip day. Many hikers either stop overnight at Barr Camp or hike to the summit one-way and are picked up on top or take the cog railroad back down. If you want to climb Pikes Peak in a day, then the Devils Playground Trail is the hike for you.

Starting in 2019, about 2.48 miles of the Devils Playground Trail is being rerouted from the Crags Trail junction near the start of the trail to the crest of the ridge west of Devils Playground, which will increase the length of the trail and the hike by approximately 1.5 miles. The existing trail is deeply eroded in places, has steep grades, has destroyed alpine tundra turf, and is unsustainable. Pike National Forest completed a trail study and archaeological and botanical surveys in 2018, allowing the Rocky Mountain Field Institute (RMFI) to begin new trail work with youth trail crews and community volunteers in the summer of 2019. Completion of the rerouted trail will be in late 2021, and the old trail will be decommissioned and rehabilitated. The new trail, not indicated on the map in this book, will climb a ridge south of the existing trail and then switchback up steep grassy slopes at timberline, joining the old trail at its 3.4-mile mark.

Start your Pikes Peak ascent at the 10,000-foot Crags Trailhead, also the trailhead for the Devils Playground Trail, on the east side of the road and opposite a large parking area (GPS: 38.873626, -105.123637). A vault toilet is at the trailhead. Cross Fourmile Creek on a good bridge and follow the trail up a couple of switchbacks on a steep hillside, then contour east above Crags Campground. After 0.6 mile the trail reaches a junction with the original Crags Trail coming in from the right, from the campground. Walk another 75 feet to another major junction and go right on the signed Devils Playground Trail (Trail #753). The Crags Trail goes left and up the main valley into the Crags area.

From this main junction to the summit, the trail is easy to follow and well worn by numerous boots. Cross Fourmile Creek again on a split-log bridge and begin hiking up the rocky trail on gentle slopes alongside a small unnamed creek and through a dense fir and spruce forest. The trail slowly gains elevation for the next 1.5 miles with a few steep sections, crossing a log bridge at 0.9 mile and passing a couple obvious granite formations on the left including Banana Rock at 1.3 miles.

After the last creek crossing over stones at 1.6 miles, the trail passes an open meadow at 10,900 feet and begins switchbacking up a steep rocky slope covered in weather-beaten limber pine trees, reaching timberline at about 11,800 feet. Take a rest here on some boulders besides the trail and enjoy the view west down the valley you just hiked up. Beyond stretches a vast panorama of mountains, including most of the fourteeners in the Sawatch Range 80 miles to the west, including Mount Elbert and Mount Massive, Colorado's two highest peaks.

From timberline the trail works up steep slopes for another thousand feet without any switchbacks to relieve your legs (this section will be closed in 2021) before finally emerging onto a high, grassy ridge at 12,750 feet. After reaching the top of the flat

The Devils Playground Trail winds along the edge of the Bottomless Pit and North Pit before climbing to Pikes Peak's summit.

64-mile-long compilation of footpaths that will eventually encircle 14,115-foot Pikes Peak. At the time of this writing in 2020, about 50 miles of the trail are complete, with a gap between Pancake Rocks and the South Slope Recreation Area needing both a trail and landowner permissions. The Ring-the-Peak Trail heads north from this junction toward the Crags on the northwest flank of Pikes Peak. Continue straight on the Horsethief Falls Trail.

The trail skirts the southern edge of the broad valley, passing placid ponds. To the north on low hills are stands of quaking aspen, the most widely distributed tree in North America. If you hike in late September, expect to see the autumn gold leaves of the aspens spreading color across the landscape. Rocky 12,527-foot Sentinel Point, a prominent pointed summit on the west side of Pikes Peak, looms east above the basin.

At 0.7 mile there is an obvious trail junction marked with an old wooden sign. Go right on the Pancake Rocks Trail (Trail #704). (*Option:* If you are only hiking to Horsethief Falls, continue straight on Trail #704B for 0.3 mile to the falls, then return to the trailhead by the same route. If you are hiking to Pancake Rocks, however, it's best to visit the falls on the return hike.)

The trail heads south and begins a sustained climb up a steep north-facing slope blanketed with dense forest. The trail section can be slow going in winter with deep, unconsolidated snow. The trail makes five big switchbacks, gaining about 800 feet of elevation, until it levels out between a couple of rocky points. Hike south on the open trail through short-grass meadows and scattered fir and spruce trees. Look for a short spur trail that climbs up left to a knobby overlook that offers views of Sentinel Point.

Continue south and then descend the trail below steeper slopes and broken cliffs (don't confuse these with the real Pancake Rocks) before huffing it up a hill to the trail's 11,088-foot high point on a ridge crest. Descend the trail for the last 0.25 mile down gradual slopes to Pancake Rocks, a collection of rock stacks on granite slabs at 10,935 feet. The granite here is fractured horizontally rather than vertically, forming the unusual layered pancake rocks. Even without syrup and butter, they are still quite a delectable sight.

The Pancake Rocks, 3.2 miles from the trailhead on CO 67, are the end of the trail, so find a comfortable rock shelf and have a sip of water and nibble on an energy bar or sandwich while you enjoy the wide views. To the east is a deep valley floored by Oil Creek. The valley's steep slopes are blanketed with aspen, forming a gorgeous autumn tapestry, while granite cliffs, including the King, Queen, Rook, and Great Dihedral, perch below a rocky ridgeline. To the south are more aspen-covered mountains and beyond are the landmark Spanish Peaks over 100 miles away, the Wet Mountains, and the sawtoothed spine of the Sangre de Cristo Mountains. A close look reveals five fourteeners (14,000-foot peaks) clustered in the range's central section—Crestone Peak, Crestone Needle, Kit Carson Peak, Challenger Point, and Humboldt Peak.

After catching your breath and rehydrating, retrace your footsteps back to Horse-thief Park. There are two short uphill sections but lots of downhill so the return hike

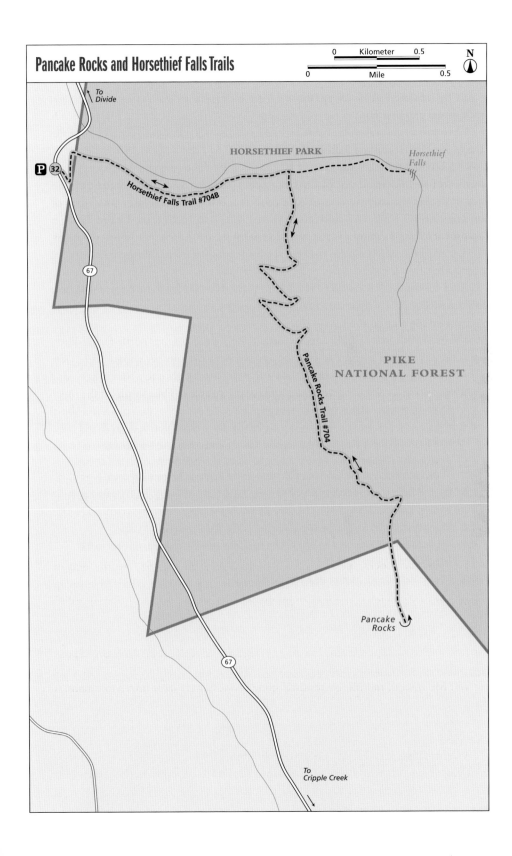

Pancake Rocks and Horsethief Falls Trails

0   Kilometer   0.5

0   Mile   0.5

N

To
Divide

HORSETHIEF PARK

Horsethief
Falls

P 32

Horsethief Falls Trail #704B

67

Pancake Rocks Trail #704

PIKE
NATIONAL FOREST

Pancake
Rocks

67

To
Cripple Creek

goes quickly. Watch your feet on a few steep trail sections since loose gravel, acting like marbles underfoot, scatters on top of hard ground.

At the junction of the two trails in Horsethief Park, go left to descend 0.7 mile back to the parking lot.

Option: For full value, go right and hike a short 0.3 mile up to Horsethief Falls. Trail# 704B heads east along the edge of the forest and the willow-filled valley floor, slowly climbing uphill to the base of Horsethief Falls. Here the chilled stream rushes over a worn boulder and cascades down a slabby cliff of granite bedrock. At the base, cross logs over the stream to sit on rocks on the north side of the falls or clamber up the hillside for 0.1 mile to a lofty perch above the falls at 10,200 feet. Either choice is ideal for a quiet picnic or a nap in the afternoon sunshine. It is best to view the falls in May and June when rapidly melting snow on Sentinel Point fills the creek. In dry years only a thin sheen of water slides down the falls.

After relaxing at Horsethief Falls, it's a quick mile hike back to the parking area and the trailhead. The trail is all downhill and goes fast.

Miles and Directions

0.0 Parking area and trailhead on the east side of CO 67 just south of closed Little Ike Tunnel (GPS: 38.834283, -105.137462).

0.6 Steep climb ends, and trail reaches Horsethief Park. Junction with Ring-the-Peak Trail (GPS: 38.83355, -105.12663). Go straight.

0.7 Trail junction with Pancake Rocks Trail (GPS: 38.83395, -105.12358). Go right on Trail #704, labeled with a Ring-the-Peak marker. Hike up a steep wooded hillside with five switchbacks. (*Option:* If you are only hiking to Horsethief Falls, continue straight on Trail 704B for 0.3 mile to the waterfall, then return to the trailhead by the same route.)

1.9 The trail flattens out at the top of the hill (GPS: 38.82572, -105.12325). Continue south, passing a spur trail that climbs to a rocky lookout to the east.

3.2 Reach Pancake Rocks and the end of the trail (GPS: 38.81343, -105.11655).

5.7 Return to the trail junction with Trail #704B to Horsethief Falls. (*Option:* Go right to the falls [0.6 mile round-trip].)

6.4 Reach the trailhead, parking area, and CO 67.

33 Mueller State Park Loop

A popular loop hike that descends Outlook Ridge past three scenic overlooks and then returns up a wooded valley past Lost Pond to the park road.

Start: Outlook Ridge Trailhead on west side of parking lot north of park visitor center
Distance: 4.3-mile lollipop
Hiking time: 1 to 2 hours
Difficulty: Moderate; some elevation gain and loss on good trails
Elevation gain: 400 feet
Trail surface: Single- and doubletrack dirt path
Seasons: Year-round. Winter trails can be icy; wear spikes on your boots.
Schedule: Park open daily 5 a.m. to 10 p.m. for day use

Other trail users: Mountain bikers
Canine compatibility: Dogs not allowed
Land status: Public land in Mueller State Park
Fees and permits: Daily fee required to enter the park
Maps: USGS Divide; Mueller State Park trail map at website
Trail contact: Mueller State Park, 21045 CO Highway 67, PO Box 39, Divide 80814; (719) 687-6867; https://cpw.state.co.us/placestogo/parks/Mueller/

Finding the trailhead: Take the Cimarron St. / US 24 exit 141 from I-25. Drive west on US 24 up Ute Pass and through Woodland Park. Continue west on US 24 to the town of Divide. Turn left (south) on CO 67 toward Cripple Creek. Drive 3.8 miles to the park entrance and turn right (west) into the park. After paying the entrance fee, follow Wapiti Road for 1.5 miles to the Outlook Ridge parking area and trailhead on the left (south) side of the road. Restrooms, picnic tables, and water are available at the trailhead (GPS: 38.881234, -105.181357).

The Hike

The 4.3-mile-long Outlook Ridge and Lost Pond Loop hike combines seven park trails into a single hike. The trail mileage can be shortened, depending on the optional hikes out to the three overlooks along the way. Each of those out-and-back trails to the overlooks is 0.6 mile long. The four main trails that the hike follows are the Outlook Ridge Trail (Trail #7), Geer Pond Trail (Trail #25), Lost Pond Trail (Trail #11), and Revenuer's Ridge (Trail #1). The entire route is easy to follow and well marked by posts with trail numbers and blue arrows.

The loop hike, divided into two distinct sections, follows a rounded ridge west from the park road past three scenic viewpoints overlooking valleys below and then returns up a wooded valley past a small pond and back to the road. The trail section along the ridge offers picture-perfect views of snowcapped Pikes Peak to the east and the surrounding landscape of wooded hills and vales, while the second segment threads up a short steep valley that is filled with tall conifers, groves of quaking aspen, birdsong, and, in summer, a colorful array of wildflowers.

The western slopes of Pikes Peak rise beyond rolling wooded hillsides along the Outlook Ridge Trail.

Mueller State Park, lying west of CO 67 south of Divide, spreads across 5,120 acres with an average elevation of 9,600 feet on the northwest side of 14,115-foot Pikes Peak. The park, a showcase of natural wonders and wildlife, offers over 45 miles of hiking on 44 trails that explore its shady valleys, humped ridges and mountains, and granite cliffs and domes. Many of the trails lead to scenic overlooks with far-ranging views of the jagged Sangre de Cristo Mountains and the Sawatch Range, home to Colorado's highest mountains.

The park's web of well-maintained trails, with generally little elevation gain and loss, can be easily linked together to form excellent loop hikes of varying lengths and difficulties. The comprehensive trail system is organized by numbers. The 45 miles of trails range from short and easy to long and challenging. Pick up the park's trail map when you enter the park, at the visitor center, or download a copy from the park's website to plan other Mueller foot adventures beyond the hikes described here.

Mueller also has 134 campsites, including 99 with electric hookups, and is renowned as the best wildlife-watching area in the Pikes Peak region, with large mammals including black bears, elk, bighorn sheep, and mule deer roaming the backcountry, as well as raptors like golden eagles and red-tail hawks. The park's sheer size and lack of roads ensure seclusion, peace, and isolation for hikers.

The Outlook Ridge and Lost Pond Loop hike begins at the Outlook Ridge Trailhead and parking area at 9,680 feet on the west side of Wapiti Road just north

Granite cliffs and slabs spill down below Raven Ridge Overlook. ▶

of the park visitor center. Picnic tables, restrooms, and water are available here. Sign the register on the trailhead kiosk and study the trail map. The smooth doubletrack trail, an old ranch road, heads west down Outlook Ridge and after 0.15 mile reaches a trail junction with Revenuer's Ridge Trail (Trail #1), the return trail for the last leg of the hike. Go straight.

The trail dips and rolls, with occasional views into Hay Creek Valley to the south, and after 0.5 mile reaches a junction with Raven Ridge Overlook Trail (Trail #8) on a slight uphill. Go left (south) on Trail #8 for great views into the valley. Raven Ridge Trail traverses a meadow and then drops steadily for 0.3 mile to a spectacular overlook of wide granite benches that drop into the valley below. Watch children since the overlook is unfenced. This is the best viewpoint on the hike, with the western slope of Pikes Peak looming to the east. After enjoying the expansive view, return 0.3 mile uphill to the Outlook Ridge Trail and turn left after 1.1 miles.

Hike down a broad ridge through aspen groves and conifers. After another 0.3 mile or 1.4 miles from the hike start is the junction with Red Tail Overlook Trail (Trail #9) on a bend. Go left (south) on Red Tail and hike 0.3 mile downhill on the doubletrack-to-singletrack trail to a timber staircase and end at another scenic overlook. This point, lower than Raven Ridge Overlook, is a smooth granite slab perched above cliffs and Brook Pond. Again, after enjoying the view, retrace your steps uphill to Outlook Ridge Trail and go left. The hiking mileage to this point is 2 miles.

The trail descends steeply for another 0.1 mile and reaches the junction with the 0.3-mile Lone Eagle Overlook Trail (Trail #10), the third overlook, at a bench after 2.1 miles of hiking. Go left on Lone Eagle, climbing a short hill and then following a level ridge to another viewpoint. Return to the junction with Outlook Ridge Trail at 2.7 miles and turn left (northeast).

Follow the doubletrack trail for 100 feet to a junction on the left with a sign that reads "Trail 7 Bypass to Avoid Steep Hills." Go left on the Trail #7 bypass—this path avoids the steep hill ahead of you and a descent on the other side by contouring northeast across wooded slopes. Follow the singletrack trail through dense spruce and fir forest for 0.2 mile to a junction with the steep alternative Trail #7. Continue straight for 0.1 miles and cross a trickling creek to a major trail junction with Geer Pond Trail (Trail #25), Beaver Ponds Trail (Trail #26) and the end of the Outlook Ridge Trail (Trail #7) after 3 miles. Go right on Trail #25.

The next 0.8-mile trail segment follows Geer Pond Trail for 0.4 mile, which then becomes Lost Pond Trail (Trail #11). The hike initially ascends a steep hill out of the drainage on a doubletrack trail. From the top of the climb, traverse above a shady valley. The rustic roadbed narrows in a swampy area fringed with deep forest, and the trail reaches Lost Pond after 3.4 miles. The small, quiet pool tucks in a pastoral pocket of forest and meadow.

Leave the pond by climbing north on the wide trail, which is now Lost Pond Trail (Trail #11), to the head of a shallow valley. Bend right and continue climbing east to

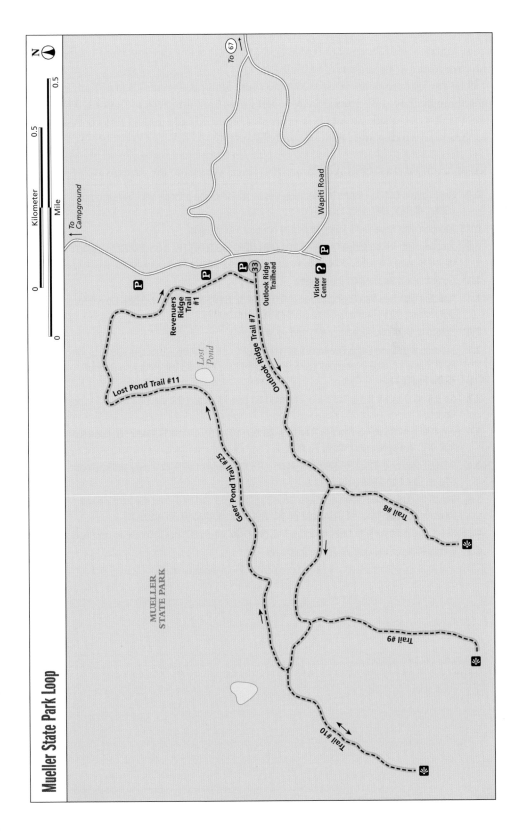

Mueller State Park Loop

N

Kilometer
0.5   0.5

Mile
0   0.5   0

To 67

To Campground

Wapiti Road

Visitor Center

Revenuers Ridge Trail #1

Outlook Ridge Trailhead

Outlook Ridge Trail #7

33

Lost Pond

Lost Pond Trail #11

Geer Pond Trail #25

MUELLER STATE PARK

Trail #8

Trail #9

Trail #10

a trail junction with Revenuer's Ridge Trail (Trail #1) below the Lost Pond Trailhead and park road. Go right (south) on Trail #1.

The last hike segment travels 0.35 mile south along Revenuer's Ridge Trail, dipping through draws and crossing tree-shaded slopes until it intersects Outlook Ridge Trail (Trail #7). Go left and hike east up Trail #7 for 0.15 mile to the Outlook Ridge Trailhead and parking area after a 4.3 mile hike.

Miles and Directions

0.0 Begin at the Outlook Ridge Trailhead on the west side of the parking area by restrooms (GPS: 38.881234, -105.181357).

0.15 Junction with Revenuer's Ridge Trail (#1) on right. Go straight.

0.5 Junction with Raven Ridge Overlook Trail (#8) (GPS: 38.879316, -105.188835). Go left on #8 to overlook (GPS: 38.876004, -105.190744). Return to Outlook Ridge Trail (#7)

1.1 Go left (west) on Outlook Ridge Trail.

1.4 Junction with Red Trail Overlook Trail (#9) (GPS: 38.879859, -105.193309). Go left for 0.3 mile on #9 to overlook (GPS: 38.87538, -105.194277).

2.0 Return to Outlook Ridge Trail (#7) and go left (west).

2.1 Junction with Lone Eagle Overlook Trail (#10) (GPS: 38.880496, -105.194939). Go left for 0.3 mile on #10 to overlook (GPS: 38.877082, -105.198316). Return to Outlook Ridge Trail (#7).

2.7 Go left on Outlook Ridge Trail. In a few hundred feet you reach the junction with #7 bypass. Go left.

3.0 Junction with Geer Pond Trail (#25)(GPS: 38.88116, -105.191887). End of Outlook Ridge Trail (#7). Go right or northeast on #25.

3.4 Reach Lost Pond (GPS: 38.882895, -105.185359). End of #25. Continue straight, northerly, on Lost Pond Trail (#11).

3.8 Reach the Lost Pond Trailhead (GPS: 38.882698, -105.181915) and the junction with Revenuer's Ridge Trail (#1). Go right on #1 and hike south for 0.35 mile.

4.15 Reach the junction with Outlook Ridge Trail (#7). Go left on #7 for 0.15 mile to trailhead.

4.3 End the hike at the Outlook Ridge Trailhead.

34 Vindicator Valley Trail

The Vindicator Valley Trail makes a 2-mile loop through what was once one of the most active and richest mining districts in Colorado. The trail explores the area's gold rush history, passing old mines including the Theresa and Vindicator Mines.

Start: Trailhead and parking lot on west side of CR 81 north of Victor
Distance: 2.0-mile lollipop
Hiking time: 1 to 2 hours
Difficulty: Easy with gentle grades
Elevation gain: 250 feet
Trail surface: Single- and doubletrack dirt trail and closed road
Seasons: Year-round; icy and snowy in winter
Schedule: Open daily
Other trail users: Mountain bikers, cross-country skiers, horseback riders
Canine compatibility: Leashed dogs only
Land status: Public and private

Fees and permits: None
Map: USGS Cripple Creek South
Trail contact: Victor Chamber of Commerce, http://ccvchamber.com
Other: The first part of the trail to the Theresa Mine is wheelchair accessible.
Special considerations: The trailhead is at 10,000 feet so altitude can cause problems. Stay hydrated by drinking plenty of water and use ibuprofen for altitude headaches. The trail crosses an unsafe mining area—stay on the trail, keep children under control, and keep your dog leashed.

Finding the trailhead: From Colorado Springs and I-25, drive west on US 24 up Ute Pass and Woodland Park to Divide. Turn left (south) on CO 67 and drive south through Cripple Creek to Victor. In the center of Victor, turn left (north) off CO 67 / Victor Avenue on Fourth Street. Drive 1 block and turn right on Diamond Avenue / CR 81, which runs east and then north out of Victor. Drive 1.7 miles north through Goldfield and turn left into a parking lot at the trailhead (GPS: 38.724972, -105.123484). An alternate trailhead (GPS: 38.727422, -105.12724) is farther north at the Vindicator Mine—continue up CR 81 another 0.4 mile and turn left on CR 831. Drive 0.4 mile to the trailhead on the left at the top of the trail loop.

The Hike

The 2-mile-long Vindicator Valley Trail, one of the Trails of Gold near Victor behind Pikes Peak, is an interpretive trail that explores the area's colorful 1890s gold rush days. The wide gravel trail, with a smooth walking surface, makes a wide loop on the southeast flank of Battle Mountain north of the town of Victor, nicknamed the "City of Mines." The easy hike, with gradual uphill grades, passes old mines and crumbling historic buildings. Numerous signs along the trail detail the area's rich mining history. The first trail section to the Theresa Mine is wheelchair accessible.

The trail has two trailheads—an upper one on Teller County Road 831 and a lower one on Teller 81. Begin your hike at the lower trailhead on the south side of a dirt parking area off the paved road just north of Goldfield.

A powder magazine alongside the trail was used by crews at the Anna J Mine.

Hike southwest on the wide trail, which is lined by a split-rail fence, toward the obvious Theresa Mine on the skyline. A trail junction is reached after 0.1 mile. Keep right on the main trail. The left trail is where you return after hiking the loop.

The trail reaches the north side of the Theresa Mine after 0.25 mile. The mine's head frame towers above the trail, its metal sheath rattling in the wind and dark with rust. An ore house adjoins the head frame. Past the mine, look up right at an old metal-sided outhouse that undoubtedly offered one of the area's best latrine views. A sign explains the photogenic mine's history.

The Theresa Mine began operating in 1895, north of Winfield Scott Stratton's famed Independence Mine, the richest gold mine in the Cripple Creek & Victor Mining District. It operated until 1915 when low gold prices caused by World War I forced it to close. The mine was idle until 1930 when it reopened with surging prices in the Great Depression and the main shaft was dug to 1,620 feet. A fire destroyed the Theresa's wood structures in 1934, and the buildings were reconstructed with steel and the metal sheath seen today. The mine operated until 1961 before closing for good, although starting in 1981 the mine's waste dump rock was removed for heap leaching, a modern process to separate gold from low-grade ore. The Theresa Mine

DATELINE 1890: BOB WOMACK DISCOVERS GOLD

Bob Womack, a 46-year-old cowboy described in *Hamptons* magazine as an "amiable, riotous, and irrepressible prospector," discovered one of the world's greatest gold bonanzas in a dry gulch southwest of Pikes Peak in 1890. Womack, aware of rumors that there was gold near Pikes Peak, herded cows across grassy hills along Cripple Creek, always keeping his eyes on the ground as he rode his horse. Bob looked for telltale rocks and outcroppings that might indicate the presence of gold or silver. In 1878 he had a piece of gray rock assayed—it came back as gold at $200 a ton. But no one believed the assay, especially after an 1884 gold claim on nearby Mount Pisgah proved to be a fraud, with salted ore. In 1890 Womack struck pay dirt with his El Paso Lode, located above his cabin in Poverty Gulch. While experts in Colorado Springs again greeted his claim with skepticism, other miners quietly filed their own claims on the hills.

By 1891 everyone believed Bob Womack, and the gold rush was on. Almost overnight the town of Cripple Creek sprang up in the valley below Poverty Gulch and by 1900 the area boasted a population of 50,000 and was Colorado's fourth-largest city. While Cripple Creek was the financial and social center of the mining district, its sister city Victor, dubbed the "City of Mines," was the mining center, with the area's greatest gold producers, including the Independence, Ajax, Vindicator, and Portland Mines, spread across the slopes of Battle Mountain above the town.

The Cripple Creek & Victor Mining District boasted over 500 working mines by 1900, and during its boom years, over $340 million of gold was extracted at the prevailing price of $20.67 an ounce. The district offered 150 saloons, forty-one assay offices, ninety-one lawyers, forty-six brokerage houses, and fourteen newspapers, along with dance halls, brothels, hotels, theaters, restaurants, and shops. Few gold camps in the world have surpassed the wealth dug from Cripple Creek's mines. Over half of Colorado's total gold production has come from the district, which produced more than fifty millionaires. Since 1890 over 23 million ounces of gold have been dug from the rolling hills with a 2020 value of over $40 billion.

Bob Womack would have been proud. Bob, however, never became a millionaire. He sold his interest in the El Paso Lode for $300; a few months later that interest was worth $15,000, and the mine eventually produced over $5 million in gold. Bob moved down to Colorado Springs, staying at his sister Eliza's boarding house, before dying in 1909.

produced an estimated 120,000 ounces of gold, valued at over $196 million at current gold prices.

A good viewpoint, looking southwest toward the distant Sangre de Cristo Mountains, is west of the mine as the trail bends right. In the valley below is the old town of Goldfield, now a collection of houses but a town of miners in 1900 with a population of 3,000 and two newspapers. The dilapidated Anna J Mine sits on the west side of the trail 0.1 mile west of the Theresa. Gold was dug from the Anna J from the 1890s until it closed in 1947. Weathering has exposed the mine's wooden head frame and torn much of the corrugated metal sheeting off its buildings. Piles of waste rock surround the site.

A trail junction is past the Anna J Mine at 0.4 mile. A short spur path goes right to building ruins above the Theresa. On the east side of the junction, however, is an interesting small structure used to store explosives. The stone-and-brick building, with a half-moon roof, was a storage magazine with a heavy steel door. Most mines had two magazines—one for explosives and one for detonators to lessen the possibility of accidental explosions. This magazine was used by Anna J miners.

Continue hiking uphill, passing numerous mine ruins as well as the abandoned bed of a railroad spur that served the Vindicator Mine and others on Battle Mountain. The trail is fenced to keep hikers from crossing dangerous slopes with open mine shafts since this is still considered an active mining area. Also, stay on the trail to avoid damaging the fragile historic buildings.

After 0.7 mile the trail reaches the upper trailhead and parking lot on CR 831/Independence Road. The many mine buildings at this trail high point include the towering steel head frame of the famed Vindicator Mine and the adjoining mill. The Vindicator, with multiple shafts, was a huge production. In old photographs from 1900, the humming Vindicator complex looks like a small busy city, with heaps of dump rock, a railroad line, an ore-sorting house, and a couple of enclosed head frames.

The Vindicator was the District's fourth-largest gold producer, yielding 1,244,000 troy ounces of gold with a 1910 value of $27 million or $1,608,492,000 in 2019. The Vindicator Lode was discovered in 1893 and mining began in 1895. By 1901 the mine had two shafts and over 5 miles of underground tunnels that reached depths of 2,150 feet below the surface. In 1921 over 50,000 tons of low-grade ore was crushed for use as a road base in Cripple Creek, Victor, and Colorado Springs, allowing locals to boast that their streets were literally paved with gold. The Vindicator permanently closed in 1958.

The hike continues past the trail's high point at the Vindicator by heading west across the head of the bowl-shaped valley and then gently descending open slopes

GREEN TIP:

Don't take souvenirs home with you. This means natural materials such as plants, rocks, and wildflowers as well as historic artifacts such as fossils and arrowheads.

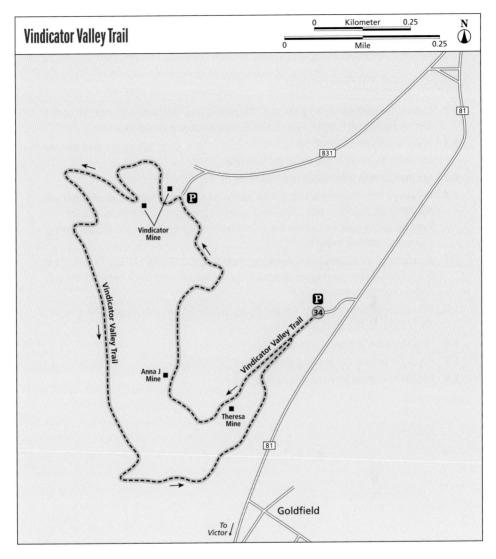

0   Kilometer   0.25

0   Mile   0.25

N

81

831

P

Vindicator
Mine

Vindicator Valley Trail

P
34

Vindicator Valley Trail

Anna J
Mine

Theresa
Mine

81

Goldfield

To
Victor

past more mine ruins and abandoned mine shafts. The western rim of the valley is the upper edge of the Cripple Creek & Victor Gold Mining Company, a subsidiary of Newmont Mining Corporation and Colorado's largest gold producer. The company is excavating a deep pit, the largest open pit mine in Colorado, below what was the old Cresson Mine, and recovering low-grade gold with grades as little as 1 gram of gold from a ton of rock. While the Cresson opened in 1892, the current pit operation began in 1995. Newmont plans to eventually dig underground shafts from the Cresson Pit into deep, unexplored terrain below the Vindicator Mine and extract more gold.

As the trail descends, stop and check out the numerous mine buildings lining the path and catch a breather at various scenic overlooks. After 1.5 miles the trail bends left and begins its return back to the trailhead by traversing gentle slopes below the Theresa Mine. At 1.9 miles you reach the original trail junction. Keep right on the broad path and return to the parking area and the end of a historic hike.

Miles and Directions

0.0 Begin at the trailhead at the south side of a parking lot on the west side of CR 81 north of Goldfield (GPS: 38.724947, -105.123505). Hike southwest on the wide trail.

0.1 Reach a trail junction (GPS: 38.724462, -105.124169). Keep right on the wide trail. The left trail is the return at the end of the loop hike.

0.25 The Theresa Mine towers above the trail (GPS: 38.723093, -105.12605).

0.4 The Anna J Mine is on the left side of the trail. In a few hundred feet, you reach a trail junction (GPS: 38.723996, -105.127301). A spur trail goes right to an overlook of mine ruins. Keep left on the main trail. Check out a stone-and-brick magazine on the east for storing explosives. Continue hiking up the trail.

0.7 Reach the upper trailhead and parking area on CR 831 (GPS: 38.727422, -105.12724). The Vindicator Mine head frame and building ruins are just west of the trailhead. The trail begins descending here.

1.5 After passing many mine ruins, the trail bends sharply left and crosses gentle slopes (GPS: 38.721581, -105.128937).

1.8 Pass below the Theresa Mine.

1.9 Reach the original trail junction. Keep right on the main path.

2.0 End the hike at the trailhead and parking area.

35 Florissant Fossil Beds National Monument Trails

The Petrified Forest Loop Trail, along with the optional wheelchair-accessible Ponderosa Loop Trail, explores the Florissant Fossil Beds National Monument's unique fossil record, passing massive petrified tree stumps and old quarries that have yielded some of the world's best fossil insects, butterflies, and leaves.

Start: Trailhead west of Florissant Fossil Beds National Monument visitor center
Distance: 1.0-mile loop
Hiking time: About 1 hour
Difficulty: Easy
Elevation gain: Minimal
Trail surface: Dirt trails
Seasons: Year-round
Schedule: Open daily. Day use only; Memorial Day to Labor Day, 9 a.m. to 5 p.m.; early Sept to late May, 9 a.m. to 5 p.m.

Other trail users: Hikers only
Canine compatibility: Dogs not permitted
Land status: National Park Service
Fees and permits: Park entrance fee required
Maps: USGS Lake George; Florissant Fossil Beds Monument trail map at park and website
Trail contacts: Florissant Fossil Beds National Monument, 15807 Teller County Rd. 1, Florissant 80816; (719) 748-3253; www.nps.gov/flfo

Finding the trailhead: From I-25 and downtown Colorado Springs, take the Cimarron Street / US 24 exit 141 and drive west for 35 miles, passing through Woodland Park and Divide, to the town of Florissant. Turn left (south) on Teller County Road 1 and drive 2 miles to the visitor center road. Turn right (west) and drive 0.2 mile to a parking area at the visitor center (GPS: 38.913562, -105.284807).) An admittance fee is charged.

The Hike

These two excellent and informative easy hikes—the 1-mile Petrified Forest Loop Trail (featured route) and the optional, wheelchair-accessible 0.5-mile Ponderosa Loop Trail—explore the unique geological record that is preserved and protected by 5,998-acre Florissant Fossil Beds National Monument, a stone repository of ancient life.

The hikes, which are easily combined into a loop that begins and ends at the monument visitor center, not only offer fun hiking, they are also educational. Interpretive signs are scattered along both trails, giving insight into both yesterday's fossil record and today's forest and grassland ecosystems. These easy walks are kid friendly and ideal for family adventures.

Florissant Fossil Beds is simply one of the best and richest fossil locales in the world. Buried beneath the meadows and woodlands is an extensive record of a lush lost world from 34 million years ago. The fossils here are of two types: the minute and

The Big Stump is the petrified remains of a giant redwood that once grew along the edge of ancient Lake Florissant.

the huge. There are the massive petrified stumps and trunks of towering redwood trees, buried by volcanic mudflows that also dammed the valley, forming Lake Florissant, that capture our imagination.

But it is small, delicate fossils of tiny insects, animal remains, and fragments of plant life hidden within thin shale layers that make the Florissant Fossil Beds singular. More than 1,500 insect species have been uncovered here, including almost all the fossilized butterflies found in the Western Hemisphere as well as the only fossil of a tsetse fly, now found only in equatorial Africa.

Start your fossil hikes at the visitor center. You can pick up a trail map and self-guiding booklet and study the fossils in the center before heading out. Exit out the back door of the visitor center to a paved path and a kiosk with safety information. Remember that you're at 8,400 feet here and may feel the altitude if you're coming from a lower elevation. Bring water, use sunscreen, and keep an eye on the weather in summer. Lightning and thunderstorms are common in the afternoon.

To hike the Petrified Forest Loop Trail, walk from the visitor center to the stump shelter. Go right (north) from the Y junction on the north side of the stump shelter. The trail goes north along the west edge of a broad valley, crossing large meadows fringed with glades of ponderosa pine. Another trail junction is 100 feet north of the fork. Keep straight on the doubletrack trail. Many interpretive signs are sprinkled along the trail, offering lots of information about the fossils, ancient ecosystems, park geology, and the national monument's history.

The trail reaches a junction after 0.4 mile and the aptly named Big Stump, one of the monument's largest fossils. Big Stump is the petrified remains of a massive redwood tree that was as tall as 230 feet and more than 750 years old when volcanic mud buried its base, smothering the tree's roots and depriving them of oxygen. Besides the twelve excavated stumps seen today, remote sensing reveals at least forty stumps that still remain buried here along the edge of ancient Lake Florissant.

(**FYI:** While it's not available on a self-guided tour, Scudder Pit is about 0.1 mile to the left. This fossil excavation site was named for early paleontologist Samuel Scudder, who collected in the pit area, amassing more than 600 fossil species of insects, most of which are now in Harvard University's Museum of Comparative Zoology. Scudder's definitive *Tertiary Insects of North America*, detailing Florissant's astonishing fossil record, was published in 1890. You're not allowed to collect any fossils here. To see Scudder Pit, you must take a ranger-led tour.)

After viewing the colorful Big Stump, head east on the trail, passing a couple more stumps, to a hillock dotted with ponderosa pines. The trail turns right here and heads southwest back to the visitor center and parking. More signs detail the area's early history, when competing fossil pits vied for customers, who paid to view the stumps or to dig fossils. Near the visitor center is a junction with an obscure trail that cuts sharply left and leads to the Hornbek Homestead. Keep straight to the hike's end at the parking lot and visitor center.

Miles and Directions

0.0 Start of Petrified Forest Loop (GPS: 38.913829, -105.286467).

0.3 Trail junction to Scudder Pit on left (GPS: 38.918142, -105.286025). Visit only on ranger-led tour.

0.4 Reach Big Stump on the left (GPS: 38.918384, -105.286089).

1.0 Finish the loop at the paved trail at the backside of the visitor center (GPS: 38.913702, -105.285830).

Options

The wheelchair-accessible Ponderosa Loop Trail has plenty of interpretive signs, some benches, and a couple of buried petrified stumps. Follow the short 0.5-mile trail counterclockwise, passing big petrified stumps and exploring the wooded hillside above. The first stump is straight ahead under a protective canopy. Continue to the next stump pavilion for more interesting exhibits and two large redwood stumps, including one with three trunks that grew from a common root system. After climbing stairs out of the stump pit or taking the paved walkway around the pit, follow the trail for 50 feet to a Y junction. Go left on a smooth gravel path. A signpost between the trails points the way.

The rock-lined, doubletrack trail travels up and left across a gentle hillside covered with fir, spruce, and pine. At the only trail junction, keep left on the wide trail. The right fork connects to longer loop hikes, including the Sawmill Trail and Hans Loop.

Florissant Fossil Beds National Monument Trails

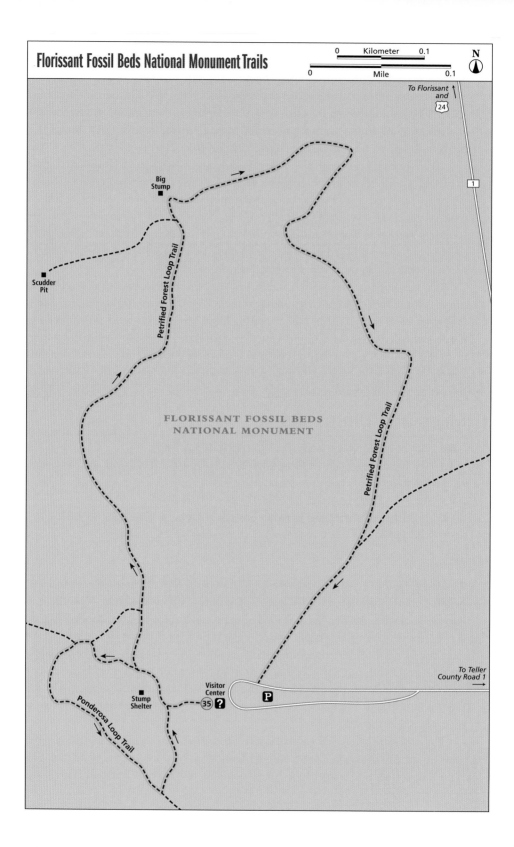

Return on the path to the large stump shelter and amphitheater and hike back to the Y fork on its north side. Keep straight to return to the trailhead on the west side of the visitor center.

Ponderosa Loop Trail Miles and Directions

0.0   Start at the trailhead behind the monument visitor center (GPS: 38.913491, -105.285657).

0.1   Reach a Y trail junction north of stump shelter (GPS: 38.913835, -105.286475). Go left on the marked Ponderosa Loop Trail.

0.4   End the Ponderosa Loop hike at the inverted Y junction north of the large stump shelter. Go straight to return to the visitor center. (**Option:** Go left at the junction to start the 1-mile Petrified Forest Loop.)

0.5   Finish the hike at the visitor center.

More Florissant Fossil Beds Trails

For extra credit, Florissant Fossil Beds offers nine excellent trails that total over 15 miles. You can pick up a detailed trail map and get hike info from a park ranger in the visitor center. All the trails are well maintained and moderate in difficulty. They have minimal elevation loss and gain, making all the trails ideal for kids or beginning hikers. Among the trails are the 3.8-mile Hornbek Wildlife Loop (keep an eye out for elk); the 2.8-mile Boulder Creek Trail, which ends at a jumble of granite boulders; and the 2.3-mile (one-way) Twin Rock Trail (Hike 36), with its aspens, meadows, and rock formations.

36 Twin Rocks Trail

This moderate out-and-back hike explores broad grassy valleys and humped ridges coated with a pine and fir woodland. It follows a good trail to the far northeastern boundary of Florissant Fossil Beds National Monument and South Twin Rock, a rounded granite dome.

Start: Trailhead on west side of Florissant Fossil Beds National Monument visitor center

Distance: 7.0 miles out and back

Hiking time: 2 to 4 hours

Difficulty: Moderate because of length

Elevation gain: About 500 feet. Total round-trip cumulative elevation gain is 1,100 feet.

Trail surface: Dirt trail

Seasons: Year-round. Best months are Apr through Oct. The trail is icy and snowy in winter; good for snowshoeing and cross-country skiing.

Schedule: Open daily. Day use only; Memorial Day to Labor Day, 9 a.m. to 5 p.m.; early Sept to late May, 9 a.m. to 5 p.m.

Other trail users: Hikers only

Canine compatibility: Dogs not allowed

Land status: National Park Service

Fees and permits: Park entrance fee required. Pay at the visitor center.

Maps: USGS Lake George and Divide quads; National Monument trail map (available at visitor center or on the park website)

Trail contacts: Florissant Fossil Beds National Monument, 15807 Teller County Rd. 1, Florissant 80816; (719) 748-3253; www.nps.gov/flfo

Finding the trailhead: From I-25 and downtown Colorado Springs, take the Cimarron Street / US 24 exit #141 and drive west for 35 miles, passing through Woodland Park and Divide, to the town of Florissant. Turn left (south) on Teller County Road 1, and drive 2 miles to the marked visitor center road. Turn right (west) and drive 0.2 mile to a parking area at the visitor center (GPS: 38.913562, -105.284807). An admittance fee is charged. The hike begins on the west side of the visitor center before the first stump pavilion.

The Hike

The Twin Rocks Trail is a wonderful hike that explores the backcountry at Florissant Fossil Beds National Monument. The 7-mile out-and-back hike, following four separate trails, sees little hiking traffic, with most walkers doing the shorter Ponderosa Loop and Petrified Forest Loop Trails. The hike traverses broad grasslands and shallow valleys lined with ponderosa pines and quaking aspen glades and finishes up a wide valley to South Twin Rock, double granite domes perched on the national monument's northeast boundary.

The hike offers easy walking with minimal elevation gain except for an uphill section above Grape Creek; the moderate difficulty rating is due to the length of the hike. The trails are singletrack dirt paths that mostly follow old ranch roads that are now covered with grass. Carry drinking water, since no potable water is found along

The slabby face of South Twin Rock, the highest point at Florissant Fossil Beds National Monument, towers above the Twin Rocks Trail.

the trail, and a raincoat, since drenching thunderstorms can occur on summer afternoons. A pair of binoculars is also a good addition to your pack since elk, mule deer, and other wildlife are often seen on this lonesome hike.

The Hornbek Homestead, which lies on the west side of CR 1, is a must-stop either before or after you do the Florissant hikes. The house and surrounding buildings, listed on the National Register of Historic Places as a prime example of a nineteenth-century homestead, were built in 1878 for Adaline Hornbek, who settled here as a widowed rancher with four children. The two-story log house had glass-pane windows; outbuildings included a milk house, chicken coop, and stable.

The hike begins on the west side of the visitor center, just past a half-moon-shaped plaza and before the first stump shelter. Go right (north) between two ponderosa pine trees on the Petrified Forest Loop Trail and hike northeast across a wide flat meadow, passing the top of a petrified stump that juts out of the ground. Reach a Y junction after 0.2 mile and go right on Hornbek Wildlife Loop Trail. The next 0.9-mile section follows this trail to its junction with Shootin' Star Trail.

The singletrack trail heads northeast through a grove of pines on a hillock and descends to Teller County Road 1 at 0.3 mile. After crossing the road, the trail gently drops down to a wooden bridge over trickling Grape Creek at 0.45 mile, swings left under a low granite cliff, and climbs a wooded hillside over a ridge to a higher ridge-line and a trail post at 0.9 mile.

Descend the cooler north side of the ridge through a Douglas fir forest and reach a signed trail junction after 1.2 miles. The Hornbek Wildlife Loop goes left here for 0.7 mile to the Hornbek Homestead. The hike, however, continues straight on the marked Shootin' Star Trail. The trail runs northeast along the edge of a ponderosa pine forest on the right and wide grasslands on the left.

Hike on the level trail and reach another major trail junction after 0.2 mile and keep left on the Twin Rocks Trail, which begins at this junction on the east side of an old dam built for a stock pond by early ranchers. The Shootin' Star Trail, named for elegant shooting star flowers found along the path in summer, goes right (southeast) for 1.6 miles to Barksdale Picnic Area off Lower Twin Rocks Road.

The singletrack Twin Rocks Trail heads northeast from the junction on a gradual grade. The trail continues along the edge of the pine forest and broad meadows, which dip gently westward to the historic Hornbek Homestead and Teller County Road 1. The trail crosses the grasslands and passes through open piney woods. Stop to enjoy good views west across the national monument to the Puma Hills and the rough Tarryall Range in Lost Creek Wilderness Area to the northwest. Also watch for herds of elk and mule deer grazing in the meadows west of the trail and in the open valleys farther east.

After hiking 0.7 mile from the last trail junction, you dip into a shallow valley and cross a small creek on a wooden bridge. The last leg of the Twin Rocks Trail heads east up this valley along an unnamed creek for 1.7 miles to the eastern boundary of Florissant Fossil Beds National Monument and the end of the trail.

Hike east on the north side of the shallow valley through open meadows. The floor of the valley on your right is bound by the west-flowing creek, lined with willows and groves of aspen. After hiking 0.3 mile from the bridge, you reach an old stock pond, the creek blocked by a small earthen dam. Cattails and willows clot the dam, while the pond's still water reflects sky, clouds, and, in autumn, golden quaking aspen trees.

Continue hiking east up the widening valley, passing pine-clad hillsides studded with granite boulders. At 2.7 miles the trail passes beneath an 80-foot-high granite out-cropping capped by an overhanging block. Look at the bottom of the cliff for a thick band of white quartz. The next 0.5 mile of hiking gently climbs the wide valley through open meadows, passing overgrown roads that once led to now-abandoned ranches and homesteads, to a boardwalk that crosses a short marshy section along the creek.

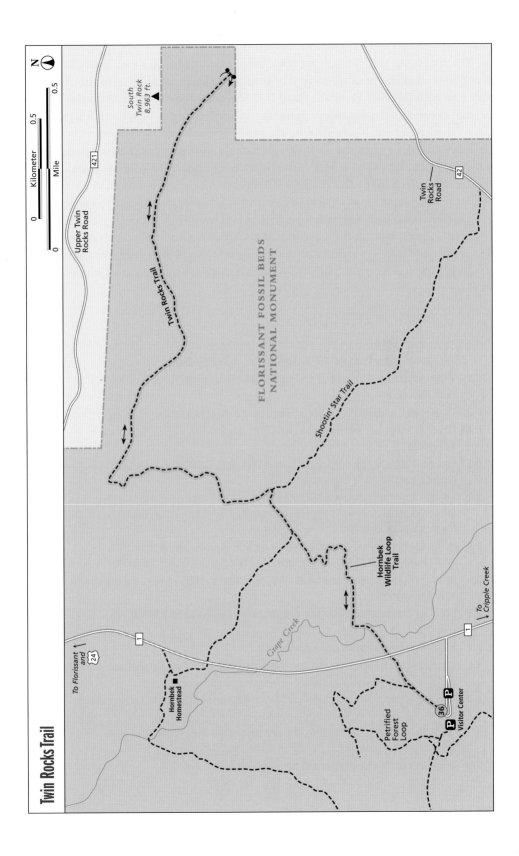

Twin Rocks Trail

N

Kilometer
0   0.5
Mile
0   0.5

Upper Twin Rocks Road

421

South Twin Rock 8,963 ft. ▲

Twin Rocks Trail

FLORISSANT FOSSIL BEDS NATIONAL MONUMENT

Shootin' Star Trail

Twin Rocks Road

42

To Florissant and
24

Hornbek Homestead ■

Grape Creek

Hornbek Wildlife Loop Trail

1

To Cripple Creek

1

Petrified Forest Loop

36

Visitor Center

P

P

The trail heads east through an open meadow toward 8,963-foot South Twin Rock, a rounded granite dome cleaved by vertical cracks separated by steep slabs. The rock, the high point of Florissant Fossil Beds National Monument, rises in the far northeast corner of the monument property. Just north of South Twin Rock is Upper Twin Rocks Road and North Twin Rock, an 8,975-foot knob that overlooks US 24.

Pass south of the rugged dome and walk through an aspen grove. This is especially gorgeous in autumn when golden leaves shimmer on the quaking aspens. Continue on the trail under a slabby cliff and, after 3.5 miles of hiking, reach the end of the trail at a fence and gate that mark the northeastern boundary of the national monument. A sign notes "Trail Ends: Private Property Beyond This Point."

This is a great spot to sit on dense grass alongside the trail and munch on sandwiches or a snack or on a granite slab on the hillside above. After a proper rest, shoulder your pack and return to the visitor center, retracing your steps along the three trails for a 7.0-mile-long, round-trip hike.

Miles and Directions

0.0 Start at the trailhead on the west side of the visitor center. Go right from the paved trail on the Petrified Forest Loop Trail (GPS: 38.913704, -105.285824).

0.2 Reach a Y junction. Turn right on the Hornbek Wildlife Loop Trail (GPS: 38.914945, -105.283688).

0.3 Cross Teller County Road 1. Descend east across a valley to a bridge.

0.45 Cross the bridge over marshy Grape Creek (GPS: 38.917334, -105.279847) and begin hiking uphill.

0.9 Reach the top of a high ridge marked with a post (GPS: 38.919248, -105.276067), then descend forested north-facing slopes.

1.2 Reach a major trail junction (GPS: 38.920750, -105.274266). Go straight on the Shootin' Star Trail. Follow the edge of a wide valley. The left turn is the continuation of the Hornbek Wildlife Loop Trail.

1.4 Reach another major trail junction on the east side of an old earthen dam (GPS: 38.921892, -105.271702). Go left on marked Twin Rocks Trail. Right is Shootin' Star Trail.

2.0 Reach a wooden bridge over a creek (GPS: 38.929569, -105.271187). The trail bends east up a wide valley.

2.3 Reach an old stock pond lined with cattails and willows (GPS: 38.928560, -105.267547).

2.7 Trail passes below a south-facing granite cliff.

3.1 Cross a boardwalk across a short marshy area or scramble across a granite slab above it (GPS: 38.926862, -105.253259).

3.3 Pass through an aspen grove below South Twin Rock and continue east below a cliff.

3.5 Reach a gate on the eastern boundary of the national monument and the end of the trail (GPS: 38.923750, -105.246886). The land beyond the fence is private property. Turn around here and hike back.

7.0 Arrive back at the visitor center and the hike's end.

37 Goose Creek Trail

An excellent out-and-back hike on Goose Creek Trail up a scenic valley to historic buildings and a spectacular overlook in the heart of Lost Creek Wilderness Area.

Start: Goose Greek Trailhead (#612) just west of Mutakat Road / Park County Road 211
Distance: 9.2 miles out and back
Hiking time: 6 to 8 hours
Difficulty: Moderate
Elevation gain: 900 feet
Trail surface: Singletrack dirt trail
Seasons: Year-round. Trail is snowy and icy in winter. The access road to the trailhead may be impassable in winter.
Schedule: Open daily
Other trail users: Equestrians, backpackers. No mountain bikes or motorized vehicles allowed in the wilderness area.

Canine compatibility: Dogs are allowed off-leash.
Land status: Public land in Lost Creek Wilderness Area, Pike National Forest
Fees and permits: A free permit for each group is at the trailhead and must be filled out and deposited in a steel box. No fees are required.
Map: USGS McCurdy Mountain
Trail contact: South Platte Ranger District, Pike National Forest, 30403 Kings Valley Dr., Suite 2-115, Conifer 80433; (303) 275-5610; www.fs.usda.gov/detail/psicc/about-forest/districts/

Finding the trailhead: Drive west on US 24 from Colorado Springs through Woodland Park and Divide to Lake George. Continue west from Lake George on US 24 for 1.2 miles and turn right (north) on paved Park County Road 77. Follow CR 77 for 7 miles and turn right (north) on FR 211 / Mutakat Road. Follow dirt FR 211 for 11 miles to FR 558. Turn left (west) and drive 1.9 miles to the Goose Creek Trailhead and a large parking area on the eastern edge of the Lost Creek Wilderness Area (GPS: 39.173143, -105.375299).

The Hike

The popular and wildly scenic Goose Creek Trail travels west up a gorgeous mountain valley into the heart of the Lost Creek Wilderness Area from its eastern trailhead for 9.4 miles to its northern trailhead in Wigwam Park. This hike, 4.6 miles one-way, is half of the trail's total distance, making it a great day-hiking excursion from Colorado Springs. The trail is often busy, especially on weekends, with hikers and backpackers, so come during the week for more solitude, quiet, and inspiration.

The 119,790-acre Lost Creek Wilderness Area protects most of the 25-mile-long Tarryall Range, a swath of wooded mountains west of Colorado Springs. Only a couple of mountains in the Tarryalls break the above-timberline elevation mark—12,432-foot Bison Peak, the range high point, and 12,164-foot McCurdy Mountain. The magic of the Tarryall Range and the wilderness range, however, is not in majestic snowcapped peaks but in bold outcroppings of pink Pikes Peak granite. The range is a metropolis of architectural forms—castles, spires, spikes, domes, minarets, mosques, house-size boulders, and cliff-lined corridors.

The Lost Creek Wilderness Area, an enclave of deafening silence an hour west of the bustle of Colorado Springs, is named for Lost Creek, one of Colorado's most unusual water courses. Lost Creek, originating on the west side of the Tarryalls, twists through wide willow-filled valleys and down rocky canyons and in at least nine places disappears underground or becomes "lost" beneath huge jumbles of fallen boulders. After its final disappearance, a 0.5-mile forested stretch that this hike crosses to a scenic viewpoint, Lost Creek emerges from the boulder sink and becomes Goose Creek.

The ancient Pikes Peak granite, a rough, coarse-grained granite, was deposited over a billion years ago in a huge batholith beneath the earth's crust. The molten rock slowly solidified and cooled underground. Later this bedrock was uplifted by the Ancestral Rocky Mountains and today's Rocky Mountains, and then ensuing eons of erosion stripped away surface layers, exposing the granite core. Weathering and erosion, including frost-wedging and flowing water, chiseled and sculpted the granite, leaving today's fanciful wonderland of rock forms and shapes.

Begin the hike at the 8,220-foot Goose Creek Trailhead after walking 250 feet southwest from the parking lot at the end of the Goose Creek Trailhead Road. Before starting the hike, fill out a wilderness permit at a register box at the trailhead. Deposit the lower portion of the permit in a metal box and keep the other half in your possession while in Lost Creek Wilderness Area. The free permit allows the national forest to keep an accurate count of wilderness users.

Past the permit station is a sign marking the wilderness boundary as well as a 1979 plaque designating Lost Creek Scenic Area, an area within the wilderness, as a prestigious National Natural Landmark. A two-panel interpretive sign has an area map, rules and regulations, safety info, what to bring on your hike, and the basic Leave No Trace ethic.

The singletrack trail (Trail #612) descends from the wilderness boundary, heading southwest down a mountain slope covered with dead tree snags. The area at the trailhead and to the south and southwest up Hankins Gulch was decimated by the Hayman Fire in 2002. The hillside is slowly regenerating with shrubs and wildflowers filling across the slope. Dead snag trees, still black from the fire, gauntly stand tall, although many have snapped off in high winds. Beware of toppling snags if you are hiking in the burn area when it's windy.

After descending for 0.25 mile, the trail crosses Hankins Creek on a slippery log. Continue a few feet to a trail junction. Go right on the signed Goose Creek Trail. A left turn goes up Hankins Pass Trail to Hankins Pass in the south part of the wilderness area. The trail heads north above the creek and in 0.5 mile reaches the edge between the burn area and the forest. Enter the pine and fir forest and turn left on the trail at Goose Creek. At 0.7 mile the trail crosses to the north bank of the creek on a sturdy steel bridge with plank flooring and turns toward the northwest.

The old engine at the shafthouse is all that remains of a proposed dam project on Lost Creek.

The next 0.4 mile of trail threads through a mixed conifer forest of ponderosa pine, Douglas fir, and Engelmann spruce beside Goose Creek. In spring the creek swells with snowmelt, but usually it's a pleasant tumbling stream; trout swim in its deep holes. Eventually the valley widens and the creek meanders among boulders and pools in still beaver ponds lined with willows. Granite slabs and faces stair-step up a couple of unnamed mountains that tower to the south.

After 1.3 miles the trail leaves the creek and begins climbing steep slopes above Goose Creek on the north side of the valley. The next 3.5-mile trail segment gently climbs for a couple of miles to 8,700 feet before dipping and rolling through a series of dry shallow valleys that drain south into Goose Creek. The initial hill is steep and rutted in occasional places before traversing mountain slopes.

At about 2 miles look up left through a gap in the trees toward a big sweeping slab with a thin pinnacle called the Organ Pipe beside it. On the right side of the slab and pinnacle at 8,960 feet is one of the Tarryalls' most unusual rock formations: Harmonica Arch (GPS: 39.19100, -105.39483). One of the longest unsupported granite arches in the United States, Harmonica Arch is 85 feet long, 30 feet high, 18 feet wide, and 15 feet thick. The arch is reached from the trailhead by a 4.8-mile round-trip hike that gains a net 740 feet. The trail to it leaves the bottom of the valley where the Goose Creek Trail begins going uphill.

Continue west on the wide, well-used trail along the north side of the valley. Occasional overlooks allow good views up the valley into the heart of the wilderness area. The trail descends hills, crosses shallow valleys, and climbs back over ridges.

After 3.9 miles the trail reaches a junction in the bottom of a shallow valley. A wooden sign designating the Goose Creek Trail also points left to a spur trail that leads to "Historic Buildings." Go left down this rocky path for 0.1 mile to a collection of dilapidated buildings alongside a meadow and the junction with the Shafthouse Trail, which you will take shortly.

These ramshackle buildings were built in the 1890s to house workers for the Antero and Lost Creek Reservoir Company, which between 1891 and 1910 attempted to build a dam at the boulder jumble just to the south of here. The largest was a two-story bunkhouse with plank floors and a stone fireplace on the first floor. The walls were made of big logs, hewn to a square shape, with the gaps between logs chinked with mortar. The back of the house was apparently a kitchen and dining room for feeding the hungry employees. Next door is another, smaller log cabin, and across the trail on the east side of the meadow are the remains of other cabins. Nearby is the gravesite of a 1930s prospector named Palmer, his grave outlined with rough chunks of white quartz.

The last leg of the hike goes 0.7 mile from the historic buildings to the shafthouse site and on through boulders to a spectacular overlook on top of giant boulders. From the signed trail junction at the north side of the bunkhouse, go west on the trail marked "Shafthouse."

The singletrack trail heads west, crosses a trickling creek, then bends southeast and traverses a gravelly hillside to a high point below a granite dome. Descend the trail through giant boulders to the bottom of the valley, which at this point is the top of a massive jumble of boulders covered with soil, gravel, trees, and grass. Lost Creek tumbles through secret rock passages over 100 feet below the surface here.

The trail heads west here, 0.6 mile from the buildings, and reaches the site of the old shafthouse. A rusted piece of machinery—an old steam engine—sits here on a gravel pad below a cliff. This was the site of a cable pulley used to raise and lower tools, supplies, workers, and waste tailings from a shaft that was dug here to the creek far below the ground surface. Between 1891 and 1913, the workers housed in the buildings were hired by the Antero and Lost Park Reservoir Company to drill a shaft through the bedrock to Lost Creek. The idea was to pump the underground void full of concrete to dam the creek and form a proposed Lost Park Reservoir in the gorgeous valley just upstream. Technology in 1900, however, was not up to the task and the project failed. Just imagine the work that it took, though, to haul all the bits of the steam engine back to this remote spot.

Beyond the shafthouse the trail winds through boulders and then crosses a quiet meadow surrounded by towering cliffs and domes. Continue through a catacomb of giant boulders and either scoot down a big log in a narrow corridor on the left or squeeze through a slot into another narrow corridor on the right. Both passageways lead west for a couple hundred feet to the hike's end at 4.6 miles and a dramatic

Towering granite formations rise above Lost Creek.

THE HAYMAN FIRE

The Hayman Fire, the largest in Colorado's recorded history, began south of Lost Creek Wilderness Area and Goose Creek near Lake George on June 8, 2002, and wasn't under control until July 18. The fire torched 138,114 acres in the South Platte River drainage between Lost Creek Wilderness Area and CO 67 north of Woodland Park. Fortunately, the fire only burned along the eastern edge of the wilderness area, saving the area's old-growth forests and beauty from ravaging flames. Most of the river canyon east of the wilderness boundary was severely burned, although the area is slowly regenerating, with groves of colonizing aspen spreading across hillsides and riparian growth along creeks. An ongoing study found that 80 percent of the forest understory, including perennial flowers like Front Range beardtongue, Fendler's ragwort, and some exotic species including mullein, quickly regenerated within a couple of years on the burned forest floor.

overlook perched on the edge of a cliff. Be careful scrambling onto the rounded viewpoint above the cliff since there are deep drops in wide cracks as well as a precipitous cliff to the west. This is not a good spot for unsupervised children or those with an aversion to heights. Be prepared for route-finding dilemmas and possible backtracking to find the best way to the overlook.

The scenic view is simply spectacular. Lost Creek twists across the valley floor, meandering between banks clotted with dense willows. Steep mountain slopes blanketed with fir and spruce climb south above the creek. Immense granite domes, abrupt cliffs, compact outcrops, and boulder piles cover the mountainsides and line the valley's edge. This hidden valley, not seen from the final trail section, is a fitting end to one of the best and wildest hikes in Pikes Peak country. It's a mysterious place that doesn't readily give up its secrets except to those willing to walk into the wilderness.

After savoring the view and enjoying your packed lunch, retrace your steps for 0.8 mile back through the boulder field to the shafthouse ruin and on to the cabins and trail junction. Go right on Goose Creek Trail and hike 3.8 miles down the valley to the trailhead and your car. Most of the trail is downhill so the hike goes quickly. There are few key junctions on the way, so stick to the well-worn path and you'll be back in a couple of hours.

Miles and Directions

0.0 Begin at the Goose Creek Trailhead west of the parking area (GPS: 39.172640, -105.376266).

0.25 Descend through a burn area and cross a bridge over Hankins Creek to a junction with Hankins Pass Trail. Go right on the west side of the creek (GPS: 39.171997, -105.379996).

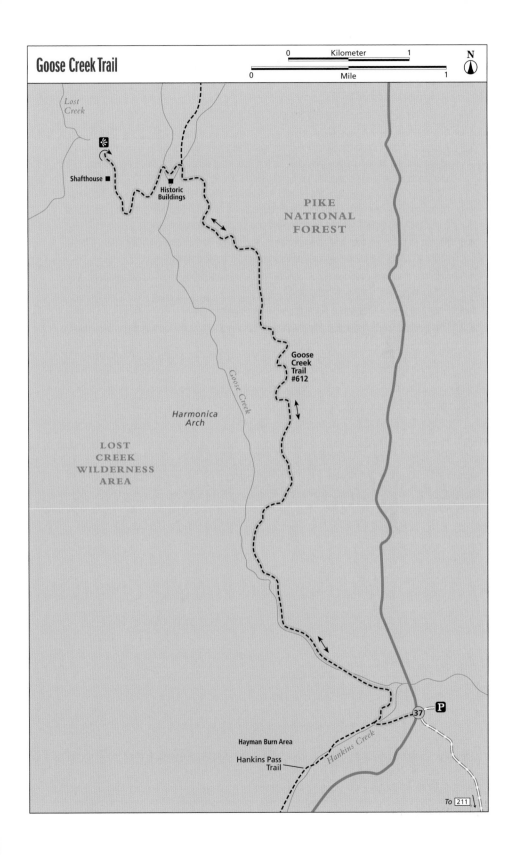

Goose Creek Trail

0 | Kilometer | 1
0 | Mile | 1

N

Lost Creek

Shafthouse ■

Historic Buildings ■

PIKE NATIONAL FOREST

Goose Creek Trail #612

Goose Creek

Harmonica Arch

LOST CREEK WILDERNESS AREA

Hayman Burn Area

Hankins Pass Trail

Hankins Creek

37 P

To 211

0.5 Reach edge of forest after a burned area in lower Hankins Gulch.

0.7 Cross Goose Creek on a bridge to the north bank and go north/northwest (GPS: 39.175296, -105.381742).

1.3 Reach meadows along the creek and start hiking uphill above the creek (GPS: 39.181905, -105.389631).

3.9 Junction of the Goose Creek Trail and the side trail (GPS: 39.208469, -105.397790) to the historic buildings and overlook. Go left down the valley to the buildings. When you reach the historic buildings, go right toward the overlook (GPS: 39.207586, -105.397718) or straight to the buildings. (**Option:** If you continue down a trail from the buildings to Goose Creek and then walk upstream a few hundred feet, you can see where Lost Creek emerges from the boulder sink and becomes Goose Creek.)

4.5 Return to the main trail and turn left (west). Reach the old shafthouse (GPS: 39.207310, -105.402288). Continue through a meadow and a boulder field.

4.6 Reach a dramatic overlook (GPS: 39.208953, -105.403264) above Lost Creek and a rocky valley. Turn around to head back.

5.4 Return to Goose Creek Trail. Go right (east) on the main trail.

9.2 End the hike at the trailhead. The parking lot is to your left at the end of the access road.

38 Blodgett Peak Trail

A steep hike up a rough trail leads to the summit of Blodgett Peak, an unranked summit that looms over the suburbs of northwest Colorado Springs.

Start: Trailhead at Blodgett Peak Open Space parking area on west side of Woodmen Road

Distance: 6.4 miles out and back

Hiking time: 4 to 6 hours depending on physical condition

Difficulty: Strenuous. Trail is steep, eroded in parts, and has uneven footing.

Elevation gain: 2,681 feet

Trail surface: Closed gravel road; double- and singletrack dirt trail

Seasons: Year-round. Trail has snow and ice in winter. Bring micro-spikes.

Schedule: Open daily, dawn to dusk

Other trail users: Hikers only

Canine compatibility: Leashed dogs allowed on the lower trail section in the city parkland

Land status: City of Colorado Springs and Pike National Forest

Fees and permits: None

Map: USGS Cascade

Trail contact: Colorado Springs Parks, Recreation and Cultural Services, 1401 Recreation Way, Colorado Springs 80905-1975; (719) 385-5940; https://coloradosprings.gov/parks

Finding the trailhead: From I-25 in Colorado Springs, exit west at the Garden of the Gods Road exit 146. Drive west on Garden of the Gods Road for 1.1 miles to Centennial Boulevard and turn right (north). The next driving leg follows Centennial north for 4.8 miles to the trailhead. Follow Centennial north through the Piñon Valley subdivision to Vindicator Drive, a major road that goes east to I-25 to Woodmen Road and the Woodmen Road exit 149. Continue north on Centennial, which becomes West Woodmen Road at Orchard Valley Road. Continue driving on West Woodmen another 0.5 mile to the obvious parking lot and trailhead on the left (west) side of the road for Blodgett Peak Open Space (GPS: 38.948994, -104.886342). Overflow parking is on the side of the road by the trailhead.

The Hike

Blodgett Peak, rising to a rocky 9,423-foot summit on the northwest edge of Colorado Springs, offers a steep trail to a small summit with spectacular views of the city spreading out below, the Air Force Academy, and Pikes Peak towering to the southwest. The 3.2-mile trail, gaining almost 2,700 feet of elevation from parking lot to summit, is a strenuous hike for most people.

Expect parts of the trail to be difficult to follow, particularly with numerous social trails branching off; slopes eroded from too many footsteps; and loose gravel and rock sections. The upper part of the mountain also has lots of dead trees that were torched in the 2012 Waldo Canyon Fire, which swept across high ridges and the mountaintop. Use caution and watch for falling branches if you are hiking in windy conditions. Some hikers will prefer using trekking poles for balance on the difficult trail sections. Take care not to knock loose rock on hikers below.

Before fitness seekers began inundating the Mount Manitou Incline for a stair-stepping workout, there was Blodgett Peak. The hike up Blodgett, once commonly used by Air Force Academy cadets for training, is still a great workout hike and, better yet, has none of the Incline's crowds. The peak has a loyal following of local hikers who regularly trek to its summit. Anyone who considers themselves an experienced Pikes Peak country hiker needs to climb Blodgett Peak at least once.

The hike starts at a trailhead at a small parking lot on the west side of Woodmen Road on the edge of Blodgett Peak Open Space, a 167-acre Colorado Springs city parkland. There are ten parking spaces plus a spot for people with disabilities and a toilet and information kiosk at the trailhead parking lot. Additional parking is found along the paved shoulder on the west side of West Woodmen Road, beside the parking lot.

Begin your Blodgett summit adventure from the obvious trailhead at the west end of the parking area. A bench facing toward Blodgett Peak honors Patrick Niedringhaus, an 18-year-old climber and hiker who died in an avalanche on Torreys Peak in the Colorado Rockies in 2004. Blodgett was one of Patrick's favorite local hikes. Before taking your hike, take a minute to sit on the bench to remember young Patrick and to scout the hike ahead of you.

Look northwest from the bench and trailhead to Blodgett Peak, the obvious high, pointed mountain with tall granite cliffs on its south-facing slopes. The true summit of Blodgett is behind the false summit you see from here. Note several obvious landmarks on the south flank of the mountain that mark the hiking route. Scouting the hike in advance allows you to locate the landmarks so that you are not lured off the best trail by social trails that usually end in brush and boulders.

To stay on track, these are the landmarks to locate on the trail: a round green water tower; a steep unnamed canyon on the south side of Blodgett Peak; a cliff band halfway up the canyon that ascends the mountain slope to the right; a large boulder field that spills down below the largest cliffs below Blodgett's summit; and a high south-facing cliff on the ridge west of the summit.

From Patrick's Bench and the trailhead, hike west for 0.6 mile up the wide closed road (which provides utility access to the water tower) to the fourth and last switchback before the tower. Go left on the doubletrack Hummingbird Trail at a junction on the left side of the switchback.

The Hummingbird Trail makes a wide bend to the south before contouring north across shady slopes clad with pine, fir, and spruce. At 1.4 miles this pleasant trail section ends at a wide gravel spot in the bottom of a dry canyon. A couple of trail options are found here. Do not go straight up the steep slope to the north, although a popular social trail heads up this way to an old road. If you go this way, be prepared for serious bushwhacking through dense scrub oak thickets if you lose your chosen path or when it ends. Instead, go left on a singletrack trail up the bottom of the canyon. A

Blodgett Peak towers above a closed road near the water tower. ▶

large granite boulder with a slabby south face and vertical face above the trail is 100 feet up the trail.

The next trail segment continues up the steep canyon for almost a mile to a steep cliff band and a 50-foot-high waterfall. This continuously steep trail section is easy to follow but has some eroded sections with unsure footing. A pair of trekking poles and a few tree branches to grab are handy to keep your balance. Water often runs across bedrock in the upper part of the canyon and down the waterfall. Avoid getting sidetracked from this trail and going onto scree slopes on the north side of the canyon on social trails and shortcuts. They are more difficult to follow and overuse of them will lead to continued erosion. The trail up the canyon could use some trail love in the form of rebuilding eroded sections and placing rock steps and water bars to lessen erosion.

After reaching trickling Blodgett Falls and the cliff band at 2.3 miles, go right on a steep trail section at the base of the cliffs, which runs north up the mountainside. To your right here is Blodgett's infamous boulder field. Some hikers prefer to boulder-hop up the long, steep boulder field, but it is best to keep left of it to avoid shifting boulders and twisted ankles.

Above the cliff band and after climbing a steep 0.1 mile, the trail goes left and contours across a hillside with open woods for about 300 feet. Again, some hikers will go right above the cliff band and clamber up the upper boulder field, which is hemmed in by cliffs on either side, to a false summit east of Blodgett's main summit. The easier alternative is to keep left and follow the well-beaten trail.

Past a large pointed boulder, the trail bends right and begins zigzagging up a steep mountain slope studded with ponderosa pines and Douglas firs. At 2.6 miles the trail enters the Waldo Canyon Fire burn scar. During the massive wildfire in June 2012, the upper slopes of Blodgett Peak were toasted by flames, killing almost all the trees from here to the summit. Pick your way up the steep trail, stepping over loose rocks and fallen trees and keeping right of a high broken cliff to your left. At 3.0 miles the trail reaches a broad saddle. The summit of Blodgett Peak is directly east from here.

The last 0.2-mile trail segment heads northwest from the saddle, scrambling up through boulders surrounded by tall burnt trees. It's advisable to use extreme caution or turn around if you are on the upper section of Blodgett Peak in high winds since the dead-snag trees can topple or break, which could be fatal if one hit you. After 3.2 miles of uphill hiking, the trail ends on Blodgett's rock-strewn summit.

The mountaintop offers spectacular panoramic views of the Pikes Peak region. Below you spread the northwest suburbs of Colorado Springs, while the city center's blocky buildings rise to the southeast. Pikes Peak, usually snow covered much of the year, towers 11 miles to the southwest. The reservoir and dam visible to the northwest is Rampart Reservoir, a popular fishing and recreation spot and part of the Colorado Springs water supply. The Air Force Academy lies to the north, tucked

Blodgett Falls spills down a vertical granite cliff.

against the soaring escarpment of the Rampart Range. The twisted wreck of a C-49 twin-engine transport plane is scattered on the northern slope of Blodgett below the summit. The plane crashed on the night of February 23, 1942, killing the pilot and two crewmen.

Take a few minutes to relax on Blodgett Peak's summit, enjoy the great view, and have a hearty drink of water or sports drink. Now it's time to head back down. Follow the same route down the mountain. Watch your footing since you will encounter gravel and loose rock. Allow about half the time it took you to climb the mountain to get back to the trailhead and your car.

Miles and Directions

0.0 Trailhead at parking lot on West Woodmen Road (GPS: 38.948995, -104.886334). Hike west up a closed gravel road, gradually gaining elevation toward a round water tower.

0.6 Before reaching the water tower, turn left on Hummingbird Trail, a broad doubletrack trail, on the outside of a wide switchback. This junction is marked with a sign on a post for Hummingbird Trail and Blodgett Peak Trail (GPS: 38.94780, -104.892866). (See "Options" below.)

1.4 The doubletrack Hummingbird Trail ends at a wide gravel area in the bottom of a dry canyon. A social trail goes straight up the brushy hill ahead—avoid going this way since several trails begin and end on the steep slopes above. Instead, go left and follow a singletrack trail up the bottom of the canyon, passing a large boulder 100 feet up the canyon (GPS: 38.953636, -104.897178).

2.3 Reach a 50-foot-high waterfall and cliff band that blocks the canyon after following the steep trail along a mostly dry creek bed (GPS: 38.953965, -104.904639). Go right below the falls and hike up a steep trail section between the cliff on the left and the boulder field on the right.

2.4 The trail reaches a knoll where the cliff band ends. Go left and follow the trail through woods for a few hundred feet to a pointed boulder. The trail goes north up steep wooded slopes here.

2.6 Reach the Waldo Canyon wildfire burn area. Continue up the steep trail through a burned forest with blackened tree trunks.

3.0 The trail reaches a wide gravelly saddle in the burned area (GPS: 38.957847, -104.907382). Hike northeast along the rocky trail, which can be easily lost among boulders, through more burned forest.

3.2 Summit of 9,423-foot Blodgett Peak (GPS: 38.959627, -104.907629). After enjoying the view, descend the same trail back to the parking area.

6.4 End the hike at the Blodgett Peak Open Space parking lot.

Options

Don't want to make the arduous trek up Blodgett Peak? You're in luck if you don't since Blodgett Peak Open Space offers plenty of easy trails in the foothills above the trailhead and parking lot. It's easy to hike up the first 0.6 mile of the twisting Blodgett Peak Trail, a closed utility road, to the water tower. Take the Ponderosa Trail back

Blodgett Peak Trail

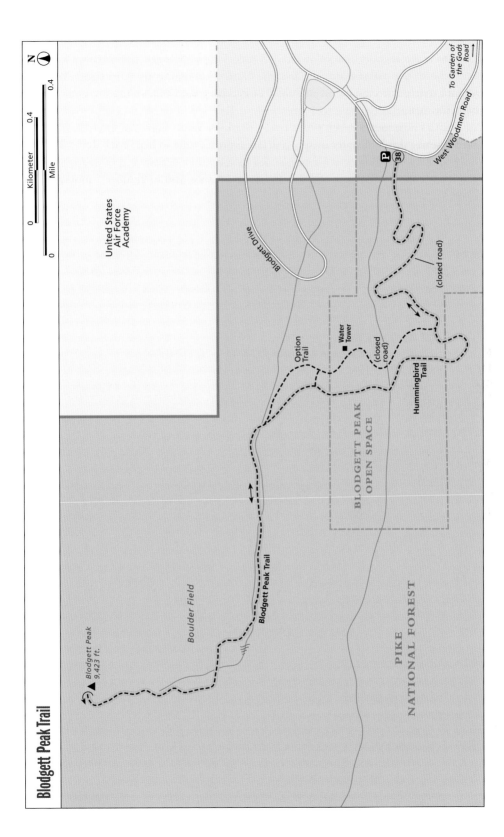

down to make an easy loop hike. The 0.5-mile-long Chickadee Trail makes a loop southwest of the parking lot or follow the Chickadee Trail to the Dry Creek Trail, which loops back to the parking for a 0.75-mile hike.

A less scenic alternative to Hummingbird Trail is to continue up the road for another 0.4 mile to the green water tower. Scramble up a steep singletrack trail left and above the tower, then follow the trail north through forest until it meets up with the Hummingbird Trail at a flat gravel area in the canyon floor. A side path (GPS: 38.95142, -104.89448) goes west for 250 feet to Hummingbird Trail in a scrub oak forest.

39 Mount Herman Trail

The Mount Herman Trail climbs the southwest flank of the 9,063-foot mountain on the eastern edge of the Rampart Range north of Colorado Springs and west of the town of Monument. The hike is popular and steep and yields spectacular views of the Front Range from its rocky prominence.

Start: Parking lot on west side of Mount Herman on Mount Herman Road
Distance: 2.2 miles out and back
Hiking time: 2 to 4 hours
Difficulty: Moderate
Elevation gain: 800 feet
Trail surface: Singletrack dirt surface
Seasons: Year-round but Mar through Nov is best; can be cold and icy in winter
Schedule: Open daily

Other trail users: Mountain bikers and equestrians allowed but rarely seen
Canine compatibility: Leashed dogs only
Land status: Pike National Forest
Fees and permits: None
Map: USGS Palmer Lake
Trail contact: Pike National Forest, Pikes Peak Ranger District, 601 S. Weber St., Colorado Springs 80903; (719) 636-1602; www.fs.usda.gov/detail/psicc/about-forest/districts/?cid=fsm9_032731

Finding the trailhead: Drive north from Colorado Springs on I-25. Take exit 161 at Monument and drive west through the small town of Monument, following signs for Mount Herman, for 0.7 mile to Mitchell Avenue. Turn left on Mitchell and drive another 0.7 mile to Mount Herman Road. Turn right (west) and drive about 7 miles to the trailhead. About a mile past the road's junction with Red Rocks Road, Mount Herman Road gets rough. The road edges shelf-like around the south side of Mount Herman. Look for the parking lot, which holds about eight vehicles, and trailhead for Trail #716 on the right (GPS: 39.071206, -104.932106). The distance from the Pike National Forest boundary to the trailhead is 4.3 miles.

The Hike

The popular Mount Herman Trail, ascending the southwest flank of Mount Herman, climbs just over a mile to the peak's 9,063-foot-high summit on the eastern edge of the Rampart Range, north of Colorado Springs and the Air Force Academy. The hike is steep in parts but is short and scenic. The summit views are spectacular, including Pikes Peak to the southwest and the Black Forest spreading to the east of the mountain. The trail is generally easy to follow, although a number of social trails can lead you astray. Stick to the wide well-traveled path to reach the summit.

The hike, following Pike National Forest Trail #716, begins from the trailhead at a small parking area on the north side of Mount Herman Road (FR 320), a rough dirt road that connects Monument and I-25 on the east with the Rampart Range Road (FR 300) and Woodland Park to the west. Another trailhead for Trail #715 is 0.1 mile farther west, but it is the wrong one for climbing Mount Herman.

Granite bedrock offers expansive views across the Rampart Range from Mount Herman's summit.

The mountain is likely named for nineteenth-century German settler Herman Schwanbeck. Another rumor states that it was named by Father John Dyer, the famous "Snowshoe Itinerant," a preacher who traveled between Fairplay and Leadville to the west, for his church friend Mr. Hermon. Another unsubstantiated story says it was named for a similar Mount Hermon in Syria.

Begin your hike by following the trail as it heads north up a shallow ravine following a trickling creek, its banks lined with thick matted grass. A mixed woodland of quaking aspen, Douglas fir, Engelmann spruce, and ponderosa pine blankets the hillsides above the trail. After 0.1 mile the trail reaches an open glade and bends right up another valley.

Much of the hike is through shady forest, providing important habitat for wildflowers including Hall's alumroot, an endemic saxifrage that grows among rose-colored boulders, as well as penstemon, daisies, and Rocky Mountain columbines, the Colorado state flower, which was first described on nearby Pikes Peak in 1820 by botanist Edwin James.

The trail heads northeast below tall white granite cliffs scattered across the mountainside, to the right of an intermittently flowing creek in a rocky draw. It climbs into a pocket meadow tucked among aspens and conifers. The aspens blaze golden in late September, offering a swath of color with summer's last gasp.

Granite slabs, creased by water streaks,
rise above the Mount Herman Trail. ▶

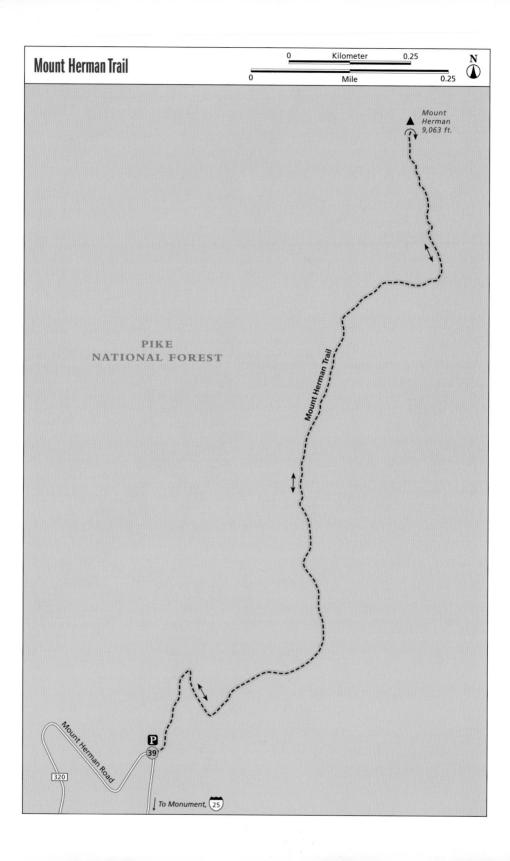

0 Kilometer 0.25

0 Mile 0.25

N

Mount
Herman
9,063 ft.

PIKE
NATIONAL FOREST

Mount Herman Trail

Mount Herman Road

320

P
39

To Monument, 25

Continue hiking through the meadow, slowly gaining elevation until the trail turns east and climbs sharply up a steep slope strewn with rounded boulders. At 0.8 miles the trail reaches a broad wooded bench on the south side of the mountain and heads north up steeper slopes on the west side of the mountain.

After 1.1 miles the trail emerges from the forest and clambers up the rocky trail to the open, windswept summit of 9,063-foot Mount Herman. A windsock used by paragliders who jump off this lofty point marks the rocky top. Look for a register tucked among the summit rocks to sign your name and jot a comment about your hike, the weather, or your traveling companions.

Mount Herman actually has two summits, with the north one being the higher point. The rarely visited south summit is a jumble of granite blocks and boulders and a strange geologic oddity called the Bottomless Pit. The pit is a deep fissure in the rocks that plunges steeply down like a vertical mine shaft; not a good place to venture into without climbing equipment.

Mount Herman has been a popular Pikes Peak region hike since the start of the Colorado Mountain Club in 1912. At that time the local club chapter, including trip leader Lucretia Vaile, often walked about the Palmer Lake area. One of their usual outings was an ascent of Mount Herman. The hikers would take the Denver & Rio Grande Railroad to access the trailhead below Fern Glen. A description of a scheduled hike for June 13, 1920, led by Miss Vaile said, "The view from Mount Herman is magnificent, from the Bottomless Pit, indescribable. . . ."

The view is still magnificent and far reaching. The bulk of 14,115-foot Pikes Peak looms to the southwest, while the Rampart Range's wild landscape of valleys, canyons, and wooded mountains surrounds Mount Herman, the highest peak in the immediate vicinity. Below to the east is the white sandstone pillar of Monument Rock and the communities of Monument and Palmer Lake; beyond stretches the Black Forest, its dark wooded hills forming a divide between the Arkansas and South Platte River watersheds.

Miles and Directions

0.0 Start from the trailhead and parking area (GPS: 39.071171, -104.932114) at a switchback on Mount Herman Road.

0.1 Go right on the trail up a steep draw.

0.4 Reach a grassy pocket meadow on the west side of Mount Herman.

0.8 The trail reaches gentle wooded slopes on the broad south ridge of the mountain.

1.1 Reach the summit of Mount Herman, with spacious views, a windsock, and register (GPS: 39.081798, -104.926395).

2.2 Arrive back at the trailhead on Mount Herman Road.

40 Palmer Reservoirs Loop with Cap Rock Option

This excellent lollipop hike, following three different trails, explores scenic canyons and mountains in the Rampart Range west of Palmer Lake. The hike passes two reservoirs, climbs along a boulder-filled canyon, and, for extra credit, scrambles up Cap Rock, an optional hike to a spectacular local landmark.

Start: Reservoir Trailhead on Old Carriage Road in Palmer Lake
Distance: 3.9-mile lollipop
Hiking time: 4 to 5 hours
Difficulty: Moderate
Elevation gain: 1,950 feet overall
Trail surface: Doubletrack dirt road and single-track dirt and rock trail
Seasons: Year-round. The trail is snowy and icy in winter. Bring spikes and trekking poles for additional traction.
Schedule: Open daily
Other trail users: Hikers only
Canine compatibility: Leashed dogs allowed on the trail to the reservoirs. Dogs are not allowed in the water. Dogs are allowed without leashes on the Pike National Forest land northwest of the reservoirs.

Land status: Public and private land in Pike National Forest and town of Palmer Lake watershed
Fees and permits: None
Map: USGS Palmer Lake
Trail contacts: Pike National Forest, Pikes Peak Ranger District, 601 S. Weber St., Colorado Springs 80903; (719) 636-1602; www.fs.usda.gov/detail/psicc/about-forest/districts/?cid=fsm9_032731. Town of Palmer Lake, PO Box 208, 42 Valley Crescent St., Palmer Lake 80133; (719) 481-2953; www.townofpalmerlake.com/.
Other: The lower canyon and reservoirs are part of the Palmer Lake watershed. The area is for pedestrian use only. Rules include: All dogs must be leashed (strictly enforced); no firearms, horses, motor vehicles, camping, swimming, or pets in the water.

Finding the trailhead: From Colorado Springs drive north on I-25 to Monument and take exit 161. Drive west on CO 105 for 3.5 miles to Palmer Lake. Turn left (west) on South Valley Road in Palmer Lake and drive west for 0.35 mile. Turn left (south) on Old Carriage Road and drive 0.2 mile to a large roadside parking area and the trailhead in the valley below (GPS: 39.118669, -104.921208).

The Hike

This 3.9-mile-long hike follows three trails—Palmer Reservoir, Swank, and Ice Cave Creek Trails—and makes a lollipop route west of the Town of Palmer Lake along North Monument Creek and Ice Cave Creek. Half of the hike follows a closed road

Winter ice and snow covers Upper Palmer Reservoir below the trail. ▶

that allows utility access to two reservoirs for the Town of Palmer Lake, while the other half threads through Ice Cave Creek's narrow, boulder-filled canyon before climbing over a wooded ridge.

Most of the hike is moderate and includes walking on the reservoir access road, hiking on rough terrain along the creek, and following an old jeep road. Grades are generally moderate with few steep uphill sections. The first half of the hike gains elevation, while the second half loses that elevation.

Option: For extra credit, do the Cap Rock loop hike (see below) by wandering farther up Ice Cave Creek before scrambling through a boulder field and up granite slabs to the airy summit of Cap Rock, a local landmark. This short loop is the most difficult route in this book.

The Palmer Reservoirs Loop hike begins at a trailhead signed "Reservoir Trailhead," on the west side of a switchback on Old Carriage Road, on the north side of North Monument Creek, and at the entrance to a steep-walled canyon. Plenty of parking is available at the trailhead and along the south side of the road just east of the trailhead. A sign at the trailhead details the area rules—all dogs must be leashed, no pets in the water, and no swimming, firearms, or horses.

The first hike segment goes 0.8 mile up Palmer Reservoir Trail from the trailhead to its junction with Ice Cave Creek Trail at the first reservoir.

Hike west on the trail up the narrowing canyon and, after 0.25 mile, climb steeply up a short slope to a closed utility road at 0.3 miles. Follow the road up the bottom of the canyon, passing through a large gate, which is usually open. The hike climbs steadily up the road and reaches the dam at Lower Reservoir at 0.6 mile. A concrete dam, split by a spillway, forms a picturesque lake tucked into the narrow canyon and surrounded by a pine and fir forest. Enjoy the scenic view of the lake from the road but remember that people and dogs are not allowed in the reservoir and fishing is prohibited.

Continue up the road along the north edge of the lake and in another 0.1 mile cross over Ice Cave Creek, which tumbles through a mass of fallen boulders in its lower canyon before emptying into a wetland at the west end of the reservoir. Past the creek, follow the road up around a corner and look right at 0.8 mile for the start of the Ice Cave Creek Trail. The next trail segment follows Ice Cave Creek northwest for 0.6 mile to its junction with Swank Trail.

The next trail section follows Ice Cave Creek Road for 0.6 mile from the road to Swank Trail. The narrow singletrack trail, rebuilt by the Colorado Mountain Club in 2013, traverses slopes covered with fir and spruce above the creek's rocky canyon. Numerous boulders of all sizes have fallen into the creek, creating watery caves and grottos beneath the granite blocks. The caves, receiving little direct sunlight, often hold ice formations in their dark depths through late May, giving the creek its name.

Chisel Point is a dramatic granite pinnacle west of Cap Rock.

Palmer Reservoirs Loop with Cap Rock Option

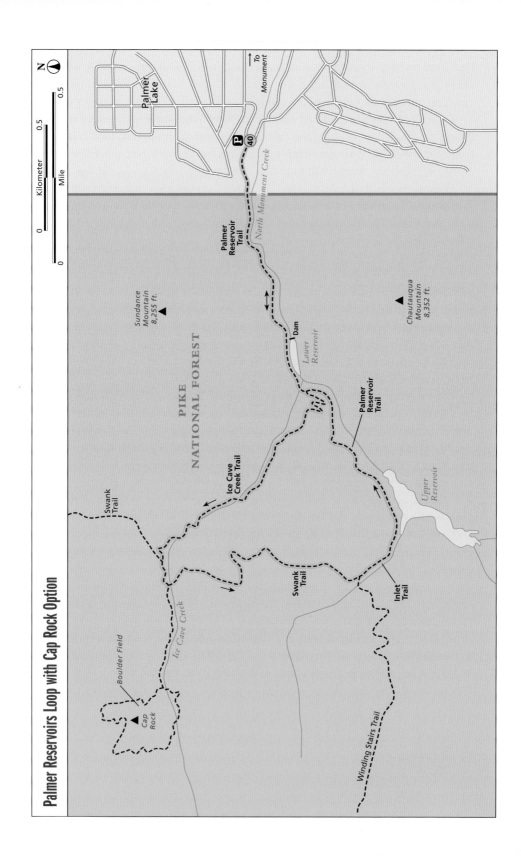

Palmer Lake

To Monument

North Monument Creek

Palmer Reservoir Trail

Sundance Mountain 8,255 ft.

PIKE NATIONAL FOREST

Dam

Lower Reservoir

Chautauqua Mountain 8,352 ft.

Palmer Reservoir Trail

Ice Cave Creek Trail

Upper Reservoir

Swank Trail

Swank Trail

Inlet Trail

Boulder Field

Ice Cave Creek

Cap Rock

Winding Stairs Trail

Kilometer

Mile

N

This trail section is snowy and icy in winter so come prepared with spikes on your boots for traction.

After you hike 0.4 mile from the road, the trail splashes across the creek and follows the open north bank in a northwesterly direction. Dense willows and grass clot the creek's banks and a couple of openings through the trees give views northwest to Cap Rock, a pointed rock formation that towers above the canyon. After another 0.2 mile the trail bends away from the creek and reaches a junction with Swank Trail, an abandoned old road. Go left at this junction, 1.4 miles from the start of the hike.

Swank Trail heads across a hillside and descends to an open grassy meadow along Ice Cave Creek and a trail junction on the north side of the meadow. Swank Trail goes south here across the creek. The Cap Rock Trail continues west up the canyon. Landmarks are a tall ponderosa pine that stands sentinel on the west side of the meadow, and a squat granite boulder sitting next to the creek.

While the standard hike continues on Swank Trail, this is where you decide if you want to climb Cap Rock. (See Cap Rock Trail Option below.)

From the junction of the Cap Rock and Swank Trails, go south on Swank. Step across the creek and follow the old rutted jeep road up a shallow valley blanketed in a spruce and fir forest. The trail slowly climbs and after 0.5 mile reaches the top of a ridge and a junction with the Winding Stairs Trail, which follows the ridge west for almost 3 miles to Winding Stairs Road and the crest of the Rampart Range.

Descend the southwest side of the ridge on Swank Trail. The old road drops steeply down the mountainside before leveling out in a valley filled with grass and willows. At 0.35 mile from the ridgetop, the Swank Trail ends when it reaches Reservoir Trail and Inlet Trail on the north shore of the Upper Reservoir.

The last hiking segment runs 1.5 miles from the inlet on the reservoir back to the trailhead. Follow the Palmer Reservoir Trail, a closed utility road, east along the north shore of the upper lake. The trail climbs up from the shoreline and runs across the hillside above a curved concrete dam. Continue hiking past the lake and downhill, passing the junction with Ice Cave Creek Trail at 3 miles and the first dam at 3.2 miles. The road drops quickly down the lower canyon, passes through the gate, and reaches the first junction. Go right and descend a short singletrack trail to the bottom of the canyon. Follow the wide trail through piney woods back to the trailhead and parking lot.

Miles and Directions

0.0 Start from the trailhead on Old Carriage Road in Palmer Lake (GPS: 39.118669, -104.921208). Hike west on Palmer Reservoir Trail, a closed road, up North Monument Creek's canyon.

0.3 Climb a short singletrack trail and reach a utility road (GPS: 39.118686, -104.925534). Hike up the road (Palmer Reservoir Trail), pass through a gate, and continue up the steep road.

0.6 Reach the dam at Lower Reservoir (GPS: 39.117136, -104.931337). Hike west on the road along the north side of the lake.

0.7 Reach the west end of the lake and cross over Ice Cave Creek.

0.8 Reach Ice Cave Creek Trail on the right (GPS: 39.115932, -104.933794) at 7,600 feet. Go right on the singletrack trail on steep slopes above the creek.

1.2 Dip down and cross Ice Cave Creek.

1.4 Cross Swank Creek. After a couple hundred feet, reach a junction with Swank Trail (GPS: 39.12228, -104.94193). Go left across a hillside and then west to an open meadow.

1.5 Reach the junction of Swank Trail and Ice Cave Creek Trail on the edge of a meadow (GPS: 39.12195, -104.94372). Go left on Swank Trail and cross Ice Cave Creek. Continue south uphill on the rutted old road.

2.0 Junction with Winding Stairs Trail on top of a ridge (GPS: 39.11780, -104.94193).

2.4 Junction with Palmer Reservoir Trail and Inlet Trail on the north side of the Upper Reservoir (GPS: 39.11393, -104.94322). Continue south and then east on the wide Palmer Reservoir Trail above the north side of the lake.

3.0 Junction with Ice Cave Creek Trail. Continue straight on the road.

3.2 Reach the first dam.

3.6 Leave the road and descend to the trail in the bottom of the valley.

3.9 Reach the trailhead and parking area.

Cap Rock Trail Option

The Cap Rock Trail is a rough backcountry hiking adventure and the most difficult hike in this book. Hikers should be skilled at route-finding, able to execute easy rock-climbing moves, and willing to make judgment calls for the group's safety. It adds 1.5 miles, 450 feet of elevation gain, and as much as 3 hours to the Palmer Reservoirs Loop.

The trail is hard to follow at times since it winds among boulders along the creek before scrambling up a steep hill to a boulder field below Cap Rock's east face. A good sense of direction and strong route-finding skills are essential. Bring a map and compass or use a GPS unit and plug the "Miles and Directions" coordinates in it to stay on route. The return hike from the summit descends the west side of Cap Rock before returning down a crude path along the creek to Swank Trail.

Start the Cap Rock Trail at the meadow where Swank Trail crosses Ice Cave Creek. Locate the Ice Cave Creek Trail, which goes west from the meadow and Swank Trail past a tall ponderosa pine. The trail winds among boulders on the hillside north of the creek and after 0.3 mile reaches a large blocky boulder on the right above the trail.

Scramble past the big boulder and then up the hillside, keeping left of the boulder field. Aim for a couple tall pines left of a huge pointed boulder below the southeast corner of Cap Rock, which looms above. Scramble and climb across boulders below the pointed block; use caution if there is snow on the rock surfaces. A couple places require careful foot placements and perhaps even a fixed rope to use as a hand line

Appendix B: Restaurants, Brewpubs, and Accommodations

Restaurants

Colorado Springs offers well over 1,000 restaurants, from the Broadmoor Hotel's five-star option, including the Penrose Room and Charles Court, to humble curbside trucks that vend burritos with homemade tortillas. There are numerous standout restaurants in the Springs that offer a huge variety of cuisines, styles, and prices. This listing is the beginning of your culinary exploration and includes the author's favorite dining experiences. Try any of these restaurants after your day of hiking and you will surely be satisfied, happy, and ready to hit the trail again tomorrow. Bon appétit!

Adam's Mountain Café
26 Manitou Ave.
Manitou Springs 80829
(719) 685-1430
adamsmountaincafe.com
A Manitou Springs tradition serving breakfast, lunch, and dinner with lots of vegetarian and vegan meals, no prepared foods, no microwaves, and organic local ingredients.

Amanda's Fonda
3625 W. Colorado Ave.
Colorado Springs 80904
(719) 227-1975
amandasfonda.com
Popular Mexican restaurant with creekside dining in west Colorado Springs. Thirty-five flavors of tequila, lunch and dinner, and gluten-free menu available. Also at 8050 N. Academy Blvd.

Green Line Grill
230½ Pueblo Ave.
Colorado Springs 80903
(719) 964-1461
greenlinegrill.com
Chef Bobby serves up a tasty onion-"fried" burger straight out of central Oklahoma, topped with El Reno Slaw and served with hand-cut fries. Also, a great veggie burger.

Hungry Bear Restaurant
111 E. Midland Ave.
Woodland Park 80863
(719) 687-5912
hungrybearcolorado.com
Hiking behind Pikes Peak? Visit the Hungry Bear, a family-style diner with traditional breakfasts and salads, burgers, and soups for lunch.

Il Vicino
5214 N. Nevada Ave.
Colorado Springs 80903
(719) 590-8633
ilvicino.com
Contemporary pizzeria with wood-fired artisan pizzas, calzones, flatbread sandwiches, salads, and award-winning ales.

King's Chef Diner
131 E. Bijou St.
110 E. Costilla St.
Colorado Springs 80903
(719) 636-5010, (719) 634-9135
www.cosdiner.com/
One phrase describes this classic down-town diner: green chile. It's hot and tasty, plus there's a vegetarian version. Open for breakfast and lunch. Eat at the tiny purple-castle diner on East Costilla for old-time ambience.

La Baguette Downtown
117 E. Pikes Peak Ave.
Colorado Springs 80903
(719) 636-5020
labaguettedowntown.com
Informal and affordable French country dining with authentic French onion soup, crusty baguettes, croissants, and delectable desserts in the heart of Colorado Springs.

La Casita Mexican Grill
306 S. Eighth St.
4295 N. Nevada Ave.
3725 E. Woodmen Rd.
Colorado Springs
(719) 633-9616; (719) 599-7829;
(719) 536-0375
lacasitamexigrill.com
Basic tasty Mexican food with three locations, daily specials, great salsa bar, and patio dining. Muy sabroso!

Luigi's Homemade Italian Food
947 S. Tejon St.
Colorado Springs 80903
(719) 632-7339
luigiscoloradosprings.com
Luigi's is a popular and traditional Colorado Springs' Italian eatery with red-checkered tablecloths, hearty servings of pasta, and fresh Italian bread.

Paravicini's Italian Bistro
2802 W. Colorado Ave.
Colorado Springs 80904
(719) 471-8200
paravicinis.com
Paravicini's, located in Old Colorado City, serves perhaps the best Italian food in the Springs with classic dishes and neo-Italian creations along with complementary wines, appetizers, and desserts.

Penrose Room
Broadmoor Hotel
1 Lake Circle
Colorado Springs 80906
(866) 381-8432, (719) 577-5733
broadmoor.com/penrose-room
Simply the best restaurant in Colorado Springs and the only five-star and Five-Diamond restaurant in Colorado. Dine on the top floor of Broadmoor South with views of the mountains, excellent food, great presentation, huge wine list, superior service, and, of course, prices to match.

Poor Richard's Restaurant
324½ N. Tejon St.
Colorado Springs 80903
(719) 578-5549
poorrichardsdowntown.com
Longtime downtown restaurant with delicious pizzas, veggie meals, sandwiches, and salads. Sidewalk and patio dining. Next door is Little Richard's Toy Store, Rico's Café and Wine Bar, and Poor Richard's Books.

Santana's Vegan Grill
3220 Austin Bluffs Blvd.
Colorado Springs 80918
(719) 694-9331
http://santanasvegangrill.com/
Perfect lunch and breakfast spot for healthy vegan food, including delicious burgers, hot dogs, breakfast sandwiches, and the best basket of hand-cut fries in the Springs.

The Rabbit Hole
101 N. Tejon St.
Colorado Springs 80903
(719) 203-5072
rabbitholedinner.com
This subterranean restaurant, great for late-night eats, offers a hip decor, diverse menu, inventive drinks, super service, and a cool vibe. Try it, you'll like it for an after-hike meal.

Uchenna
2501 W. Colorado Ave.
Colorado Springs 80904
(719) 634-5070
uchennaalive.com
Uchenna, the only Ethiopian restaurant in the Springs, is also the number-3 ranked restaurant on Trip Advisor (2020). Fabulous African food with great service and ambience; it's not fancy but you're treated like family. Try the rosewater lemonade too.

Brewpubs

What better way to celebrate your latest local hike than quaffing a few pints of craft beers in a Colorado Springs brewpub? Colorado Springs is simply one of America's best beer towns with more than twenty local breweries that create exquisite and tasty microbrews for all you trekking hopheads. There are, of course, award-winning beers like Laughing Lab from Bristol, a mildly sweet, nutty Scottish ale, and the broad beer selection at Phantom Canyon, the Springs' original brewpub started in 1993 by former Colorado governor John Hickenlooper. There are also lots of small brewpubs and taprooms scattered around the Pikes Peak region. Sample my favorites below and then try others, including Smiling Toad, Ute Pass, Rocky Mountain, and Bierworks breweries.

Bristol Brewing Company
1604 S. Cascade Ave.
Colorado Springs 80905
(719) 633-2555
bristolbrewing.com
The brewery, housed in the historic
Ivywild School, offers a taproom and
restaurants. Their iconic beers are
Laughing Lab Scottish Ale and Beehive
Honey Wheat.

**Colorado Mountain Brewery at the
Roundhouse**
600 S. 21st St.
1110 Interquest Pkwy.
Colorado Springs
(719) 466-8240, (719) 434-5750
cmbrew.com
Colorado Mountain Brewery off US 24
is a convenient stop after a mountain
hike. Taste its handcrafted brews and
Colorado cuisine and enjoy views of
Pikes Peak from the patio.

**Phantom Canyon Brewing
Company**
2 E. Pikes Peak Ave.
Colorado Springs 80903
(719) 635-2800
phantomcanyon.com
Popular Phantom Canyon, one of the
Springs' oldest brewers, is located in the
heart of downtown. Classic beers, special
releases, small-batch bomber series to
wash down pub food. Also pints and
pool upstairs.

Trail's End Taproom
3103 W. Colorado Ave.
Colorado Springs 80904
(719) 428-0080
www.trailsendtaproom.com/
Hit up Trail's End Taproom after a long
day on the trails. There's a big selection
of craft beers, cider, wine, and kombu-
cha at the first self-pour taproom in the
Springs. Try an ounce or a glass from
forty taps and then move on to the next
one. They also support local outdoor
nonprofits like Friends of Red Rock
Canyon and the Pikes Peak Climber's
Alliance.

Trinity Brewing Company
1466 W. Garden of the Gods Rd.
Colorado Springs 80907
(719) 634-0029
trinitybrew.com
Convenient to the Garden of the Gods,
Trinity was a 2014 gold-medal winner
at the Great American Beer Fest for its
Elektrick Cukumbahh. Eclectic and
busy pub with mountain views from its
small patio.

Accommodations

Since its 1871 founding, Colorado Springs has been a destination for travelers and has offered a wide range of accommodations. Visiting hikers find a broad spectrum of hotels, motels, and bed-and-breakfast inns with an equally wide range of prices. Stay in a basic no-frills hotel like Motel 6 to save cash or indulge yourself and bed down for a few nights in one of the Pikes Peak region's many B&Bs where you're treated like family. Here's a listing of some of the most popular accommodations. For more B&Bs, visit bedandbreakfast.com, pikespeakareabnbs.com, and tripadvisor.com for suggestions, reviews, and contact information.

Bed & Breakfast Inns

Adobe Inn at Cascade
4675 Hagerman Ave.
Cascade 80809
(719) 684-2194
adobeinnatcascade.com

Avenue Hotel Bed and Breakfast
711 Manitou Ave.
Manitou Springs 80829
(719) 685-1277 or (800) 294-1277
avenuehotelbandb.com

Carr Manor Historic Inn
350 E. Carr Ave.
Cripple Creek 80813
(719) 689-3709
carrmanor.com

Glen Eyrie Castle
3820 N. 30th St.
Colorado Springs 80904
(800) 944-4536
gleneyrie.org/lodging

Holden House 1902
Bed and Breakfast Inn
1102 W. Pikes Peak Ave.
Colorado Springs 80904
(719) 471-3980 or (888) 565-3980
holdenhouse.com

The Hotel St. Nicholas
303 N. Third St.
Cripple Creek 80813
(719) 689-0856 or (888) 786-4257
hotelstnicholas.com

Hughes Hacienda Bed & Breakfast
12060 Calle Corvo
Colorado Springs 80926
(719) 576-2060 or (800) 576-2060
hugheshacienda.com

Old Town Guest House
115 S. 26th St.
Colorado Springs 80904
(719) 632-9194
oldtown-guesthouse.com

Red Crags Estates
328 El Paso Blvd.
Manitou Springs 80829
(719) 685-4515
redcragsestates.com

St. Mary's Inn
530 N. Nevada Ave.
Colorado Springs 80903
(719) 540-2222
thestmarysinn.com

A Room with a View Bed and Breakfast
528 E. Bijou St.
Colorado Springs 80903
(719) 633-3683
arwav.biz/1.html

Silver House Bed & Breakfast
355 S. Second St.
Cripple Creek 80813
(719) 689-5558
silverhousebnb.com

Hotels

Colorado Springs offers plenty of hotels for footsore hikers to rest their dusty boots, including all the major chain hotels like Best Western, Comfort Inn, Hilton, Holiday Inn, Hyatt, La Quinta Inn, Marriott, Radisson, and Ramada. Check out your favorite booking site like Orbitz, Expedia, Kayak, or Hotels.com to find accommodations that agree with your pocketbook. Here are five great Colorado Springs hotels that will not only massage your feet and back but also clean your boots.

Antlers Hilton Hotel
4 South Cascade
Colorado Springs 80903
(719) 955-5600
antlers.com

The Broadmoor Hotel
1 Lake Ave.
Colorado Springs 80906
broadmoor.com

Cheyenne Mountain Resort
3225 Broadmoor Valley Rd.
Colorado Springs 80906
(719) 538-4000
cheyennemountain.com

The Cliff House at Pikes Peak
306 Canon Ave.
Manitou Springs 80829
thecliffhouse.com

The Mining Exchange Wyndham Grand Hotel
9 S. Nevada Ave.
Colorado Springs 80903
wyndham.com

Campgrounds

Despite its easy access to the great outdoors, Colorado Springs is not exactly camper friendly. There are a few local campgrounds, but most cater to RVers rather than tenters. The best campground close to the Springs is at Cheyenne Mountain State Park on the southwest edge of the city. It's easy to reach and offers scenic campsites with expansive views. You will have to drive farther away to find more rugged camping options in Pike National Forest north of Woodland Park and at Mueller State Park.

Cheyenne Mountain State Park
410 JL Ranch Heights
Colorado Springs 80926
(719) 576-2016
cpw.state.co.us/placestogo/Parks/
cheyennemountain
61 campsites in five campgrounds

Echo Canyon Campground
45044 US Hwy. 50
Cañon City 81212
(866) 341-7875
echocanyoncampground.com

Garden of the Gods RV Resort
3704 W. Colorado Ave.
Colorado Springs 80904
(719) 475-9450
https://gardenofthegodsrvresort.com/

Mueller State Park
21045 CO Highway 67 South
Divide 80814
(719) 687-2366
cpw.state.co.us/placestogo/parks/
Mueller
132 campsites in seven campgrounds;
three cabins

Pike National Forest
601 South Weber
Colorado Springs 80903
(719) 636-1602
www.fs.usda.gov/activity/psicc/recre
ation/camping-cabins/Campsite
reservations at recreation.gov

Pikes Peak Ranger District
Colorado Campground, 80 sites
The Crags Campground, 17 sites
Meadow Ridge Campground, 19 sites
Painted Rocks Campground, 18 sites
South Meadows Campground, 64 sites
Springdale Campground, 13 sites
Thunder Ridge Campground, 21 sites
Wye Campground, 21 sites

South Park Ranger District
Eleven Mile Canyon Recreation Area
Four campgrounds with 61 sites

About the Author

Based in Colorado Springs, Stewart M. Green has hiked, climbed, photographed, and traveled across the American West as well as the United States and the world in search of memorable images and experiences to document. Stewart, a freelance writer and photographer for Globe Pequot Press and FalconGuides, has written and photographed forty-five travel and outdoor adventure books, including *Best Easy Day Hikes Colorado Springs*, *Scenic Driving Colorado*, *Scenic Driving California's Pacific Coast*, *Best Climbs Moab*, *Best Climbs Denver and Boulder*, *KNACK Rock Climbing*, *Rock Climbing Colorado*, *Rock Climbing Utah*, *Rock Climbing Arizona*, and *Rock Art: The Meanings and Myths Behind Ancient Ruins in the Southwest and Beyond*. His photographs and  writing are also published in many magazines, books, catalogs, and websites. Stewart is a professional rock climbing guide with Front Range Climbing Company. Visit him at green1109.wix.com/stewartmgreenphoto for images and information.